RESTARTING THE FUTURE

RESTARTING THE FUTURE

HOW TO FIX THE INTANGIBLE ECONOMY

Jonathan Haskel and Stian Westlake

PRINCETON UNIVERSITY PRESS
PRINCETON AND OXFORD

Published by Princeton University Press
41 William Street, Princeton, New Jersey 08540
99 Banbury Road, Oxford OX2 6JX

press.princeton.edu

First Australian paperback edition, 2022
ISBN 9780691241098

The Library of Congress cataloged the U.S. edition of this book as follows:

Names: Haskel, Jonathan, author. | Westlake, Stian, author.
Title: Restarting the future : how to fix the intangible economy / Jonathan Haskel and Stian Westlake.
Description: 1st Edition. | Princeton, New Jersey : Princeton University Press, 2022. | Includes bibliographical references and index.
Identifiers: LCCN 2021032784 (print) | LCCN 2021032785 (ebook) | ISBN 9780691211589 (hardback) | ISBN 9780691236025 (ebook)
Subjects: LCSH: Intangible property—Economic aspects. | Intellectual capital—Management. | Investments. | Business planning. | Organizational change.
Classification: LCC HF5681.I55 H375 2022 (print) | LCC HF5681.I55 (ebook) | DDC 338.5—dc23
LC record available at https://lccn.loc.gov/2021032784
LC ebook record available at https://lccn.loc.gov/2021032785

British Library Cataloging-in-Publication Data is available

Editorial: Hannah Paul, Josh Drake
Jacket/Cover Design: Karl Spurzem
Production: Erin Suydam
Publicity: James Schneider, Kate Farquhar-Thomson

This book has been composed in Adobe Text Pro and Trade Gothic

Printed in Australia

CONTENTS

FIGURES AND TABLES

Figures

Tables

PREFACE AND ACKNOWLEDGMENTS

This book has its origins in the thought-provoking conversations we had after the publication of *Capitalism without Capital: The Rise of the Intangible Economy* in 2017. We are very grateful for the insightful and generous comments we received from Martin Brassell, Stephen Cecchetti, Tyler Cowen, Diane Coyle, Chris Dillow, Daniel Finkelstein, Martin Fleming, Rana Foroohar, Bill Gates, John Harris, Constance Hunter, Richard Jones, John Kay, William Kerr, Saul Klein, Arnold Kling, Baruch Lev, Yuval Levin, Ehsan Masood, George Molloan, Ataman Ozyilidirim, Robert Peston, Reihan Salam, Michael Saunders, Dan Sichel, David Smith, Tom Sutcliffe, Bart Van Ark, Callum Williams, Martin Wolf, and many others.

We thank our collaborators for their continual inspiration: Sam Bowman, Carol Corrado, Janice Eberly, Harald Edquist, Peter Goodridge, Massimilliano Iommi, Cecilia Jona-Lasinio, Paul Mizen, Gavin Wallis, and Giles Wilkes. We are grateful to our generous funders: Ericsson; the UK Economic & Social Research Council (ESRC); McKinsey & Company; the Programme on Innovation and Diffusion, ES/V009478/1; the

Productivity Institute, ES/V002740/1; and to our employers, the Bank of England, the Department of Business, Energy and Industrial Strategy, Imperial College, and the Royal Statistical Society, who have both supported our endeavours and provided us with countless practical insights into the matters discussed in the book. Our views in this book are ours and not theirs.

This book would not have been possible without the assistance and input of a range of people, including Brian Anderson, Azeem Azhar, Alina Barnett, Sandra Bernick, Matt Clifford, Simon Cox, Dan Davies, Ned Donovan, Alex Edmans, David Edmonds, John Fingleton, Tom Forth, Marco Garofalo, Sam Gyimah, Anton Howes, Jonny Kitson, Mark Koyama, Alice Lassman, Jamie Lenney, Paul Lewis, John Myers, Ramana Nanda, Martin O'Neill, Sophie Piton, Petra Sarapatkova, Ben Southwood, Marilyne Tolle, Rachel Wolf, Ben Yeoh, and the team at Princeton University Press (especially Josh Drake and Hannah Paul). Particular thanks to Sue Haskel and Steve Rigolosi, who read the entire manuscript.

As ever we thank Kirsten, Sue, and our families for their endless love and support. We are delighted to dedicate this book, with love, to our parents: Stian, to Marit and Robert, and Jonathan, to Carole and Simon.

Introduction

HOW TO RESTART THE CENTURY

The twentieth century ended in a flurry of optimism. New technologies and new ways of doing business would, it was hoped, soon usher in great advances in prosperity and human flourishing. But the reality has proved very different. Over the past twenty years the performance of advanced economies has been a study in disappointment. This book proposes a new explanation for what went wrong, suggesting how we can fix the problems and create an economy that not only grows faster but is fairer and more sustainable, too.

Postponing Tomorrow: Selden's Brass Plaque and Lorenzetti's Fresco

Sometimes a future that in retrospect seems inevitable was at the time a close-run thing. And sometimes a future that seems desirable and likely does not happen at all. One way of thinking about this is by considering two old objects: a brass plaque in the case of the automobile and a seven-hundred-year-old painting.

Perhaps more than any other technology, the automobile defined the twentieth century. For better or worse, it influenced our lifestyles, our economy, our cities, and our climate. Even at the very beginning of the century, people saw it as an icon of the future. But if you look at vintage American automobiles from around 1900, you'll see that many of them share an unusual feature: a brass plate stating that the car is the design of a man named George Selden. If you have not heard Selden's name alongside automotive pioneers Karl Benz or Henry Ford, there is a reason for this. Selden was not an engineer but a patent attorney, and at the time he had not produced a single car. But he did file a patent in 1879 that he claimed covered all gasoline-powered cars (US patent 549,160).[1] He made the most of this patent, forming in due course a cartel with a number of other businesses to demand royalties from every car sold—a precursor of the patent trolls who acquire obscure patents and use them to shake down tech companies today. A dynamic industry looked like it might fall victim to a greedy collective. Several years later, Henry Ford challenged the patent, eventually prevailing after an eight-year lawsuit, and the rest was history. But the situation could have turned out differently, moving the American auto industry onto a different path and affecting the wider history of the motorcar, too. The brass plaque is a reminder that the development of the automobile was not, in fact, a sure thing.

Patent wars have not been limited to the auto industry. America's aviation industry was defined, and nearly derailed, by a similar patent war only a few years later. Hollywood is synonymous with cinema in part because early moviemakers went there to escape the legal constraints of Thomas Edison's Motion Picture Patents Company. These patent wars are examples of the broader historical lesson that the evolution of many new technologies, and their economic consequences, depended on good fortune in terms of rules, laws, and institutions.

Selden's brass plaques are a reminder of a lucky economic escape from bad rules that nearly held back a major technology in its earliest days. But sometimes society is not so lucky, and bad institutions bring material progress grinding to a halt. A popular attraction in the city of Siena is a set of stunning frescoes by Ambrogio Lorenzetti (active approximately 1317–48) depicting the city as it was in the fourteenth century, with towers and marketplaces picked out in rose pink and mauve, delicately painted merchants plying their trade in the streets, and happy citizens dancing. The title is *The Effects of Good Governance on Siena and Its Territory*. It is located in the Palazzo Pubblico, on the wall of the chamber where the city's ruling council sat, and it makes a basic political point: good governance helps an economy flourish. And where better to paint it? In the early 1300s, it must have seemed that Siena and the surrounding cities of northern Italy had pulled off a remarkable economic feat. By supporting trade, finance, and investment, they had begun to break out of the trap of subsistence in which most of western Europe had been stuck for centuries. But even as the paint on the fresco was drying, the economic tide was beginning to turn. The institutions that had helped Siena prosper turned out to be inadequate for the new economy. Like many other northern Italian cities, Siena began to stagnate and then decline. The frescoes in the Palazzo Pubblico stand as a melancholy reminder of what had been.

The Sienese experience raises an important question that we will explore in chapter 3: What institutions, norms, and strategies does the economy need as it grows and changes?

The Great Economic Disappointment and Its Symptoms

When we think about the state of the economy today, it is hard not to think, *it wasn't supposed to be like this*. The world is richer than it has ever been, remarkable technologies are transforming every facet of our lives—and yet, everyone seems to know that, from an economic point of view, *something is wrong*.

In Britain in the late 1970s, the *something wrong* was so obvious that it earned itself a name: Britain was described as "the sick man of Europe." No one has given a name to the problems that the economies of rich countries face today, but we see five symptoms in country after country: stagnation, inequality, dysfunctional competition, fragility, and inauthenticity. These symptoms are noteworthy not only because they are objectively undesirable but also because they are all somewhat hard to explain, defying traditional economic explanations or exhibiting unexpected paradoxes. We introduce them briefly here and explain them in more detail in chapter 1.

Stagnation. Productivity growth has been dismally slow for over a decade. As a result, rich countries earn about 25 percent less per capita than they would have earned if twenty-first-century growth had continued at trend rates. Periods of low growth are not in themselves unusual, but our current slump is both protracted and puzzling. It has proved resistant to ultra-low interest rates and a host of unconventional attempts to stimulate the economy. And it coexists with widespread enthusiasm about new technologies and new businesses that exploit them.

Inequality. Whether you measure it in terms of wealth or income, inequality has increased considerably since the 1980s and has stayed constant. But inequality today is not simply a matter of haves and have-nots. Rather, it is complicated by what we might call *inequality of esteem*: a perceived divide between high-status elites and low-status people left behind by cultural and social change. Although there is some correlation between esteem and material affluence, this correlation is not perfect. Many people who feel left behind by modernity are asset-rich retirees, while the liberal elite includes plenty of impecunious, debt-saddled graduates.

Dysfunctional Competition. The lifeblood of market economies, competition does not seem to be working as it should. The fortunes of firms seem to be more entrenched. Trillion-dollar businesses such as Amazon and Google consistently outperform laggards, earning sky-high profits. Fewer new businesses are set up, and people are less likely to change employers or move to find work. Here, too, we see a paradox as many people complain of a growing sense of frenetic, stressful, and wasteful contestation in economic life, with the objectively affluent, and even the rich, seeming to have to work harder and harder to keep up.

Fragility. The COVID-19 pandemic has shown that even the world's richest economies are not immune to natural forces. Indeed, the damage caused by the pandemic is linked to the complexity and sophistication of the economy. Our large, dense cities, our complex international supply chains, and the unprecedented interconnectedness of our global economy allowed the virus to leap from country to country and increased the cost of the lockdowns needed to control it. Even fifteen years ago, a pandemic outbreak in a remote area of China would be at most a minor news story for the rich world. Now, thanks to globalisation, supply chains, and the internet, we seem to be increasingly exposed to the mere flap of a butterfly's wings on another continent.

For many, the ruinous human impact of COVID-19 offers a forewarning of the havoc that climate change will cause in the years to come. The combined actual impact of the pandemic with the expected impact of global warming illustrates the vulnerability of the economy to big, ecosystem-level threats. Both problems share another feature: the curious gap between knowing how to solve them and actually doing so. Countries from Taiwan to Thailand have shown that the right policies can help to reduce the number of COVID-19 deaths and the amount of economic damage. Likewise, detailed and credible plans for decarbonising the economy exist. But the gap between knowing and doing is wide, and most countries seem unable to bridge it.

Another indication of fragility is the declining ability of central banks to offset economic shocks. In the nine US recessions leading up to the COVID-19 pandemic, the Federal Reserve cut interest rates by an average of 6.3 percentage points.[2] In the United Kingdom, the cut was 5.5 percentage points in the five pre-COVID-19 recessions. But since 2009, average interest rates set by the Central Bank in the United States, the United Kingdom, and Continental Europe have been 0.54 percent, 0.48 percent, and 0.36 percent, respectively (data to April 2021). On interest rates, so-called policy space for central banks seems severely limited.

Inauthenticity. The final disappointing feature of the economy in the twenty-first century is not something that economists talk about, but it looms large in laypeople's discussions. We call it *inauthenticity* or *fakeness*: the idea that workers and businesses lack the grit and authenticity they should have, and that they once had. Consider anthropologist David Graeber's critique of "bullshit jobs": "Through some strange alchemy, the number of salaried paper-pushers ultimately seems to expand" even while "the lay-offs and speed-ups invariably fall on that class of people who are actually making, moving, fixing, and maintaining things."[3]

Graeber's critique follows in the footsteps of postmodernists such as Jean Baudrillard, who argued that the modern world is dominated by "simulacra": imitations and symbols that, like Disneyland, take on a new life of their own that is detached from the underlying reality.[4] Likewise, the conservative commentator Ross Douthat has argued that one of the characteristics of modern decadence is the prevalence of imitation rather than originality in culture, media, and entertainment. The modern world is remixed, narrated, and curated in a way that the past was not.[5]

This view resonates with the public, too. Manufacturing, along with the idea that governments should do more to promote it, is perennially popular with voters. Bringing back manufacturing jobs to the United States was one of Donald Trump's most resonant electoral promises in 2016. Successive British governments promised to respond to the global financial crisis with "New Industries, New Jobs" and a "March of the Makers." None of these promises were kept, but the fact that they were made at all strongly indicates the popularity of the idea that we should return to "making things" and the suspicion that a lot of modern economic activity is somehow not genuine.

Economies and societies have often gone through periods of unease. But the coexistence of the five problems listed here is particularly puzzling and paradoxical. Economic stagnation has affected us before. But today it coexists with low interest rates, high business profits, and a widespread belief that we live in an age of dizzying technological progress. The rise of material inequality has slowed down, but its consequences and sequelae—inequality of status, political polarisation, geographical divides, blighted communities, and premature deaths[6]—continue to grow. And, as we discuss in chapter 7, competition seems to have decreased, with fewer new firms and more persistent performance gaps between leader and laggard businesses. But working life for managers and workers alike feels more frenetic than ever.

This book answers two key questions: What is causing all these symptoms, and what can we do about it?

Explaining the Great Economic Disappointment: Conduct versus Circumstance versus the Transformed Economy

When things go terribly wrong, there is rarely a shortage of theories to explain why. As we discuss in chapter 1, the explanations offered for the Great Economic Disappointment tend to fall into two groups: theories that blame conduct and theories that blame circumstance.

Conduct explanations hold that we could have avoided our problems if we had acted better. Critics on the left argue that we should have undone neoliberalism with higher taxes or stricter competition law; critics on the right blame the decline in entrepreneurial spirit and lament a lost culture of "building." *Circumstance* explanations are more fatalistic. Some of them argue that the issues we face today are just the manifestation of long-standing failings, the chickens of capitalism coming home to roost. Others maintain that stagnation is the inevitable consequence of progress, perhaps because historical growth rates depended on technological good luck—for example, transformational inventions such as the internal combustion engine, electrification, television, and indoor plumbing—and we are simply not so lucky in the technologies available to us today. Some circumstantial explanations are pessimistic, maintaining that the past two decades represent a new normal; others are more optimistic, predicting an improvement in the future as we discover ways to make new technologies productive.

We are sceptical of theories that rely on the assumption that humanity has simply gotten worse or that providence or the great unfolding of technology has simply turned against us. This book provides an alternative explanation. We believe that the economy is partway through a fundamental change from one that is largely material to one that is based on ideas, knowledge, and relationships. Unfortunately, the institutions on which the economy depends have for the most part failed to keep pace. The problems we see are the morbid symptoms of an economy caught between an irrecoverable past and a future that we cannot attain.

We documented the transformation from a largely material economy to one based on ideas, knowledge, and relationships in our 2017 book, *Capitalism without Capital*. There we noted the shift towards investment in intangible assets (such as software, data, R&D, design, branding, training, and business processes). This shift has been ongoing for more than four decades. As we show in this new book, this change in itself explains some of the features of the Great Economic Disappointment, from rising inequality of esteem to the persistent gap between leader firms and laggard firms.

As we were writing *Capitalism without Capital*, we became aware of a totally unexpected aspect of the story of intangible capital. It seemed that around the time of the financial crisis, the long-running growth of intangible investment was beginning to slow. This slowdown was totally unexpected. After all, intangible investment had been growing reliably for decades. Intangible investments, such as software and R&D, and the intangible benefits of platforms, networks, and strong brands were only becoming more important to businesses. Intangibles-rich firms were increasing their dominance of the world's stock markets, and at a micro level the demand for intangible investment showed no sign of waning. Initially we assumed that the slowing growth of intangible investment must be a temporary consequence of the global financial crisis. But as more data became available, it became clear that the downturn was not temporary. It has now been with us for a decade, and we believe that it explains a significant proportion of the decline in productivity growth over the period.

An Unfinished Revolution

Our proposition, which we detail in chapter 3, is that the underlying problem is one of *inappropriate institutions*. Economists and laypeople alike generally accept that economic activity depends on institutions, what Douglass North described as "the humanly devised constraints that structure political, economic, and social interaction" or what Arnold Kling and Nick Schulz called the "operating system" of the economy. Sound institutions enable exchange: trade, investment, and specialisation that make the economy progress. Sound institutions have to solve four problems in exchange: ensuring sufficient *commitment*, solving *collective-action* problems, providing *information*, and restricting wasteful *influence activities*.

The key problem is that because intangible capital has unusual economic properties, institutions have to change to accommodate them. Consider, for example, the increased need for collective action: public institutions that fund intangibles that businesses are reluctant to fund, such as basic scientific research or vocational training, become more central to economic policy. Also consider the increased need for information: capital markets and banking systems must be able to lend to firms whose assets are difficult to use as security for loans.

Simultaneously, wasteful influence activities increase: there are more lawsuits around intellectual property, which grants ownership over certain intangible assets, and dysfunctional arguments over planning and zoning occur in the densely populated areas where intangible investment seems to thrive. Without the right institutions, two problems result: (1) worthwhile intangible investments are not made, resulting in slower growth, and (2) the potential downsides of an intangibles-rich economy go unchecked.

We can use the metaphor of a catalyst in chemistry to think about why institutions that were adequate for increasing intangibles to around 15 percent of a country's GDP cannot support a further increase. (We apologise to economic purists who object to this metaphorical reasoning, while noting that economics is loaded with metaphorical concepts already.) Brewers and winemakers know that yeast produces zymase, an enzyme that catalyses a reaction that turns sugar into ethanol and carbon dioxide. However, once the alcohol concentration of a fermenting liquid creeps up beyond 15 percent, the yeast dies and the zymase on which the reaction depends is no longer produced. Yeast will make wine, but not brandy; beer, but not whisky. Chemical engineers speak of the more general phenomenon of catalyst poisoning, in which catalysts are rendered less effective by impurities or the by-products of the reactions that they enable.

The institutions on which the intangible economy relies seem to behave in the same way. In some cases, intangible-friendly institutions exist only in small parts of the economy and are impractical to scale up. One example is the venture capital industry, which provided early-stage finance for many of the largest intangible-intensive firms. In other cases, flaws and kludges that were only minor problems when intangibles represented a small part of the capital stock become more problematic as intangible capital becomes more important. Patent wars caused by poorly designed intellectual property regimes, research fraud by academics trying to meet publication targets, and planning disputes that prevent clusters from growing are all bigger problems in today's world than they were in 1980.

In other cases, the consequences of a more intangible economy—such as rising inequality or the political consequences of the growing gap between liberal elites and the left-behind masses—serve to weaken the institutions on which an intangible economy relies. Voters angered by the rise of intangibles-rich elites elect populist governments, which cut funding for institutions that produce intangible investment, such as scientific research. Businesses that have achieved market dominance through valuable software or networks fund lobbying to make life harder for competitors, discouraging those competitors from investing. As a result, the cost of inadequate institutions rises.

As intangibles become more important, the institutions on which our economy depends begin to look like the legacy software systems found in large banks or government departments: outmoded in their architecture and increasingly costly, a situation that software developers call *technical debt*. At first, the shortcuts, architectural compromises, and workarounds can be lived with, but over time their costs increase, and eventually the system fails if the debt is not paid down. Technical debt rarely intrudes into the public consciousness—perhaps the most famous example is the Millennium or Y2K Bug, which cost hundreds of billions of dollars to fix—but it lurks in countless pieces of software on which we all rely daily. The growing importance of intangibles has created a bigger and more pervasive version of technical debt that we call *institutional debt*.

Paying Down Our Institutional Debt

In the second half of this book, we look at four areas where our institutional debt is greatest, holding back future intangible investment and exacerbating the problematic effects of the intangible investment that already takes place.

Public Funding and Intellectual Property. The most obvious problem relates to institutions whose explicit purpose is to encourage intangible investment. Intellectual property (IP) laws and public bodies that fund research, training, or cultural content all work to solve one of the main quirks of intangible capital: the fact that it generates spillovers, reducing the incentive for private firms to invest as much as they otherwise would. Accordingly, as we discuss in chapter 4, governments create IP laws to limit these spillovers, or they subsidise or directly fund the investments themselves.

Unfortunately, finding the right balance is difficult, and existing institutions, designed for a tangible-intensive economy in which the stakes are lower, are increasingly challenged. Notably, our existing systems often struggle to encourage high-return intangible investments rather than junk. Everyone is familiar with stories of researchers incentivised to produce papers that nobody ever reads and young people earning degrees that employers do not value. This problem derives from a fundamental property of intangibles: compared with tangible capital, their value is more variable, more heterogeneous. Sorting the wheat from the chaff places an unusually large burden on governments, especially because government systems for funding research or administering patents usually rely on rules, which are not good at making this distinction. Furthermore, our existing systems can potentially deliver publicly supported funding, but promoting the variety of ideas that are increasingly needed for successful projects can be challenging.

Finance and Monetary Policy. Equally severe challenges exist not only in the financial markets and banking systems that provide finance to private-sector businesses but also in the monetary policy regimes that underpin them. Most external finance for businesses takes the form of debt. But intangible-intensive businesses are not well suited to debt finance. Intangible assets are difficult to pledge as collateral, and the winner-takes-all nature of intangible assets makes assessing creditworthiness more difficult. These realities weaken central banks' ability to manage economic cycles by altering interest rates. The solution is institutional change in how we regulate financial institutions, increasing their ability to invest in intangibles-rich businesses, combined with tax and regulatory rules that favour debt over equity.

It is also time to examine the traditional role of central banks of lowering the cost of credit when an economy needs a boost, which has become much harder with interest rates close to zero—a phenomenon caused in part by rising risk premiums as the economy becomes more intangible. We discuss these issues in chapter 5.

Cities. Traditionally, intangible-intensive businesses clustered in dense, thriving cities, from Silicon Valley to Shenzhen to Soho. Intangibles generate spillovers and exhibit synergies, and the best way to take advantage of these, COVID-19 notwithstanding, seems to be through some face-to-face interaction. But the planning and zoning rules in most rich countries militate against city growth, putting veto power in the hands of homeowners to block it. This veto power gets more and more costly as intangible capital becomes more important. In chapter 6, we examine the evidence for this problem, discuss the political challenges of fixing it, and suggest solutions that not only allow homeowners and communities to share in the benefits of city growth but also help maximise the benefits of remote working in an intangibles-rich economy.

Competition Policy. It is increasingly argued that the rise of large, dominant businesses—from tech platforms like Google to retail chains like Walmart—is the result of weakened competition policy and that the right response is a return to the more aggressive competition rules of the 1960s and 1970s. As we discuss in chapter 7, we believe this argument is misguided. The growth in the gap between leaders and laggards is mostly a result of the growing importance of intangibles, and it should be addressed not by arbitrary corporate breakups but rather by ensuring that barriers to market entry are low. More insidious and troubling is a different aspect of competition, specifically the growing competition between individuals—also driven by the growing importance of intangibles—that results in greater investment in gratuitous signalling qualifications such as unnecessary graduate degrees and superfluous professional licencing. Discouraging this type of zero-sum competition among individuals is not something that most governments worry about, but it ought to become a political priority.

Two common themes underpin these institutional problems and point to solutions. The first theme is the importance of building capacity in our governments and the organisations that support our institutions, particularly in the functions that relate to intangible investment. In some cases, this is a matter of spending more money on things that have not traditionally been government priorities, such as R&D. But more often it is about investing in the ability to exercise good judgment and to get things done. Functional intellectual property regimes, effective funding of scientific research or education, and deep and liquid capital markets for intangible-intensive businesses all require specific competencies. These competencies are scarce, especially within government, where they have often been hollowed out in the name of efficiency or austerity. Patent examiners, court administrators, and research funding officers are perhaps among the least glamorous public servants, and their jobs are the first to go when politicians vow to cut bureaucracy and management. But building these particular forms of state and institutional capacity is especially important for building a thriving intangible economy.

The second theme is the idea that if we want to fix institutions, we need to identify and strike political bargains. Our institutions are inadequate not because we don't have enough smart ideas but rather because the status quo suits plenty of people, and change is politically and socially costly. Homeowners do not want more housing built, and they like rules that allow them to block it; IP regimes benefit rights holders, who lobby to extend and strengthen their rights. Improving these institutions requires more than efficient technocracy. It requires deals to make the new institutions work. For example, street-level zoning (discussed in chapter 6) provides homeowners with incentives to support new housing, and increased political capital can help politicians justify increased public spending on elite projects such as scientific research.

These requirements may seem like a tall order, politically. Rebuilding state capacity is a tough electoral sell, and doing the deals necessary to make the new institutions stick requires creativity, cunning, and willingness to challenge vested interests. They necessitate a mind-set of practical optimism, a belief that things can actually get better. But unlike other explanations for the Great Economic Disappointment, the story we are telling and the solutions we are proposing are grounds for optimism.

If the big economic problem that we face were, as some commentators suggest, a general moral decadence or an inexorable, exogenous change in the productivity of new technologies, fixing it would be a great imponderable. But if our problem is that we have failed to update and improve our institutions to keep up with the changing structure of the economy, then there is a solution, even if it is difficult to implement. Institutional renewal has happened before, and it can happen again. If we are successful in its implementation, we can increase growth and prosperity, tackle ecological threats from pandemics to global warming, and find a way out of the unhappy halfway house in which the economy has been stuck for nearly two decades.

PART I

What's Gone Wrong, and Why?

1

The Great Economic Disappointment

Since the early years of the twenty-first century, developed economies have been wrestling with a host of big problems: stagnation, inequality, fragility, dysfunctional competition, and a general sense of what we might call inauthenticity. In this chapter we describe these problems and some of the standard narratives used to explain them. These narratives are characterised by nostalgia, fatalism, or both. We offer an alternative explanation: that the problems should be seen as the result of the difficult transition of advanced economies from a reliance on tangible assets to a reliance on intangible assets.

Right now it is hard to view the modern economy other than through the prism of the COVID-19 pandemic and its aftermath. So much is wrong and different that the world's problems before COVID-19 seem like a sepia photo of a vanished world.

But cast your mind back to 2019 and you will recall that even then there was a widespread feeling that something was wrong in advanced economies. This worry was ubiquitous and multi-faceted. From the keynotes of Davos to the rallies of populist politicians, it formed a sort of wallpaper for how we talked about modern life. It expressed itself in the big-picture stories we tell about our national economies (Why is economic growth so low? Why don't we *make* anything anymore?) and the way we think about our personal lives (Why is working life ever more stressful? Why does my job involve so much bullshit?). It united unimpeachably mainstream economists debating secular stagnation and market concentration with critical voices asking whether capitalism is destroying our planet and creating an unbridgeable gulf between rich and poor. When people talked about the economy, they did so with a sense of disappointment, as if we lived in an age of lead.

Faced with the challenges of recovery from a global health crisis, these concerns may seem quaint and dated. Who cares about secular stagnation when output has fallen by 25 percent? Who cares about the structure of the economy when the immediate challenge is to protect public health and consumer and investor confidence? But we must continue to care because these long-term concerns have not gone away. They have a common cause that is grounded in long-run changes occurring in our economy. Our ability to understand and respond will determine our ability to rebuild our economy. Like a lightning storm on a dark night, the COVID-19 crisis helps illuminates some of the long-standing problems we face, making hidden issues clear. It also provides an opportunity to put them right. Furthermore, COVID-19 illustrates the vital necessity of getting right the long-run features of the economy. Just as innovation in World War II built on the stock of basic research before the war, such as radar, COVID-19 vaccines are based on past discoveries, such as Katalin Kariko's research into synthetic messenger RNA.[1] And, of course, paying down the debt buildup created by COVID-19 will require faster economic growth.

Five Symptoms of the Great Economic Disappointment

Sometimes the most familiar and ubiquitous phenomena are unexpectedly difficult to recognise and describe. We must ask the same questions that a doctor treating a patient with many symptoms asks: Which symptoms are linked? Which ones should we disregard as extraneous? Our first task, then, is to itemise the long-run concerns about the twenty-first-century economy.

As noted in the introduction, we propose that people are concerned with five negative characteristics of the twenty-first-century economy: *stagnation*, *inequality*, *dysfunctional competition*, *fragility*, and *inauthenticity*. We'll explain each of these in turn.

Stagnation

The dramatic fall in output following the COVID-19 outbreak in 2020 is the most dramatic shock to economic growth in living memory. But the rich world was hardly in good economic health beforehand.

Figure 1.1 shows what output per capita would have been if growth had continued at its trend from the start of the century to the financial crisis: advanced economies would have been 20 to 30 percent richer.

The disappointment is all the more acute if we look over a longer period. For most of the second half of the twentieth century, developed countries could rely on average real GDP growth of over 2 percent a year. The turn of the century saw a drastic 50 percent reduction in economic growth. Between 2000 and 2016, growth in real GDP per capita in the United States was around 1 percent per year (see table 1.1 later in the chapter). If we focus on the period of the global financial crisis

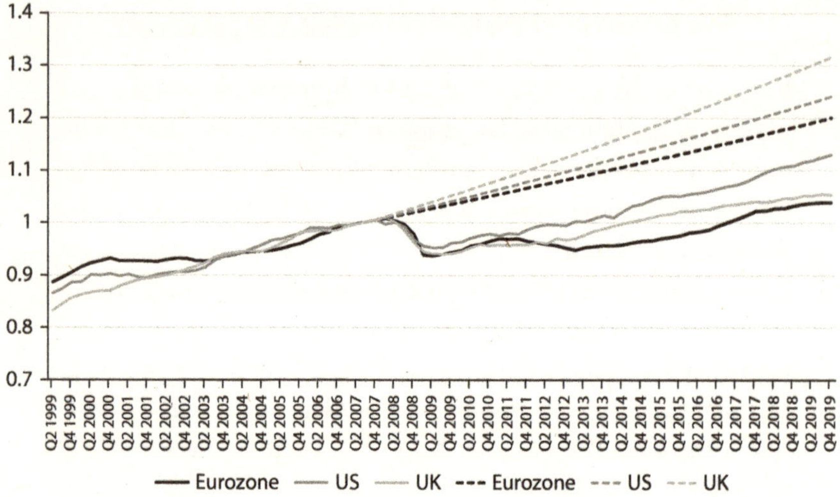

FIGURE 1.1: Output per Capita Relative to Prefinancial Crisis Trends. *Source*: Authors' calculations using Organisation for Economic Co-operation and Development data.

and afterwards, the figures are even worse, with growth from 2006 to 2016 at a feeble 0.6 percent per year. European countries experienced similarly low levels of growth. Towards the end of 2019, the United Kingdom's Royal Statistical Society selected low productivity growth as its statistic of the decade.

Low growth is so familiar to us now that even before COVID-19, experts took it for granted. But it would have been truly shocking to observers as recently as twenty or thirty years ago. One vivid way to get a feel for how disappointing current levels of growth are is to look at long-range economic forecasts prepared in the early years of this century and earlier. The last report of the US Congressional Budget Office before the start of the global financial crisis predicted growth of 2.5 percent per year in the mid-2010s.[2] Most other central banks seem to have assumed the same.

A decade earlier, pundits seem to have been even more optimistic. A detailed survey by the Organisation for Economic Co-operation and Development (OECD) from 1992 set out several scenarios for US economic growth in the 2010s. Its two business-as-usual forecasts predicted the American economy would grow between 3.1 percent and 3.4 percent per year. Even its gloomiest case (called, with some prescience, "Global Crisis") predicted growth of 2.3 percent per year. Peter Schwartz, the father of scenario planning, provided an even more optimistic perspective in a widely read piece in *Wired* magazine in 1997, predicting the US economy would grow at 4 percent per year until 2020.[3] Paul Krugman's explicitly downbeat book *The Age of Diminished Expectations*, reprinted several times in the 1990s, was overoptimistic too, presenting a base-case forecast that the US economy would grow at just over 2 percent a year in the coming decades.[4] Even Keynes would have been disappointed. In 1930, when he wrote "Economic Possibilities for Our Grandchildren," he estimated that GDP would grow eightfold between 1930 and 2030.[5] Based on growth to date, even excluding the effect of the COVID-19 pandemic, the UK and US economies have managed to grow by a factor of 5 and 6.4, respectively.

But the problem with economic growth is not just that it has slowed down. It has slowed down in a way that has defied many standard economic explanations. The weak growth of the early twenty-first century coexisted with low interest rates and, until the COVID-19 crisis, high corporate valuations. Economists call this phenomenon *secular stagnation*. We can see those high valuations in figure 1.2: Tobin's Q (a measure of how optimistic investors are about future corporate profits) is not quite at the dizzying heights of the dot-com boom, but it is way above its 1980s lows.

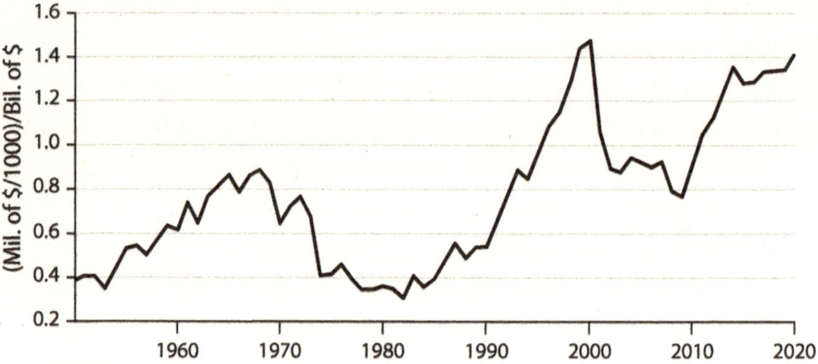

FIGURE 1.2: Tobin's Q in the United States. *Source*: Federal Reserve Economic Data.

This state of affairs is surprising. Normally, high corporate profits are a sign that businesses are reaping good returns from their investments. If money is cheap, then we would expect businesses to raise funds and invest more in the opportunities available to them, which would cause economic growth to recover. But interest rates have been low for over a decade, and growth remains low. What's more, this slow growth is happening during a period of widespread belief that a lot of exciting technological progress is being made. If this is true (a question we consider in more detail in chapter 4), then slow economic growth is the last thing we would expect.

Inequality

It is not just the size of the economic pie that is causing concern; it is how it is divided. Since the turn of the century, and especially since the financial crisis, there has been a growing concern about the gap between the richest and the rest. Wilkinson and Pickett's best-selling book *The Spirit Level* argues that inequality leads to crime, poor health, and unhappiness not just among the poor but also across society.[6] In 2011, the Occupy

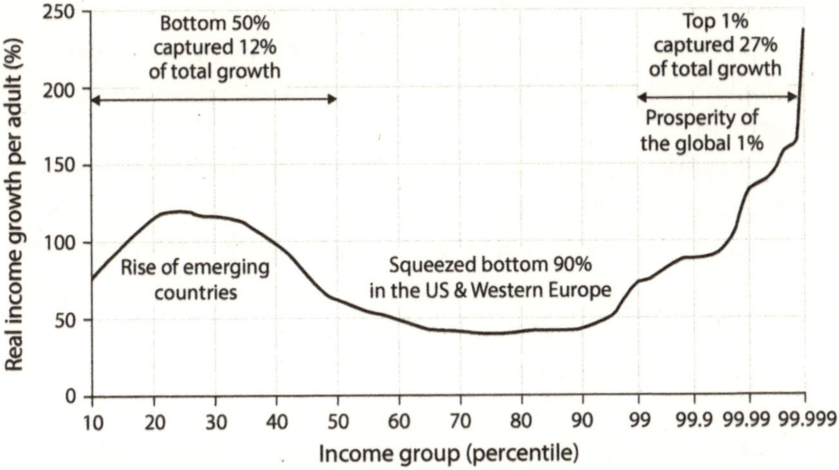

FIGURE 1.3: Growth by Income Group in the World, 1980–2016. *Source*: Figure E4 in Alvardero et al. (2020).

movement popularised the meme of "The 99%," highlighting the dichotomy between a rich elite and the population as a whole. And Thomas Piketty's *Capital in the Twenty-First Century* brought decades of empirical work on wealth inequality to bear on the public debate.[7]

We observe the material inequality in rich countries both in people's wealth and in their income. Compared with forty years ago, the richest in society are further ahead than the poorest in terms of both how much they *own* and how much they *earn*. Much of this increase seems to have happened in the 1980s and 1990s, after some measures of inequality seemed to have continued to rise while others seem to have plateaued.

Figure 1.3 gives a sense of these numbers. It shows, for the world, the rise in income per adult from the poorest to the richest in the period from 1980 to 2016. On the left side of the figure, we see that the rise of emerging countries has grown incomes for those at the bottom of the world distribution. But this increase is outweighed by the growth at the top, where the top 1 percent has captured 27 percent of total growth (while the bottom 50 percent has captured only 12 percent of total growth).

Like the failure of economic growth, the rise of inequality was not something that the future-gazers of the twentieth century predicted. Looking back at grand narratives of the future written a quarter of a century ago, we find great concern about the very poor and about social exclusion, but not about the super-rich or about the liberal elite. In Hamish McRae's best-selling *The World in 2020*, the author sees that social disruption, including crime, drug use, and family breakup, "primarily affect the poorer socio-economic groups" as a threat to the United States in 2020, but he has nothing to say about the gap between the elite and the masses that dominates the narrative today.[8]

Modern-day inequality is not just an economic phenomenon. In the 2000s and 2010s, the familiar material sorts of inequality were joined by an increase in *inequality of status* between liberal, educated, urban elites and so-called left-behind inhabitants of less favoured places, from postindustrial towns in the United Kingdom to the US Rust Belt. This aspect of contemporary inequality is about something other than money. It involves differences in openness, in education, in rootedness, and in respect. It has a strong geographical component, and it is sometimes orthogonal to economic inequality. Plenty of underpaid, indebted college graduates might find themselves described as liberal elites, while the left-behinds include comfortable retirees with homes and pensions.

Economist Enrico Moretti called the geographical dimension of this divide the "great divergence," presenting evidence on the differences between prosperous and left-behind US cities on everything from graduate rates and graduate salaries to divorce and mortality rates.[9] Will Jennings and Gerry Stoker, two British political scientists, observed a divide emerging in the early 2010s between what they called "the Two Englands"—one cosmopolitan and outward-facing, the other illiberal and nationalistic.[10] A similar divide in the United States became the dominant political fact of the late 2010s, delivering the votes that put Donald Trump in the White House, removed the United Kingdom from the European Union, and launched the careers of populist politicians around the world.

This type of inequality may well be a matter of life and death. Anne Case and Angus Deaton link it to the epidemic of "deaths of despair," the wave of deaths from suicide, opioid overdose, and alcoholism among middle-aged white Americans that began in the late 1990s and has continued to grow.[11] This epidemic and other manifestations of status anxiety have continued to grow even as inequality of income and wealth has remained stable.

Dysfunctional Competition

The next element of the twenty-first-century economic malaise relates to the competitive forces that make markets work. A host of important measures that economists use to gauge the health of markets have been behaving in strange ways for a long time.

First, the gap between the most successful businesses and the rest seems to be growing inexorably. In sector after sector and country after country, the gap between the most profitable, productive businesses and the rest has grown dramatically over the past few decades, as shown in figure 1.4. The fact that the information and communication technology (ICT) services firms gap has risen may not be surprising, but the gap is pervasive in other industries, too.

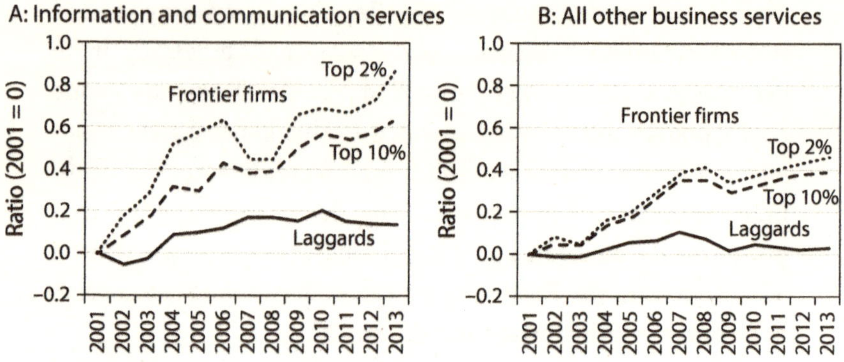

FIGURE 1.4: Performance Gaps. *Note*: In panels A and B, the global frontier group of firms is defined by the top 5 percent of companies with the highest total factor productivity levels within each two-digit industry, while all the other firms are identified as laggards. *Source*: Andrews, Criscuolo, and Gal 2016.

At the same time, the tendency for unproductive firms to shrink and productive ones to grow—the phenomenon that economists call *business dynamism*—has gone through what Ryan Decker and colleagues call "pervasive decline" since 2000.[12] Research also shows that fewer new businesses are being set up, with a significant reduction in high-growth entrepreneurship.

In addition, in recent years economists have documented an increase in the markup between prices and marginal costs that firms appear to be earning (figure 1.5).[13] This work is nicely summarised in an excellent book, *The Great Reversal*, by the economist Thomas Philippon.[14]

At the level of individual workers, the data show signs of declining dynamism. Contrary to popular myths about job-hopping millennials, younger workers change employers significantly less frequently than previous generations did. They are also less likely to move from one city to another for work. Economist Tyler Cowen describes these tendencies as

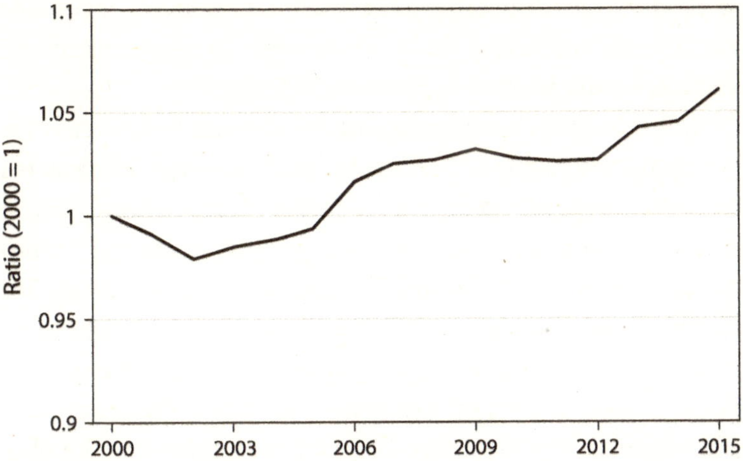

FIGURE 1.5: Average Global Markup, 2000–2015. *Source*: Diez, Fan, and Villegas-Sanchez 2019.

symptoms of an emerging "complacent class" that is "working harder than ever to postpone change."[15]

But there's something incongruous here. If you present the average worker or manager with evidence that markets are becoming less competitive and workers more complacent, they will respond with something ranging from surprise to disbelief. For all that business competition and dynamism appear to be declining, the business environment in which most firms find themselves did not feel complacent even before the COVID-19 pandemic threw the business world into turmoil. Firms do not feel particularly "fat, dumb, and happy," to use US commerce secretary Malcolm Baldrige's forthright description of American companies in 1981.[16]

Nor do workers feel particularly happy with their jobs or working conditions. The intensity and unforgiving performance management of low-paid jobs such as those in Amazon warehouses are a regular source of stories for investigative journalists. Conditional benefits systems designed to encourage the jobless to rejoin the labour force mean that even unemployment is harder work than it was decades ago.

It is not clear that working life has become less intense for well-paid and highly skilled workers either. Daniel Markovits's *The Meritocracy Trap* documents how "frenzied competition now dominates top jobs," contrasting it with the sleepy corporate world of the 1950s and William Whyte's 1956 book *The Organization Man*, in which Whyte noted that the chief executive did not have to be "ruthless or compulsively driven to succeed."[17] Top executives' struggles begin not at the office door but rather in kindergarten, as aspiring members of the elite jump through a never-ending series of hoops to prepare themselves for highly competitive jobs in a high-class cake-eating contest where the prize is more cake. Similarly, the economist Peter Kuhn has documented that although working hours for US males are falling on average, they are rising for top earners and bottom earners.[18]

Fragility

The COVID-19 pandemic dramatically demonstrated that even the richest economies are not immune to natural forces. Indeed, the damage caused by the pandemic is linked to the complexity and sophistication of the economy. Our large, dense cities, our complex international supply chains, and the unprecedented interconnectedness of the global economy allowed the virus to leap from country to country.

To a certain extent, such interconnected fragility is a natural consequence of specialisation in a global economy. Another dimension of this fragility is the sense that there is little that governments can do to offset some of the shocks that we face.

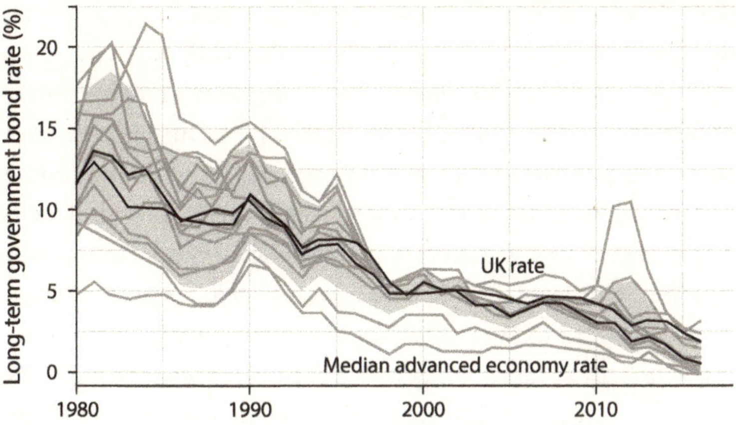

FIGURE 1.6: Interest Rates since 1980, Advanced Countries. Gray area shows ninetieth to tenth percentile across seventeen advanced economies. Data from Jorda, Schularick, and Taylor (2017), quoted in https://bankunderground.co.uk/2020/06/03/theres-more-to-house-prices-than-interest-rates/.

European economies in general have relied on the state to cushion the blows from economic shocks, or, more prosaically, to provide social insurance to their citizens. Some of that insurance comes from the welfare state and so is fiscal. But, importantly, some of that insurance comes from monetary policy. In previous times, central banks could stabilise the economy by cutting interest rates in the face of adverse shocks, thereby reigniting economic activity and restoring growth. But, as figure 1.6 shows, interest rates have been declining for nearly forty years. With interest rates very close to zero, there seems to be a limit on how much cushion central banks can provide.

Economists Jason Furman and Lawrence Summers emphasise this lack of policy space. As mentioned in the introduction to this book, they calculate that in the nine US recessions leading up to the COVID-19 pandemic, the Federal Reserve cut interest rates by an average of 6.3 percentage points.[19] We have done a similar calculation for the United Kingdom. Over the four recessions before COVID-19, the bank rate was cut on average 5.5 percentage points—for example, from 17 percent to 12 percent between July 1980 and March 1981. During loosening, there was an average cut of 0.5 percentage points per month for eleven months. As of this writing, the UK Bank Rate is 0.1 percent, which means that current UK rates have one week's worth of cuts available (before they hit zero).

In addition, COVID-19 is not the only example of the modern economy's vulnerability to big natural forces. The fairy-tale magic at the heart of industrial society is abundant energy. Keeping the lights of civilisation burning requires over one hundred thousand terawatt-hours of energy a year, and by the greatest stroke of luck, we live in the vanishingly small sliver of human existence to date in which we have been able to generate this amount of energy. But all good fairy tales have a curse, and our tale's curse is this: generating about 80 percent of this energy involves creating invisible and superficially harmless pollution that over time is causing cataclysmic damage to the planet.

Not only is the reality of climate change depressing, but so is our apparent inability to tackle it. Low-carbon energy technologies exist, and their price has fallen rapidly in recent years. Vast numbers of the world's smartest people dedicate their careers to fixing the problem. The economics of how to reduce carbon emissions is to a great extent a solved problem. Most governments have long-standing policies for reducing carbon emissions and mitigating the effects of climate change. In short, reducing carbon emissions is a *hard* problem, but compared with the problem of increasing economic growth, it does not seem like a *mysterious* one. And yet, despite widespread awareness of the problem and considerable political energy, the transition to a low-carbon economy seems to be happening far too slowly.

Whether the shock is an acute, unexpected one like COVID-19 or a slow-motion one like climate change, there is a widespread belief that today's rich economies are unusually vulnerable to disruption and somehow unable to take steps to prevent the problem.

Inauthenticity

The final disappointing feature of the twenty-first-century economy is what we might call its *fakeness*. Although we do not often hear this critique from economists, it is widely cited by laypeople and by commentators in other academic disciplines who seem to share a belief that what goes on in today's economy lacks the "realness" and authenticity that it should have and that it once had. The idea that the modern economy is unsatisfyingly fake is a recurrent theme in conservative critiques of modernity. We see it in investor Peter Thiel's lament that "we wanted flying cars, instead we got 140 characters." Commentators make clear their belief that a lot of modern economic activity is somehow fake, inauthentic, or even fraudulent.

This discontent became acute during the COVID-19 pandemic, when many Western countries found themselves short of ventilators and personal protective equipment and without the wherewithal to make them rapidly. How, many people asked, had rich economies lost the ability to make these important things?

These feelings of fakeness and inauthenticity are compounded by the online experience we mentioned above. Although the internet can be a treasure trove of free information, it also seems to be plagued by charlatans, misleaders, and hucksters. A 2019 study documented that "Ryan's World" was the sixth-most-watched YouTube channel for children, with more than nineteen million viewers. On it, the seven-year-old vlogger Ryan Kaji reviews children's toys and games. He reportedly received $22 million in 2018 in payments.[20]

To recap: the economies of the developed world in the early twenty-first century have five problems. First, growth has been slow for two decades, even though money is cheap, businesses have done well for most of the period, and technologies seem abundant. Second, the material gap between the rich and the poor has increased, and it is accompanied by hardening forms of social and cultural division. Third, there is a perceived lack of competition, although people's working lives seem to be dominated by a paradoxical mixture of enervating, productivity-sapping sluggishness among firms and a febrile, exhausting competition in our lived experience. Fourth, the economy seems fragile and vulnerable. Our ability to rely on monetary policy to support the economy likewise seems to be ebbing away. We are dependent on unsustainable fossil fuel consumption, and although we have a fairly clear idea of the remedies, making sweeping changes is proving very hard. Fifth, there is widespread sentiment that much of what goes on in our economy is inauthentic and unreliable.

The Golden Age and the Great Divide: Two Stories about the Great Economic Disappointment

Faced with this unsettling combination of economic events, commentators and academics have come up with a variety of explanations.

In a recent book, Nobel Laureate Robert Shiller makes a powerful case for the importance of *narratives* in economics.[21] Ed Leamer has written similarly, as have Yuval Noah Harari and John Kay and Mervyn King.[22] Humans cleave to narratives,

Shiller argues, to understand and describe how the economy works. These narratives tend to be archetypal; there are a few recurrent stories to which we are naturally drawn, and which we seek to recognise, just as our eyes recognise a man's face in the shadows and craters of the moon. And, for Shiller, these stories have economic power. They don't just help people describe the world; they also drive human behaviour.

Indeed, when economic pundits talk about the current state of the economy in developed countries, a lot of familiar narrative elements crop up, particularly two archetypal stories. Let's call them the Lost Golden Age and the Great Divide.

The Lost Golden Age

The first popular explanation holds that we are living in an era that is somehow deficient compared with the past. This conclusion emerges fairly clearly from the data: productivity growth has been significantly lower since the financial crisis, and perhaps before. But it also taps into the much older human story of a *Lost Golden Age* when ease and prosperity reigned, and which has given way through bad luck or bad conduct to a modern age of toil and scarcity. Once the gods favoured us, but their favour has now been withdrawn, and we find it difficult to restore the golden age of prosperity.

Some economic explanations for the current productivity downturn pin the blame on exogenous events. The influential narratives of growth slowdown by Tyler Cowen (*The Great Stagnation*) and Robert Gordon (*The Rise and Fall of American Growth*) fit into this time-honoured tradition.[23] Both argue that a range of headwinds meant that growth, both from technological progress and from human factors such as improvements in education, had slowed down; Gordon in particular remains

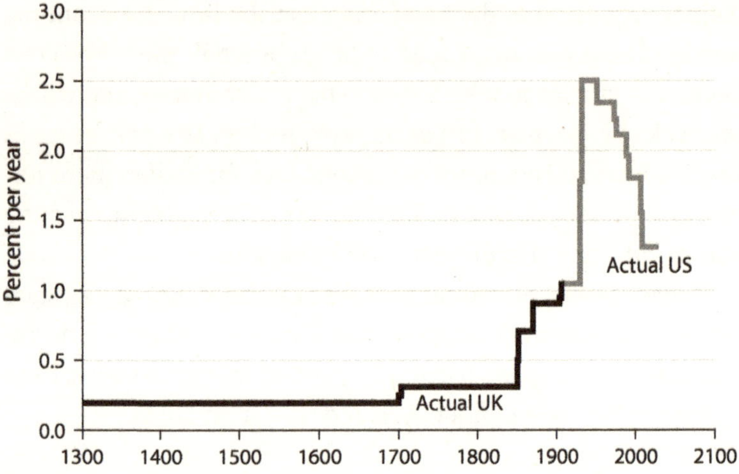

FIGURE 1.7: Growth in the Frontier Economies since 1300. *Source*: Gordon 2012.

pessimistic that it will speed up again in the future. Gordon dramatically illustrated the long-term trends in economic growth in figure 1.7, which shows growth in the frontier economies (the United Kingdom and United States) since 1300. The twentieth century, in Gordon's telling, was an economic golden age. Times have changed, and we must accept it.

The excellent book *Fully Grown*, by economic growth expert Dietrich Vollrath, makes the case in great detail that economic growth has taken a permanent downwards step.[24] According to Vollrath, the immediate contributors to growth are the increases in the physical and human capital that workers have to work with. For example, farmers can raise yields if they work with more tractors (physical capital) and better-educated and better-trained workers (human capital). Concentrating on the United States, Vollrath points to a very substantial expansion of secondary education in the latter half of the twentieth century. In 1940, 60 percent of the age twenty-five-plus population had completed elementary school but had no further education, and less than 10 percent had completed college. By 2010, only 5 percent had completed only elementary school, but 33 percent had completed college. Thus, over a period of seven decades US workers became more educated. This increased human capital contributed substantially to US economic growth. GDP per capita grew 2.3 percent per year from 1950 to 2000, and multiplying the rise in human capital by its economic return (how much more productive workers become with education) contributes another 0.6 percent per year.

By 2000, however, this effect had run its course. Once everyone is educated up to the age of sixteen or eighteen, the possibility of stimulating incremental growth by sending more people to school is reduced. Specifically, the contribution of increased human capital to growth between the years 2000 and 2016 was −0.10 percent. Indeed, Vollrath shows that the fall in productivity growth after 2000 is largely explained by the decrease in human capital's contribution to growth. Vollrath advises us to be philosophical about today's lower rate of growth, arguing that it is in many respects the result of choices that we want to make in a rich society, from having fewer children to moving around less for work. But like Gordon, he suggests it is foolish to waste political energy trying to return to the growth rates of the past.

An alternative version of the Lost Golden Age story agrees that we live in an age of sluggish growth, but it claims we can be reasonably confident that growth will return—perhaps even faster than before. We may not live in the postwar golden age, but we can hope for a new economic dawn in the future, ushered in by new technology. Erik Brynjolfsson and Andrew McAfee's *The Second Machine Age* holds that we are living in an age in which growth is low because new technologies are bedding in.[25] Our economic fields look bare, but wait a bit and a bumper harvest will come in, delivered by rapidly increasing computing power and its application to every domain of human endeavour. According to this *retooling hypothesis*, a period of slow growth reflects businesses and workers gearing up to make use of radically different new technologies.

But this narrative raises several questions: Why does productivity growth *fall* as we wait? Why doesn't productivity growth remain unchanged until the new wave boosts it again? The answer lies in how we measure productivity. Think of the driverless car. Very large amounts of money have been spent on the software, hardware, and testing of driverless cars. But at the time of this writing, driverless cars are not in common use. Now consider the measurement of productivity, which is defined as output per unit of input. In developing driverless cars we have greatly increased our inputs, but we have not yet reaped the benefits of the output. According to the *mismeasurement hypothesis*, this phenomenon is fairly widespread. Perhaps in many industries, such as health care and education, there has been a large amount of repurposing of the inputs without the output to show for it. This mismatch may explain why there seems to be so many technological opportunities today but so little productivity.

The Great Divide

The second ancient narrative we see recurring in modern discussions of the economy is the idea of a *Great Divide* between a prosperous, well-connected elite and the left-behind masses. The misdeeds and moral failings of the elite are the reason for the state we find ourselves in.

Like the Lost Golden Age story, the Great Divide story can be supported by the data. We have seen that inequality of wealth and income has been high for many years, and that the gulf in prosperity between richer and poorer places in the developed world is higher than ever. But this narrative is more than just a simple reflection of current data. Rather, the idea of a nefarious elite whose prosperity is wrapped up in, and perhaps dependent on, the economic impoverishment of the virtuous poor is a narrative with a long and chequered life of its own.

In some explanations of the Great Economic Disappointment, these two archetypal narratives have converged. A greedy, well-connected minority has changed the rules of the game to benefit itself at the expense of society at large, simultaneously breaking the mechanism on which we relied for steady economic growth. This explanation, which is widely held among radical Right parties, is sometimes associated with conspiracy theories and racism. But this is not just a populist talking point; various forms of it exist across the Left, from Marxist economist David Harvey's *A Brief History of Neoliberalism* to Will Hutton's *The State We're In*, both of which argue that self-serving elites took capitalism down a blind alley from the 1980s onwards with an agenda of deregulation, privatisation, and tax cuts.[26] Stephen Cohen and Brad De Long's *Concrete Economics* argues that these choices undermined productivity growth in rich countries while making the rich richer.[27]

A popular version of the Great Divide story focuses on big businesses lobbying to protect themselves from competition. Thomas Philippon's influential book *The Great Reversal* argues that large American businesses have used political influence and lobbying to chip away at antitrust law, protecting themselves from competition and reaping monopoly profits at the expense of customers, workers, and society at large.[28] For many critics, this explains both the growth of vast businesses with few strong competitors (Google in search engines, Amazon in online retail) and the decline in productivity: Why innovate when you have no credible competition? Other critics point to the legal monopolies granted by patents, copyrights, and other intellectual property rights; when patent trolls acquire old patents for the sole purpose of suing legitimate businesses, or when media companies seek to have the copyrights of profitable franchises extended on a technicality, it is hard not to think that bad behaviour on the part of the powerful is holding the economy back.

The narratives human beings are drawn to are powerful, but they are also dangerous, in that they may oversimplify or misrepresent what is really going on and contain really bad advice. In addition, historians sometimes describe certain concepts, such as "feudalism" and "revolution," as *overschematised* when they are not equal to the conceptual burden placed on them. As a result, we overgeneralise and jump to the wrong conclusions. Perhaps something similar is going on today. The lure of the narratives of the Lost Golden Age and the Great Divide is so strong that they miss important aspects of what is really going on. We explore those aspects next.

The Conventional Explanations: Some Doubts

There is no *one* cause of slow growth. For this reason, the explanations we set out above are unlikely to tell the whole story.

Technology: Is Growth Over?

The fall in productivity over the very long term, as documented by Robert Gordon, is compelling (see again figure 1.7). That said, the economist Dan Sichel has reminded us that neither economists nor technologists are very good at predicting the future.[29] Part of the difficulty is knowing to what purpose technology might be put. Joel Mokyr has advanced the view that perhaps the growth impact of ICT on health via personalised medicine, gene therapy, and other technologies is yet to play out because these areas have so much promise but are very hard to apply new technology to.[30] Technology has not yet lost its ability to surprise us for the better: early in 2020 many wondered if a COVID-19 vaccine would be years off. As it happened, not only were several safe, effective vaccines developed within a matter of months, but progress was made towards generalisable coronavirus vaccines, and an apparently effective malaria vaccine emerged, too.

Education: Is Growth Over?

A second explanation for the productivity growth slowdown is the contribution of education. Some details of Vollrath's calculation are worth discussing. As he explains, we can account for growth in output per capita by growth in inputs per capita. Table 1.1 summarises the relevant data. The US data for 1950–2000 show that US output per capita grew by 2.3 percent per year over that period. The growth in physical capital per capita contributed 0.6 percent per year, and the growth in average skill levels per capita contributed 0.5 percent per year. Everything else, labelled total factor productivity (TFP), which we can think of as the efficiency with which physical capital and human capital are used, contributed 1.1 percent per year. As the row shows, each of these factors made a fairly equal contribution. The final column shows that the growth in human capital or skill per capita was a healthy 0.8 percent over this period, reflecting the expansion in higher education in the United States.

The last row, which sets out the US data for the years 2000–2016, presents a very different picture. There is a considerable

TABLE 1.1
Sources of per Capita Growth in the Euro Area, the United Kingdom, and the United States

			Contribution			Memo
Country	Period	GDP per capita (%)	Cap services per capita (%)	Human cap per capita (%)	TFP (%)	Human cap per capita (%)
Euro area	1950–2000	3.3	1.3	0.0	2.0	0.0
Euro area	2000–2016	0.7	0.5	0.2	0.0	0.4
United Kingdom	1950–2000	2.4	1.1	0.2	1.1	0.3
United Kingdom	2000–2016	1.1	0.4	0.0	0.6	0.1
United States	1950–2000	2.3	0.6	0.5	1.1	0.8
United States	2000–2016	1.0	0.5	−0.1	0.6	−0.2

Source: Authors' calculations based on EU KLEMS and the data in Bergeaud, Cette, and Lecat (2015).

slowdown of growth in GDP per capita from 2.3 percent to 1 percent. The contribution of capital services per capita remained basically unchanged, and there is a large fall in the contribution of human capital per capita, along with an additional fall in TFP. As Vollrath notes, and as the final column shows, the decrease in human capital per capita growth was quite considerable, from 0.8 percent in 1950–2000 to −0.2 percent in 2000–2016. These data are the source of Vollrath's claim that the major explanation for the US productivity slowdown is simply that the United States has run out of years of education.[31]

Vollrath's book sets out the data for the United States. We have gathered data for the United Kingdom and the euro area, also shown in table 1.1. As the final column shows, the situation in the euro area and the United Kingdom is different. The growth in skills in the euro area did not slow down. Rather, it sped up over time, increasing from 0 percent in 1950–2000 to 0.4 percent in 2000–2016. As for the United Kingdom, the skills growth rate did fall over the same period, from 0.3 percent per year to 0.1 percent per year, but nowhere near as dramatically as the growth rate of the United States. So while the slowdown in education is important in the United States, if we are to understand what is happening in Europe, we need to look elsewhere, because skills in the euro area sped up.

Evaluating the Retooling Hypothesis

There is some evidence to support the retooling hypothesis, the idea that we might be in a necessary period of low growth while we work out how to make the most of radical new technologies. David Byrne, Carol Corrado, and Dan Sichel document that firms providing cloud computing services have been making massive investments in hardware but that official data may have missed these investments because many of these purchases are conducted internally, whereas official investment surveys mostly ask respondents to report on external purchases.[32] Such omitted cloud computing investment results are sufficient to add 0.1 percentage points to GDP growth between 2007 and 2015. That said, measurement problems existed before the financial crisis as well as after, leading Byrne and Sichel to argue that adjusting for IT prices raises productivity in the IT-intensive sector but slows it even more in the IT-extensive sector.[33]

In addition, the retooling hypothesis requires a very substantial level of unmeasured intangible investment to explain the orders of magnitude of the decreases in TFP growth. Recent work by Carol Corrado, Jonathan Haskel, and Cecilia Jona-Lasinio[34] suggests that the unmeasured intangible investment would have to be orders of magnitude more than measured, which seems unlikely.

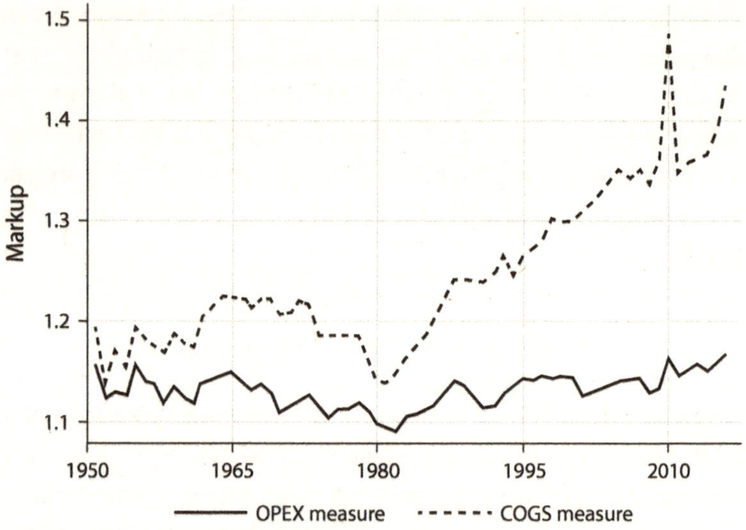

FIGURE 1.8: Estimated Markups Excluding Cost of Goods Sold (United States, Firms in Compustat). *Source*: Traina 2018.

Evaluating the Markups Hypothesis

A number of economists have strongly contested the assertion that markups have been increasing. Figure 1.8, reprinted from the work of University of Chicago economist James Traina,[35] shows that the conclusions about markups crucially depend on how one defines the variable costs that firms use as a basis for marking up prices. The rising line shows estimated price markups over cost of goods sold (COGS), whereas the flat line shows markups over COGS plus sales and general administration (SGA) costs. If SGA costs are capturing intangible spending by firms, then rising markups result from inadequate measurement of incurred costs rather than reveal a true economic tendency. Similarly, Chad Syverson has noted that if there has been a widespread increase in markups, it should have led to a widespread increase in inflation, other things being equal.[36] However, inflation has been incredibly low over the past decade.

A Different Explanation: Intangibles

Our explanation is different. We believe that the world is in the midst of an incomplete, faltering transition from one type of economy to another. This emerging economy is only superficially based on technology, the internet, big data, or whatever is on the cover of *Wired* magazine this month. In fact, it relies on long-term changes in the nature of capital and their economic implications. Specifically, we believe that our current problems exist because

- the nature of capital has changed, with businesses investing ever more in (largely unmeasured) intangible assets;
- the growth of this intangible capital has slowed in the past decades; and
- we have not yet mitigated the challenges caused by intangibles. Nor have we overcome emerging barriers to investment.

We continue our discussion by documenting the shift to intangible investment and the slowdown in recent years.

The Shift to Intangible Investment: A Reprise

The last forty years have seen an important change in the economy: *the rise of the intangible economy*, as we described in our book *Capitalism without Capital*.[37] If you're familiar with the argument and data, you may want to skip this section; if not, here is a brief summary.

An important determinant of a society's prosperity is its *capital stock*: all the things in which people, businesses, and governments have invested over time with the goal of delivering an enduring benefit. If workers are the sinews of an economy, then capital represents the joints, ligaments, and fulcrums—the mechanisms through which the muscles act, which determine how effective they are. Since the 1980s, we have seen a steady shift in the world's capital stock. Once upon a time, firms invested mostly in physical capital: machines, buildings, vehicles, computers. Today, as society gets richer, most business investment goes to things you can't touch: research and development, branding, organisational development, and software.

Consider Apple. Its market capitalisation in 2018 was around $1 trillion. Its tangible assets, mostly buildings, cash, and other savings, were valued at only 9 percent of Apple's market value.[38] A large chunk of the rest of its value resides in *intangible assets*: things that were costly to acquire, last a long time, and are valuable to the company, but are not physical. Apple's intangible assets include the knowledge gained from R&D, the design of its products, its widely trusted brands, the valuable and durable relationships with its suppliers (including both its physical supply chain and the developers who support the Apple ecosystem), staffers' internal firm knowledge and relationships, the software in its operating system, and its vast data resources.

Over the decades, intangible investment has become more and more important to the economies of the world. A longstanding research programme to infer intangible investment from existing data and from new surveys, and to value it accurately, shows that it has been growing since at least the 1980s. And, as far as we can tell from more tentative US data, the buildup of intangible capital began several decades before that. By the time of the global financial crisis in 2007–8, countries

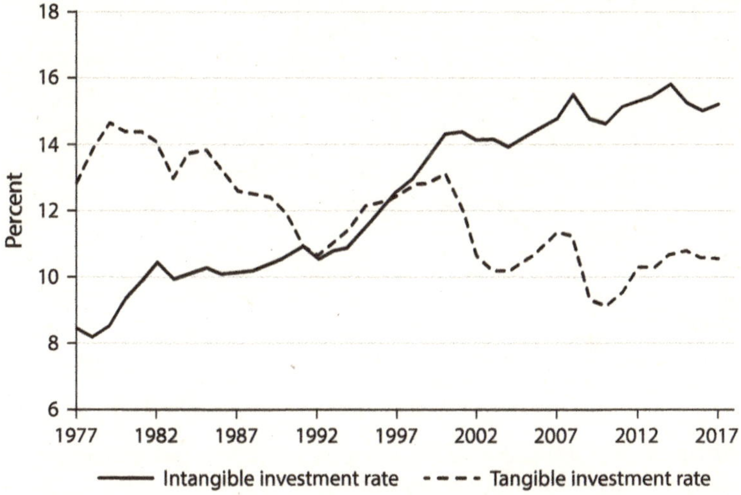

FIGURE 1.9: US Investment Rates, 1977–2017. *Source*: http://www.intaninvest.net/charts-and-tables/.

such as the United States and the United Kingdom were investing more each year in intangible assets than in tangibles ones, as shown in figure 1.9.

Figure 1.10 shows the shorter-run trends for the major developed economies. This steady increase in intangible capital is not just a rich-world phenomenon. The rapid growth of China's economy in recent decades also seems to have been accompanied by a big increase in intangible investment.

The Slowdown in Intangible Investment

This discussion brings us to an important but largely unrecognised twist in the emergence of the intangible economy. Although the time-series graphs in figures 1.10 and 1.11 show the general tendency for intangible investment to have grown, they do not reveal another important trend. Towards the end

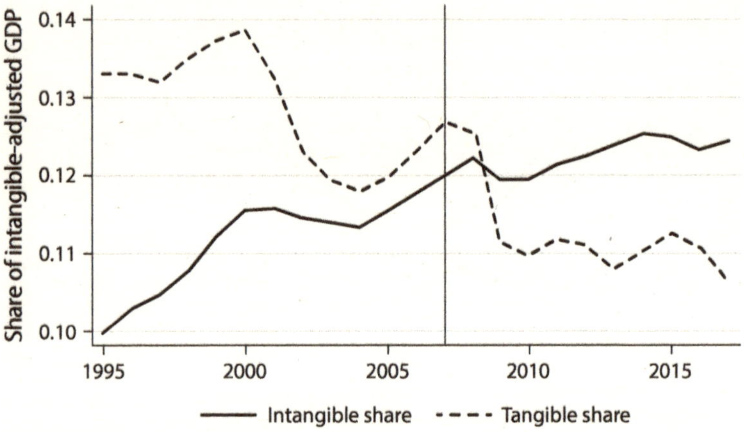

FIGURE 1.10: Tangible and Intangible Investment, Major Developed Economies. *Source*: Authors' calculations from www.intaninvest.net.

of the first decade of the twenty-first century, intangible investment as a share of GDP, which had been rising steadily for several decades, began to grow more slowly. It was initially unclear whether this slower growth was a short-lived effect of the global financial crisis, which clearly could have reduced business investment in many ways. Reliable investment data take a while to produce, so back in 2016, when we were writing *Capitalism without Capital*, it was hard to know whether this downturn was a glitch in the data, a temporary phenomenon, or something more serious.

As more recent data have emerged, it has become clear that the slowdown in intangible investment was no blip. Figure 1.11 shows the data to 2017 against a pre-2007 trend. The slowdown for Continental Europe and the United States is clear, with the United Kingdom a bit noisier. That reduced pace is also apparent when we convert investment into capital services. Figure 1.12 shows the decline in the growth of "intangible" capital

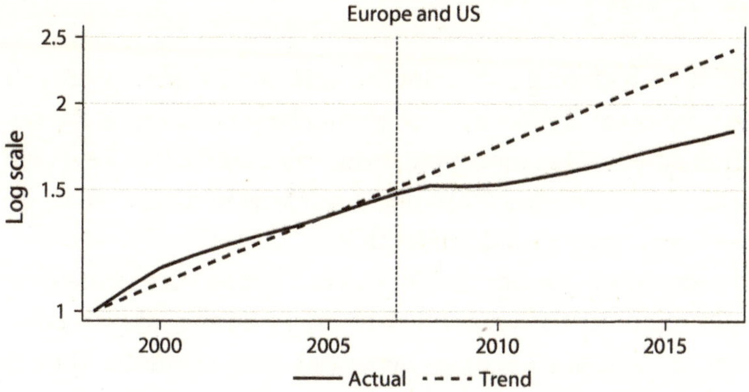

FIGURE 1.11: Intangible Investment: Actual Growth versus Trend Growth (Trend from 1997–2007). *Source*: Authors' calculations from www.intaninvest.net. Countries are Continental Europe, the United Kingdom, and the United States.

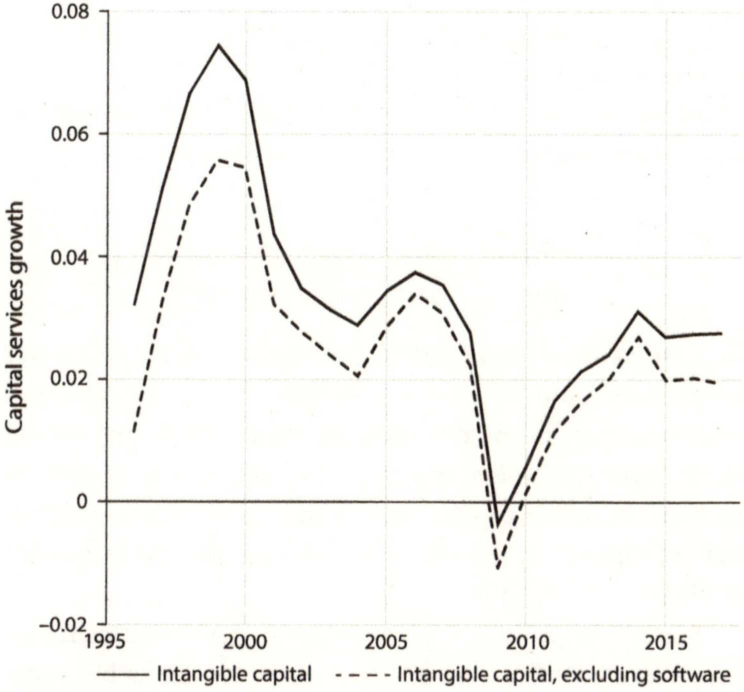

FIGURE 1.12: Capital Service Growth Trends. *Source*: Authors' calculations from www.intaninvest.net. Countries are the major advanced economies.

services, including and excluding software. The pace of growth slowed in the 2010s onwards, particularly excluding software. This slowdown in intangible investment, as we will see, is the source of its own set of problems, not least its direct impact on economic growth and productivity.

By way of analogy, consider a vat of grape juice fermenting into wine. As the yeast turns the sugar in the juice to ethanol, the solution becomes more and more alcoholic. But, as we noted in the introduction, as the percentage of alcohol creeps above 15 percent, the yeast becomes inactive and the fermenting process slows and stops. This stage has two important characteristics: the liquid now behaves differently from the grape juice it once was, because it is now alcoholic; and it is no longer fermenting and therefore no longer producing heat, carbon dioxide, or other by-products. Similarly, the current state of intangible investment is at a higher level than ever before, but it is growing much less than it did in the past.

The Properties and Consequences of a More Intangibles-Rich Economy: An Overview

You might ask why the shift to intangibles matters. Doesn't investment naturally change over time? We used to invest in canals, then we invested in railways, then in roads, and now in the internet. In *Capitalism without Capital*, we argued that the shift to intangible capital matters because intangible capital behaves differently from the physical assets that made up most business investment in the past.

Specifically, we identified four main ways in which intangible assets tend to differ from tangible assets: (1) intangible assets are often highly *scalable* (an asset like an algorithm can be used across a very large business); (2) intangibles have *spillovers* (a business investing in, say, R&D cannot be sure it will be the only entity to benefit from its investment); (3) intangibles are *sunk* costs (they are often not worth much to creditors if a business fails); and (4) intangibles have *synergies* (they are often massively more valuable when combined with other intangibles). These characteristics have a range of implications for how intangibles-rich businesses and an intangible-intensive economy behave.

Businesses that own scalable intangibles can grow very rapidly and become large, as in the case of today's tech giants. The spillover effects mean that businesses that invest in them may find that their competitors end up reaping the benefits, as defunct smartphone makers Blackberry and Nokia learnt to their dismay. They also strengthen the case for governments to subsidise investment, as almost all governments do with scientific research, training, and education.

The fact that intangibles are often sunk costs raises challenges for business finance. Especially for small businesses, debt finance is often ultimately secured against a business's assets. Businesses whose assets are worth little if the business fails are less attractive lending prospects for banks—a problem in a world where debt finance and bank lending are the main sources of external finance for most businesses.

We see the value of synergies between intangibles in the fact that J. K. Rowling became richer than P. G. Wodehouse or J.R.R. Tolkien, partly because the valuable intangibles she created in the form of the Harry Potter novels could be so effectively combined with other intangibles such as special effects and merchandising to create an immensely popular movie franchise. Synergies also matter to the extent that they increase the importance of combining the right intangibles, hence the inexorable growth of jobs involving brokering ideas, brands, or skills, and the prosperity of dynamic cities in which this kind of activity happens most easily.

These characteristics of intangibles have two types of important effects. On the one hand, in some cases they directly create challenges and problems, including increased inequality and weaker competitive dynamics. These problems form the first part of what we call the intangibles crisis. On the other hand, they change the type of institutions that a society needs for continued, healthy economic growth. In many cases, there is a discrepancy between the institutions we need and the ones we have. This institutional failure is the second part of the intangibles crisis.

What Is an Intangibles-Rich Economy? Knowledge, Relationships, and the Postindustrial Economy

Since we first wrote about the intangible economy over a decade ago, we've spoken about it to a wide range of businesspeople, journalists, investors, economists, and policy makers. One thing we have noticed is that people sometimes assume it means something that it doesn't. In particular, we found that people associated intangible investment with other modern economic phenomena, such as the knowledge economy or the postindustrial economy. They also often associated it with the tech sector, or in some cases with a sort of dystopian modernity. These associations are misleading, so let's look more closely at some key terms, trends, and phenomena.

The Knowledge Economy

The term "knowledge economy" was coined by Fritz Machlup, who first proposed measuring intangible investments in a 1962 book; it was subsequently popularised by management guru

Peter Drucker. More recently, a 2013 OECD report on intangible assets described them as "knowledge-based capital." It is true that some intangibles can fairly be described as knowledge—for example, the result of R&D to develop a new drug, a new production technique, or the results of training a worker in a new skill. And some intangibles, such as a software program or a database, consist of information, which is very similar to knowledge, if not precisely synonymous with it.

But other intangibles are about something more than knowledge or information. The value of a brand, for example, does not lie only in the informational content of the name and the logo. Instead, the brand is both relational and expressive. It is *relational* in that it is a sort of promise and a reminder of the past, tacitly referencing countless past transactions that make up the brand's reputation and purporting to offer customers a particular experience or quality. Two aspects of Apple-branded products are their sleek design and ease of use. This brand identity is not just a piece of information. Rather, its value derives from the experience of millions of customers and Apple's implied incentives when designing new products. A brand's value is *expressive* in that it conveys an emotional message about the product, one that consumers often value. When we hear "Just Do It," "Coke Is It," or "Because You're Worth It," what we are hearing is not knowledge in any normal sense of the word. It is something much more subjective.

Also subjective is the value placed on organisational capital accumulated within firms or in supply chains. Consider Marks & Spencer, a venerable UK retailer with a long-standing reputation for excellent relationships with its diverse supply chain. These relationships are widely acknowledged as an important reason for its profitability. Aspects of a supply chain can certainly be described as knowledge—the knowledge, say, that M&S will buy a certain number of strawberries from a certain set of farms at a certain price and grade according to a certain schedule. But the value of this intangible asset lies not in knowledge but in the relationship—in the expectations that the parties have of one another, and in the way those expectations systematically affect their actions. The same applies within firms. One can write down a business's operations or codify management practices such as Scrum or Six Sigma, but their implementation is about more than just knowledge. It is also about their instantiation in a set of relationships.[39]

Perhaps the reason the intangible economy is often described as the "knowledge economy" is that economists, being cerebral people, find the knowledge aspect of intangibles most salient. But equating intangibles with the knowledge economy is a misleading shorthand, obscuring the importance of relational and expressive capital in the modern economy.

The Postindustrial Economy

People sometimes describe the intangible economy as *postindustrial,* a phrase coined by French sociologist Alain Touraine and popularised by Daniel Bell in the 1970s. People sometimes infer from this description that intangible assets are mainly important to service industries and that an intangibles-rich economy is one with many services and little manufacturing.

But this too is a misleading way to think about intangible capital. If we look at manufacturing firms in rich countries, we find that, for the most part, they are heavy investors in intangible assets as well as tangible assets. They invest in R&D and design in order to produce cutting-edge products, in organisational development and training to increase factory productivity, and in software and data not only related to their own production but also as an adjunct to the physical goods they sell.

If we consider rich countries that are thought to have particularly healthy manufacturing sectors, we usually find a story of sustained and distinctive investment in intangibles. The consultant Hermann Simon's exploration of the German *Mittelstand*—Germany's cadre of profitable, globally competitive medium-sized manufacturing businesses—finds that the sources of their profitability include a commitment to research, development, and innovation; strong, durable, information-rich relationships with suppliers and customers; and excellent workforce skills and organisation: all intangible assets.[40] The success of the so-called developmental state in Japan, Taiwan, and South Korea would be impossible without heavy investment in intangibles such as R&D, process design, and training that led to the emergence of globally competitive manufacturing businesses in sectors from shipbuilding to semiconductors. It may be correct to describe the modern economy as both intangibles-rich and to some extent postindustrial, but intangibles and thriving industries—in the sense of manufacturing industries—are complements, not substitutes.

We also find that people tend to think of the intangible economy as something associated with high-tech businesses, particularly the so-called tech platform businesses such as Google, Apple, Facebook, and Amazon. In a sense, this association is fair. The value of these business giants derives mostly from the very valuable intangible assets they own. But the importance of intangible investment is not limited to the tech sector. To the extent we can measure it, we find intangible investment in all sectors of the economy. The rapid growth of vast tech companies in the past decade is an important part of the story, but it is not the whole story.

Nor is intangible investment a minor extension of R&D. Innovation in industries that were most hit by COVID-19 (retail, entertainment, hotels, and restaurants) is not included in the R&D data because those sectors do almost no R&D. Instead, they invest in intangible assets: training, marketing, design, and business processes. And the companies that do R&D do it in harness with a host of other intangible assets, such as marketing spending on new pharmaceuticals. Indeed, the change in R&D is itself remarkable, as Efraim Benmelech, Janice Eberly, Dimitris Papanikolaou, and Joshua Krieger have documented.[41] In the United States, pharmaceutical firms account for around a dollar of every ten dollars of R&D spending (up from thirty cents of every ten dollars during the 1970s). Further, about a third of R&D spending by these firms is geared toward those age sixty-five and over.

The final misapprehension of intangible capital sees it as highly commercialised, transactional, and high modernist—a kind of Marxian cash nexus where all that is solid melts into air and tradition is scorned and scrapped. Tradition can indeed be overturned because ideas are sometimes disruptive, but disruption is not a necessary component of intangible capital.

Consider the work of critics of modernism, such as James C. Scott and Ernst Schumacher. Scott, author of the anarchist classic *Seeing Like a State*, gives examples of well-intentioned but overconfident rulers and managers who tore up traditional ways of doing things—traditional forest management in Prussia, traditional cultivation in Java or Tanzania—and replaced them with new, impersonal, "scientific" systems that turned out to be far less effective than the previous systems.[42] Similarly, Schumacher's *Small Is Beautiful* observes that locally sensitive, "intermediate" or "appropriate" technology is generally more valuable than uniform, globalised products, even when those products are superficially more advanced.[43] It is tempting to see intangibles as the tools of high modernism, and the economies envisaged by Scott and Schumacher as grounded on something else. But this interpretation is mistaken. Scott's case studies describe intangibles-rich methods of production, grounded on detailed, time-honoured know-how and relationships—that is to say, intangibles—being replaced unwittingly by lower-quality ideas and practices (again, intangibles) that are more congenial to powerful, high-status people.

These inadequate definitions of intangible investment help cast light on what intangible investment actually is. If you want to think about how intangible-intensive economies differ from less intangible-intensive economies, don't think about knowledge work, small manufacturing sectors, or big tech companies. Think instead of an economy where what people do is more heavily and intimately connected in economic relationships; where activities of all sorts, from factory production to supermarket shopping, are more information rich; and where economic activity is more freighted with meaning, with association, and with emotional significance.

The Long-Run Growth of Intangible Investments—and the Recent Slowdown

In the long term, the historical growth of intangible investment seems to be intrinsically linked to the world getting richer. Intangible investment is necessary to drive growth in advanced economies that cannot simply expand their frontier, clear another forest, or mine more ore. To this extent, the move to an intangible-intensive economy is good news for anyone concerned about the planet's natural resources, as Andrew McAfee argues in *More from Less*.[44] At the same time, as people grow richer and their basic material needs are satisfied, we would expect them to demand a wider variety of goods and services, often with the kind of expressive or emotional value that intangibles can provide.[45]

Intangible-intensive businesses benefit from being in proximity to one another, because knowledge and relationships typically work better with face-to-face interaction. But our planning systems make it painfully hard to build new office space and new housing in and around the most dynamic cities, like San Francisco and London. COVID-19, which enforced remote working for many people, temporarily removed some of these planning issues, but it introduced its own problems, depriving knowledge workers of the face-to-face contact that at least some of them feel is important for their work. Both congested cities and a haphazard shift to remote working make it harder to invest in intangibles, likely slowing down long-term investment relative to what it might have been. We examine this issue, and potential solutions to it, in chapter 6.

The Post-2008 Slowdown: Why?

As we have seen, intangible investment growth slowed after the 2008 recession and, especially outside software, does not seem to have recovered its previous pace. Why? One reason is its complementarity with other forms of investment, such as ICT, which have also remained comparatively low. But there are additional reasons. Gustavo Adler and colleagues find that, in their sample of firms, intangible investment relative to tangible investment fell in firms that were particularly financially exposed before the recession (that is, they were very indebted or had debts due in 2008).[46] And intangible investment fell in the five years after the recession, suggesting more than just a cyclical downturn. Similar findings have been reported by the OECD in a study of firms across Europe.[47]

This finding suggests that rising financial "frictions" are affecting intangible investment, though it is difficult to identify those specific frictions. Many institutions are unsuited to supporting intangible investment. For example, banks are typically reluctant to lend against capital they consider to be unsuitable as collateral. But presumably this has always been the case, so for intangible investment to have slowed down because of more "frictions," something else must have changed.

One possibility is that banks and firms have become more cautious in their lending owing to a rise in uncertainty and risk after the crisis. The financial crisis, a massive shock in itself, was followed by Greece's possible withdrawal from the eurozone (Grexit) in the early 2010s, the drawn-out issues around Brexit in the United Kingdom after 2016, and the controversy around US trade policy, all of which might have raised uncertainty.[48] Importantly, intangible investment is likely highly affected by increased uncertainty because it is "sunk." (Sunk investment is spending you cannot get back: Microsoft had to write off $5 billion when its Windows Mobile program, which powered Nokia mobile phones, was retired.) By raising the option value of waiting, a rise in uncertainty particularly holds back such irreversible investment.[49]

Another possibility is synergies. Economist James Bessen and colleagues have built a (mostly US) company-level data set with both accounting and intangible data.[50] Their findings are striking—for example, the strong decline after around 2000 in lagging firms' ability to overtake leading firms. Such a decline is strongly correlated with leading firms' investment in intangibles, particularly of software written in-house. This finding makes sense as a function of the properties of intangible capital. Because intangibles have synergies, a marginal dollar spent on R&D or product design is more valuable to an intangibles-rich firm such as Facebook than to a laggard. In addition, it seems that large firms benefit particularly from the spillovers of intangible assets, to the extent that they are adept at exploiting these spillovers, copying or adapting their smaller competitors' ideas (what the tech industry has come to call the *kill zone* around big tech firms—a periphery in which competitors are routinely crushed). Perhaps, then, the years 2000–2009 marked the turning point when the synergies of intangible capital in the leading firms were sufficient to dissuade followers from investing, and the result was an overall slowdown in investment and/or lowered overall productivity growth despite ongoing investment.

Summary

We have reviewed the disappointing economic performance of economies since the turn of the century and the financial crisis and discussed the five problems of stagnation, inequality, dysfunctional competition, fragility, and inauthenticity. The conventional explanations—the Lost Golden Age and the Great Divide—seem not to explain everything. We think the turn toward intangible investment and its recent slowdown help to explain our difficulties, a theme we develop in more detail in the next chapter.

2

The Economic Crisis Is an Intangibles Crisis

In this chapter we argue that the fundamental economic properties of intangibles help explain the five failings we introduced in chapter 1. An intangible economy will have rising concentration, gaps between firms, apparently rising markups, potentially dysfunctional competition, and the air of inauthenticity.

As we define it, the *intangibles crisis* is the combination of (1) unprecedented high levels of intangible investment, (2) the slowdown in the growth rate of intangible investment, and (3) the inadequacy of institutions to deal with the challenges of an intangibles-rich economy. In this chapter, we explore how the intangibles crisis helps explain the unsatisfactory and unusual state of the economy in the twenty-first century. We begin by describing features of an intangibles-rich economy that arise from the basic economic properties of intangibles. We then discuss how these features help explain the world's five big economic problems today.

Features of an Intangible Economy

As we saw in chapter 1, intangible capital tends to behave differently than tangible capital. Specifically, intangible capital is *scalable*, it exhibits *spillovers* and *synergies*, and it often represents a *sunk* cost. These economic properties combine to produce three noteworthy features in the economy at large: the gap between the best and the rest, the benefits of clustering, and the rise of contestedness.

The Gap between the Best and the Rest

Because valuable intangible assets are scalable, a company that owns them can grow very big and very rapidly at its competitors' expense. And because intangibles have synergies, a firm with several valuable intangibles will have a disproportionately strong competitive position. In addition, intangible assets' ability to spill over to other firms can benefit market-leading businesses, to the extent that some of them are adept at capturing the benefit of their smaller or weaker competitors' intangible investments (what is often called the *kill zone* in the tech industry). Thus, the intangibles-rich economy has an "O ring" feel to it: seemingly small differences between firms can be greatly magnified so that the gap between firms becomes very large.[1]

The Benefits of Clustering

Economists have long known that people prosper when they come together to exchange ideas. When Alfred Marshall wrote about industrial clusters over a century ago, he was giving a name to a phenomenon that casual observers had known about since time immemorial. Today, the benefits of being located in dynamic cities (so-called *agglomeration effects*) have increased, and they are increasingly seen across industries. Consider the San Francisco Bay Area. It was once a semiconductor cluster, but today it is a cluster for a host of only tenuously related industries. At the same time, left-behind places and people with ties to them lose out more and more. Unfortunately, the COVID-19 pandemic made physical proximity dangerous at a time when our economies rely on it more than ever.

The Rise of Contestedness

Because intangibles have spillovers, it is difficult to prove who owns them—unlike tangible assets, whose ownership is relatively easy to prove. Accordingly, we see more high-stakes arguments, rivalry, and litigation around what belongs to whom, and even whether certain things should be owned at all. These disputes are already common in the tech sector. For example, what are Uber's obligations to its partner drivers? To what extent should YouTube respect the requests of rights holders when it comes to pirated content? Such disputes are becoming ubiquitous. Can libraries lend e-books? Can farmers repair their own tractors?

Contractual enforcement is a good thing when we are seeking to encourage trade and investment. A rise in the number of contested resources should thus be expected: it merely reflects the rise in intangible investment in the economy as a whole. If there are more patents, there will be more patent lawyers. Indeed, contestation is not always acrimonious. In addition, it gives rise to innumerable professions whose role is to smooth the transfer, combination, and separation of intangibles, from literary agents and patent attorneys to merchandising managers and ontologists.

However, not all forms of contestedness benefit the economy. Two specific forms are problematic. First, when the nature of the economy is changing and new rules of the game are being forged, there is an increase in the economic returns to political and social power—to those who can nudge the rules of the economic game in their favour. Second, intangible investment is more likely to be zero-sum, or positional, than the average tangible investment, especially when intangibles are primarily relational rather than knowledge based. For example, a new idea for treating a disease or boarding passengers onto an aeroplane does not diminish the usefulness of other ideas. But some relational intangibles may reduce the value of intangibles owned by others. An advertising campaign whose effect is to strengthen a brand at a competitor's expense in a fixed-sized market creates a valuable intangible, but only to the extent that it reduces the value of its rival's asset. The costs of setting up an international subsidiary whose only role is to avoid tax are also an intangible investment, but the value created is simply a transfer from taxpayers. Relatively few tangible assets have this characteristic, but one example is the fibre-optic cables that high-frequency traders use to shave nanoseconds off securities transactions in order to beat out rivals.

To summarise, the majority of investment in the economy is now intangible, but the growth of intangible capital has slowed significantly. This capital is highly scalable, exhibits spillovers and synergies, and is often a sunk cost. In addition, some intangible investment is zero-sum, and the average dollar of intangible investment is more likely to be zero-sum than the average dollar of tangible investment. The result is stronger agglomeration effects, making thriving cities more productive than left-behind towns or the countryside. The gap widens between the best, intangibles-rich businesses and their laggard competitors. The ownership of intangible assets is often unclear and therefore contested. And intangible assets are worth less in the event of business failure, posing a challenge for lenders and for businesses looking for credit.

Intangibles and the State We're In

Let's now return to the troubling features of the twenty-first-century economy that we described in chapter 1: stagnation, inequality, dysfunctional competition, fragility, and inauthenticity. The characteristics of the new intangible economy have made a significant contribution to each.

Stagnation

The intangibles crisis has contributed to our economic slowdown in three important ways. The first factor is the most direct: the largely unrecognised slowdown of intangible investment since around the time of the financial crisis. Businesses are investing less in intangibles than we would expect based on pre-2007 growth rates. We expect that this reduced investment will translate into lower growth in two specific ways. First, we expect that countries that have seen a sharper fall in intangibles will have experienced a worse slowdown, and indeed, the data support this conclusion. Second, we expect the slowdown to manifest itself in decreased total factor productivity (TFP), in which the spillovers from intangible investment—technical breakthroughs that advance an entire industry, new management methods that are widely adopted, new product designs that create whole new categories—show up. And, indeed, the downturn we are experiencing is predominantly one of TFP. Figure 2.1 shows that countries with the biggest slowdown in

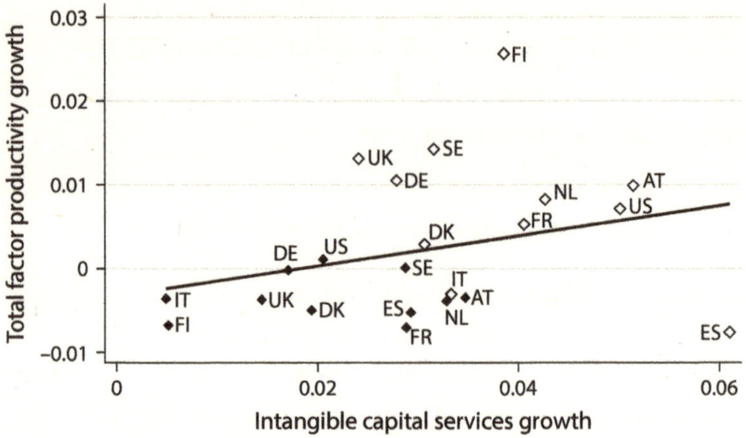

FIGURE 2.1: TFP and Intangible Capital Services Growth. *Note*: Open diamonds = 1999–2007; closed diamonds = 2008–16. Countries included are Austria, Denmark, Finland, France, Germany, Italy, the Netherlands, Spain, Sweden, the United Kingdom, and the United States. *Source*: Corrado et al. 2019.

the growth of intangible capital services have seen the largest slowdowns in TFP.

There is also a second-order effect, one that relates to the disappointments of modern technology. As we've seen, one of the peculiarities of twenty-first-century stagnation is the disconnect between low economic growth and the lavish hopes and predictions of the tech sector: the flying cars that were promised but never showed up. Economists Erik Brynjolfsson, Daniel Rock, and Chad Syverson link this state of technological disappointment to intangibles.[2] Specifically, they note that for new technologies to deliver economic benefit, they need plenty of other intangible investment alongside them to make them useful: new processes, new business relationships, new worker skills. Put another way, intangibles have particularly strong synergies when it comes to new technologies. Thus, at a time when radical new technologies are being developed, we would expect a slowdown in intangibles to have an even more dramatic negative effect on productivity growth.[3]

There may also be an effect on TFP growth not from the slowdown of intangible investment growth but rather from its historically high levels. Recall that a certain proportion of the stock of intangible investment is zero-sum because it is relational. That is, it is valuable to its owner only to the extent that it destroys value for someone else (an example is a tax-avoiding subsidiary company). We can think of this exchange as a negative spillover that will manifest itself as lower TFP. If a greater proportion of intangible investment is zero-sum rather than tangible investment (which seems plausible), then an economy with more intangible capital relative to tangible capital might see less TFP than we would expect. These three effects would combine to produce exactly the effect that we see: lower TFP in an economy in which intangible investment is abundant but growing slowly.

The intangible explanation for slow productivity growth is consistent with other findings about slowing productivity growth. It helps explain the concerns about slowing technological progress voiced by Robert Gordon, Tyler Cowen, and Erik Brynjolfsson, providing an underlying explanation for why this slowing should be happening now. It is also consistent with two explanations of declining TFP made by Dietrich Vollrath in his book *Fully Grown*. Vollrath points out that a significant fraction of the fall in US TFP between 2000 and 2016 is explained by lower business dynamism (the fact that productive small businesses grow and replace incumbents less quickly) and by the long-term shift from manufacturing (where TFP growth has historically been high) to services (where TFP growth has historically been lower).[4] Both of these causes have an intangible angle: lower business dynamism relates to the growing leader/laggard gap that intangibles are exacerbating. Further, productivity growth in services likely needs more intangible investment to grow faster, along with the introduction of IT and improvements in the difficult areas of health and education.

Dysfunctional Competition: Profits, Concentration, and Productivity Gaps

The problem of competition in the twenty-first century is a paradoxical one. Many have argued that competition among businesses and market dynamism more generally have fallen significantly. This reduction is partly a function of the large and persistent gap between leader firms and laggards, but the explanation does not stop there. Fewer new businesses are starting up, and fewer small businesses are growing large. But this picture of stagnation and complacency is not mirrored in the lived experience of workers and managers. Working life feels more ranked, more appraised, and more competitive than ever. Low-paid workers are increasingly subjected to onerous performance regimes, while high-status workers experience life increasingly as a high-stakes tournament beginning in childhood and involving the costly signalling of ability through baroque rituals of education.

We will take up these issues in chapter 7, but broadly we do not share the view that competition has declined. Although the number of competitors and leader/laggard gaps in some markets has fallen, these figures may not be good measures of rivalry in an intangible-intensive world. When companies can scale up and exploit synergies, small differences between companies with attractive intangible assets and unattractive assets are greatly magnified. Thus, the leading companies will pull away from the laggards and reap rewards from intangible investment.

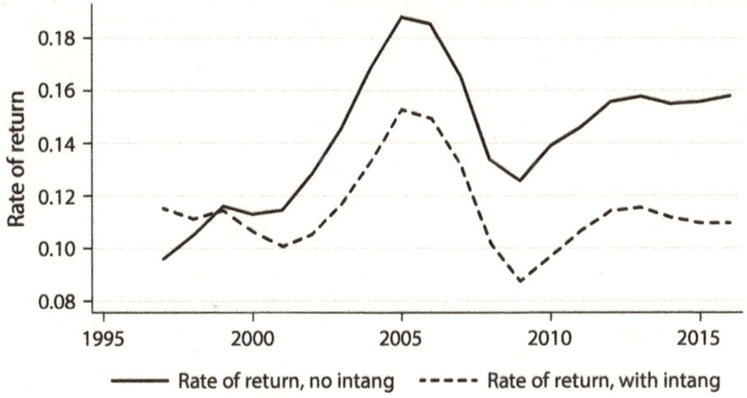

FIGURE 2.2: Rates of Return in the United States with and without Intangibles. *Source*: Authors' calculations using www.intaninvest.net data.

That doesn't necessarily mean competition is falling. Even with fewer numbers, competition between a few platforms can be very intense, and the calculation of markups needs to measure the reward to those intangibles, which is rarely done.

Three findings support this assertion. First, as we saw in chapter 1 from Traina's work, when we incorporate data that might cover intangibles, markups have not risen in the United States. However, sales and general administration spending includes other things besides intangibles. So one way forward is to calculate the rate of return in the macroeconomy with and without intangibles, measuring intangibles at the industry level though a variety of data sets not available at the firm level, as in figure 2.2. Without intangibles, rates of return are rising in the United States. With them, rates are flat. Thus, on this measure, rising returns in the United States are an illusion caused by the failure to measure intangibles properly.

Second, the Organisation for Economic Co-operation and Development has studied the correlation between changes

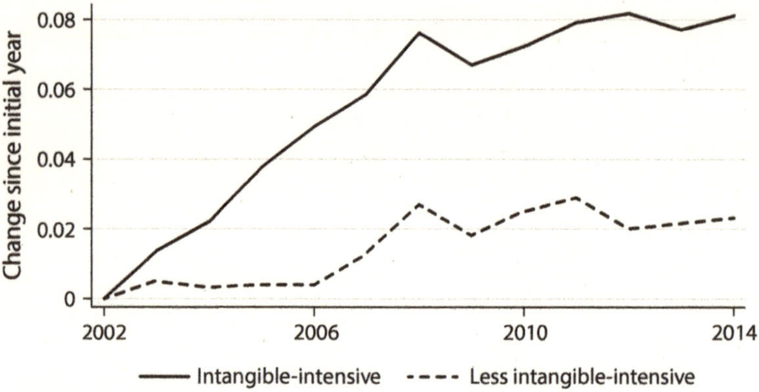

FIGURE 2.3: Evolution of Concentration (Share of Top Eight Firms) by Intangible Intensity. Countries included are Belgium, Finland, France, Italy, Japan, Spain, Sweden, the United Kingdom, and the United States. *Source*: Bajgar, Criscuolo, and Timmis 2020.

in concentration and intangible intensity. It finds that rises in concentration have occurred in the most intangible-intensive industries, as shown in figure 2.3.[5]

Third, Carol Corrado and colleagues look at the rise in the productivity gap.[6] As figure 2.4 sets out, there has been a growing productivity spread between leaders and laggards, controlling for a large number of other factors, in industries that are more intangible intensive.

Finally, what conclusions can we draw, then, about competition in our working lives? In his book *The Meritocracy Trap*, Daniel Markovits argues that, in the United States, parenting, access to education, and the "fetishisation" of credentials are becoming the key passports to good jobs and economic success.[7] Such access is denied to all but the already wealthy and excludes the middle class. We can interpret the importance of such passports in an intangibles-rich world. Positional/zero-sum investment in intangibles in the form of education (e.g., university

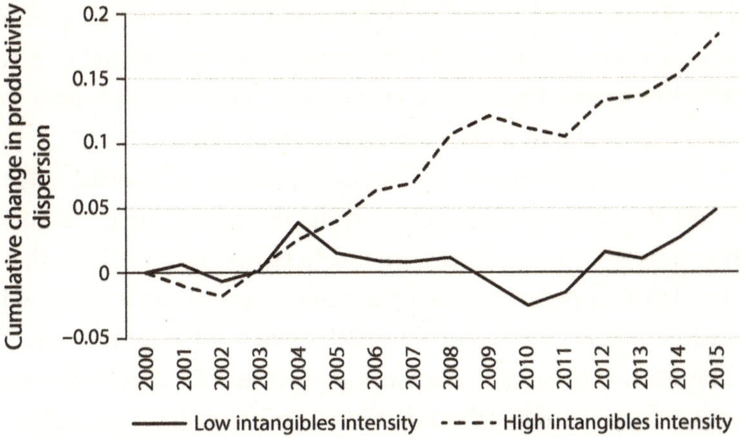

FIGURE 2.4: Evolution of Productivity Dispersion by Intangible Intensity. *Note*: The graph plots the evolution of productivity dispersion for high and low intangible-intensive industries, after controlling for other factors driving productivity dispersion, including gross output, capital and labour inputs, and capital-labour ratios. Countries included are Austria, Belgium, Denmark, Finland, France, Germany, Ireland, Italy, the Netherlands, and Portugal. *Source*: Berlingieri et al. 2021.

degrees), the use of intangibles such as software monitoring to sort workers,[8] and the value of social capital (e.g., connections) in "contesting" jobs all forge the meritocracy trap. (For more on competition, see chapter 7.)

In sum, it seems that intangibles can account for many of the trends in profits and concentration that have been observed. We discuss this topic in much more detail in chapter 7.

Inequality

We observed in chapter 1 that inequality in the twenty-first century has three characteristics: a gap between the rich and the poor, which grew significantly in the 1980s and 1990s and has stayed wide; a gap between high earners and low earners, with a similar pattern; and a divergence in esteem and social status, which is harder to measure empirically, but which appears to have continued to grow in the past two decades.

Western governments have historically made considerable effort to reduce the gap between the haves and the have-nots through progressive taxation and benefits, and the idea that the rich will get richer and the poor poorer is at least as old as the book of Matthew; so it seems safe to assume that when inequality increases, the cause is governments taking their foot off the pedal of redistribution. But there is reason to believe that the intangibles-rich economy is also partially to blame. It turns out that a significant share of observed increases in inequality can be explained by changes that are themselves driven by intangibles, particularly from the leader/laggard gap and from the effects of clustering.

Consider income inequality. Recent research on income differentials suggests that a major driver of the increase in income inequality in recent decades was the difference in salaries between staff at the most profitable firms and staff at all other firms. This finding has been observed not only in the United States but also in egalitarian Sweden. A world in which some companies do very well and others very badly is, it seems, one where the gap increases between high earners and low earners.[9]

Intangible investment by businesses seems also to have increased inequality by making it easier to observe and manage workers' performance. Economists have long studied the concept of the *efficiency wage*, the idea that employers might pay generous salaries in order to discourage shirking by employees. Part of the rationale for efficiency wages is that management relies on trust rather than on minute observation of what workers are doing all the time, which has generally been both objectionable and very costly. However, software, data analysis, and new management practices make close observation much easier, with the result that the activities of workers who once had to be trusted can now be observed in detail, compared, and assessed. Amazon's ability to monitor how many packages its warehouse staff ships per hour, how many calls call centre workers handle per hour, and how much time customer service reps spend between calls is grounded in intangibles—the software and business processes used to measure and reward employees' performance. Similar technologies and practices increase inequality among white-collar workers. For example, Luis Garicano and Thomas Hubbard showed how better systems for monitoring performance and hours billed allowed law firms to differentiate between their highest performers and the rest.[10] The stars ended up being paid more, while the laggards got left behind or were fired. Intangible investment allows professional services employers to replace egalitarian work cultures, where pay is often based on seniority, with sharply incentivised ones, where workers "eat what they kill."

The rise of intangible investment also has an indirect but powerful effect on wealth inequality. Following the publication of Thomas Piketty's landmark *Capital in the Twenty-First Century*, it became clear that a significant proportion of the increased wealth inequality that Piketty observed (almost all of it, according to Matt Rognlie)[11] derived from the dizzying increase in property prices in the late twentieth and early twenty-first centuries. These increases did not arise everywhere. Instead, they arose for the most part in dynamic cities that exhibit the clustering and agglomeration effects driven by the growing importance of intangible assets.

The link between inequality of status and the intangible economy is more obvious. As clustering has become more economically important, the economic divide between thriving cities and left-behind places has become deeper, especially because strict planning laws make it increasingly uneconomical for low-paid workers to move to take advantage of job opportunities in thriving cities.[12] This link is underscored by the implications of the contestedness of intangibles: if more and more economic activity involves negotiating and asserting claims over contested assets, then social capital will become more important, and so will markers of social capital, such as class and education.

Fragility

The idea that modern societies' vulnerability to threats such as pandemics and climate change comes from our failure to invest in intangibles is counterintuitive. Indeed, most people would assume the opposite: that fragility is caused by worrying too much about fluffy things like intangibles, and not enough about robust physical things.

When the COVID-19 pandemic began, much public debate focused on the *tangible* capital necessary to fight it. International observers were impressed with how fast China built a new COVID-19 hospital in Wuhan. Westerners nervously wondered if they could build new hospitals as quickly and worried that they might not have enough ventilators to meet peak demand or enough factories to produce protective equipment.

As it turned out, many of these tangible capital issues were under control. The United Kingdom and the United States built their own emergency hospitals and avoided breaching ICU capacity. In fact, the countries that excelled in handling the COVID-19 pandemic had made strong investments in intangible assets: effective track-and-trace and quarantine systems (which rely on software, data, and processes), functioning supply chains (to avoid the situation seen in several Western countries in which protective equipment existed but could not be delivered quickly enough to the right places), and the ability to measure, analyse, and respond quickly to epidemiological data. Some wealthy countries, such as Taiwan and South Korea, got it right, but so did much poorer places, such as Vietnam. The path out of the pandemic also required massive intangible investment: software and processes to track, trace, and quarantine people with the disease; research to develop effective drugs, treatment protocols, and vaccines; and networks, systems, and campaigns to ensure that people got vaccinated.

Strong investment in intangibles is also required to meet the longer-term challenge of reducing the world's carbon emissions. When people think of fighting climate change, they often think of the need to invest in physical assets: solar panels and wind farms, electric vehicles, and devices for capturing and storing carbon. This tangible investment is a necessary part of reducing carbon emissions, but it is not sufficient—and, in fact, it has proved the easiest part to get right. The United Kingdom, for example, has significantly reduced the amount of electricity generated by coal, replacing it with renewables and lower-carbon forms of energy. Average carbon emissions from electricity generation fell from 242 million tonnes of CO_2 equivalent in 1990 to 98 in 2018.[13] Because Britain is served by a common electricity grid, replacing dirty power with cleaner power is just a matter of building the production capability once the right incentives are in place. The grid is partly a matter of tangible capital (pylons and connections), but it is also a piece of intangible capital: putting one in place requires investment in systems, standards, and agreements. In the United States, where separate grids exist on the East and West Coasts and in Texas, the deployment of wind power has been slower, partly because the lack of a common grid makes it harder to generate power in Texas, where it is windy, and transport it to the East or West Coast, where renewable energy is in high demand. Germany, which embarked on an ambitious and expensive programme to decarbonise its electricity supply by investing in renewables, was stymied by the need to decommission its nuclear power plants. The problem was not one of physical capital but rather of social licensing and providing safety regimes that voters deemed acceptable—an intangible failure, not a tangible one.

We see more intangible failure when we look beyond electricity generation. Energy experts tend to agree that the hard part of decarbonising an economy is not electricity generation but rather transport systems and domestic heating. Making this transition relies on tangible investment: installing air-source heat pumps or hydrogen-fuelled boilers instead of gas-fired heating, or replacing internal combustion engines with electric engines, cars with buses, or roads with bicycle lanes. But as with electricity generation, the tangible capital is not the hard part. Heating and transport are hard problems because they are complex systems, and to be able to invest in the tangible capital, you also need significant intangible investments. For transport, these might include new road layouts that work, new agreements between road users to allow those layouts to be built, systems and business models that allow people to charge their cars as easily as they fill up with petrol, and battery R&D to produce electric cars with sufficient range. For heating, intangible investment means designs and plans to retrofit houses for electrical heating or hydrogen power, and systems and business models to support the changeover.

If we were building cities from scratch, many of these intangible investment problems would be eased. It is the lock-in of legacy systems that makes the intangible challenge so significant.

Fragility has another important dimension beyond health and climate. There is fragility in the sense that some of the policy levers that we have used in the past as insurance against adverse economic "shocks" seem to have withered away, notably monetary policy. In a more intangibles-rich world and with more uncertainty around outcomes, borrowing gets riskier. At the same time, precautionary behaviour by an aging society raises the demand for "safe" assets—to fund retirement, for example. Rising demand for savings and a rising wedge between safe and risky returns will lower the safe long-term real interest rate, giving central banks less room to lower their rates and boost the economy. Chapter 5 discusses the fragility of monetary policy in more detail.

Inauthenticity

The idea that our economy lacks authenticity and that we should be troubled by it has at least three dimensions. The first is Ross Douthat's observation in *The Decadent Society* that too much of our output is derivative and self-referential, the product of recombination rather than original effort.[14] The second is the concern expressed by David Graeber and a thousand politicians in rich countries that the economy involves too much fakery, too much work that does not produce useful, tangible results. In the public mind, and in political discourse, the most lamented type of lost economic activity is manufacturing. Third, there is the widespread impression that the modern economy is replete with frothy get-rich-quick schemes that lack substance and are at best risible and at worst fraudulent, such as Juicero's failed plans to make $1 billion from web-enabled juicers, the collapse of Theranos's fake blood-test empire, and the sudden liquidation of British government outsourcer Carillion. Businesses look less like the product of honest, hard work and more like Jack's magic beans.

The idea that our creative economy is increasingly dominated by remixes and recursions is, in Douthat's account, inherently unsettling: a failing that is so troubling that it must be a sign of something deep-seated and rotten. Viewed through the prism of intangible assets, though, remixing makes sense. Today's economy has an unprecedented stock of intangible assets, including creative properties from Harry Potter to the Broadway play *Hamilton* and from NASCAR to National Geographic. These assets are sometimes unusually valuable when you combine them in just the right way—a function of their synergies. In this context, the many attempts to find the right combinations, which often take the form of remixing or reworking, should not come as a surprise. It is what we expect to see in a society rich in intangibles.

The concern over the loss of "real" jobs also relates in part to the great value found in exploiting the synergies of intangibles. In fact, many of the "bullshit jobs" that Graeber identified involve attempts to exploit synergies. In the context of manufacturing, intangibles provide a different explanation. When people think about manufacturing, they often think of tangible assets: factories, machine tools, production lines. But when we look at rich countries that have been able to maintain relatively large manufacturing sectors—Germany and Japan are prime examples—we find that their competitive advantage relies mostly on intangible assets: skills and training among their workforce, R&D and design abilities that allow them to stay at the cutting edge of product technology, and constant improvement in processes (such as Lean and Six Sigma) to mitigate high unit labour costs. A failing manufacturing sector, and the loss of the physical, politically desirable jobs that it provides, is the result of a failure to invest in intangibles.

The importance of intangibles also helps explain the magic beans factor—the apparent abundance of businesses that look like high-variance bets. In a world where more and more business assets are highly scalable and where the right combination can release big synergies, we would expect to see a sort of Cambrian explosion of variety in business ideas (many of them suspect or flaky) and the possibility of very large returns when someone eventually gets it right.

Summary

This chapter has argued that the intangibles crisis is well suited to explaining the problems and paradoxes we set out in chapter 1: stagnation, inequality, dysfunctional competition, fragility, and inauthenticity. In particular, the more intangible world explains how and why these problems coexist. Stagnation coexists with dizzying technical change. Inequality, which has mostly stopped rising, coexists with rising inequality of esteem. Competition indicators show falling competition, but our personal lives are becoming more crowded. Fragility coexists with apparently better communications and travel. And inauthenticity coexists with exploding creativity across borders.

The rest of this book looks at the institutional changes needed to overcome these problems. But first we have to explain what we think institutions are. We do that in the next chapter.

3

The Intangibles Crisis

INSTITUTIONAL FAILURE

Good institutions help promote economic growth. But as we will see from the history of the lighthouse, a good institution can become a bad one as the economy changes. The unusual properties of intangible assets require specific institutional arrangements, which for the most part do not yet exist. Institutional renewal and innovation are necessary to end the slowdown of intangible investment and restore economic growth.

In the picturesque Tuscan city of Siena, you can see Ambrogio Lorenzetti's remarkable fresco *The Effects of Good Governance on Siena and Its Territory* (figure 3.1). One of the earliest secular paintings of the Italian Renaissance (c. 1338), it was painted in the Palazzo Pubblico, on the wall of the chamber where the city's ruling council sat. As noted in the introduction to this book, it makes a basic political point: good institutions make an economy flourish.[1]

In the early 1300s, Siena and other Italian cities seemed to have achieved something remarkable from an economic point of view. They had begun to break out of the trap of subsistence

FIGURE 3.1: Ambrogio Lorenzetti, *The Effects of Good Governance on Siena and Its Territory*, Public Palace, Siena.

in which most of western Europe had been stuck for centuries. By modern standards, Siena was still desperately poor, but it was slightly less poor than it had been, and that growth was in itself remarkable by historical standards. But even as the paint on the fresco was drying, the economic tide was beginning to turn. The institutions and rules that had helped the Tuscan towns become richer were not able to cope with the demands of the emerging new economy. Investment slowed. Rich townsfolk increasingly spent their money on status and display. Unwise land development led to disastrous floods. Growing inequality led to riots and disorder. Improving Siena's institutions to deal with these new challenges was difficult. Indeed, the fact that its rulers saw fit to commission costly frescoes about good and bad governance suggests that this issue was contested at the time.

The institutions that had helped Siena prosper were not adequate for the new economy that had emerged. Like many northern Italian cities, Siena began to stagnate and then to decline. The frescoes in the Palazzo Pubblico stand as a melancholy reminder of what had been.

Nonetheless, the frescoes of Siena provide three lessons that are important to our argument. First, good institutions help drive economic growth and investment. Second, the definition of a good institution can change over time as the economy changes. Third, without institutional renewal an economy can go from growth to stagnation. As the expression goes, sometimes what got you here won't get you there.

When we talk about institutions, we do not mean "grand old organisations." Rather, we use the word in the sense in which economists have come to use it: the formal and informal rules of the economic game. Douglass North, one of the pioneers of the New Institutional Economics, defined institutions more precisely as "the humanly devised constraints that shape human interaction."[2] So, for example, by this definition Harvard

University is *not* an institution (even though it is old and grand), but "academic peer review," "liberal arts education," and any other practices and norms of universities *are*.

Institutions and Economic Growth

Critics of mainstream economics often accuse economists of underestimating the importance of institutions. Economists, they argue, are too quick to accept Adam Smith's claim that prosperity depends on "little else . . . but peace, easy taxes, and a tolerable administration of justice"[3] and to overlook the sprawling and intricate infrastructure of norms, rules, and expectations that underpins a modern market economy. To borrow Marx and Engels's phrase, economists are accused of caring about "no other nexus between man and man than naked self-interest, than callous 'cash payment.'"[4]

Economists defend themselves by pointing to the decades of research undertaken by practitioners of New Institutional Economics, who examined the relationship between institutions and economic performance, combining perspectives from history, law, political science, and other disciplines with rigorous economic analysis. Elinor Ostrom, one of the winners of the Nobel Prize for Economics in 2009, wrote about the rules and norms that coastal communities use to manage fisheries; Melissa Dell, winner of the 2020 John Bates Clark Medal, looked at how forced labour rules in colonial Peru affected poverty and health centuries later. The idea that institutions are important to economic growth is now uncontroversial among economists. Indeed, Daron Acemoglu, Simon Johnson, and James Robinson,[5] in a string of highly insightful books and papers, define good institutions as those that provide "security of property rights and relatively equal access to economic resources to a broad cross-section of society." Arnold Kling and

Nick Schulz, who highlighted the importance of institutions in an intangible economy over a decade ago, describe them as "operating systems."[6]

The idea that good institutions can encourage investment and growth and that bad institutions can hold them back is intuitive. After all, the rule of law, well-functioning markets, and the provision of public goods all arise from combinations of institutions: the laws themselves, the practices of the courts that enforce them, and the norms that predispose most people to act in a law-abiding way. If noneconomists have always known that institutions are important, they might reasonably ask, "Did we really need five decades of institutional economics to confirm it?"

At the same time, some economists respond with suspicion to an explanation of economic growth that relies on institutions. Certainly, they argue, institutions *in general* are important, but they are too easily invoked to explain anything unusual and are therefore not to be trusted. When the economy is doing well, you can always thank good institutions, and when it is not doing so well, you can blame bad ones. We believe it is helpful to think about precisely *why* institutions are good for growth, because doing so forces us to set a higher threshold of proof to determine when institutions may be letting us down. And with this focus, we can set out why the intangible economy puts strain on existing institutions.

Institutions, Social Interaction, and Economic Exchange: A Road Map

We are going to advance some rather abstract ideas about institutions, so here is a brief overview of why we do so and a road map of where we are going. In the coming pages, we argue that institutions are of their time. Therefore, we need to explain why certain institutions are good in some eras and not good in others. We will argue that institutions help with some dimensions of exchange but hurt others. Thus, as the economy changes and the conditions of exchange are altered, some institutions become less appropriate.

One of the key features of our social interaction is exchange: the trade, sometimes for money, of goods and services. Such exchange is good for economic growth. Indeed, economic growth needs a particular kind of exchange called investment—broadly speaking, exchange made now for benefit in the future. Thus, we must identify the dimensions of the exchange process or, more specifically, the conditions or stages of exchange. Then we must describe which institutions support or create those conditions so that exchange can occur. Finally, we must show how a move to a more intangible economy requires a different exchange process, which in turn requires different institutions.

To illustrate our arguments, we will use the example of the history of the lighthouse. Students of lighthouses (by the end of this chapter you will be one such student) might approach studying a lighthouse in many ways. A *technological approach* studies the technical aspects of the lighthouse: its construction and illumination, for example. Other approaches might study the *conditions of exchange* around the lighthouse: What exactly does it sell? We must also look at the *institutions that support exchange*. Is the lighthouse private, public, a charity, regulated? Before we begin developing our lighthouse example, though, we must ask and answer an important question: What are institutions for?

What Are Institutions For?

To answer this question, let's start with a society with no institutions. As economist Harold Demsetz pointed out, Robinson Crusoe didn't have to worry about institutions. There were no lawyers, accountants, or police officers because he didn't have to deal with anybody else. Crusoe's world is one without exchange, but it is the exception to the rule. After suggesting that institutions are the humanly devised constraints structuring interactions, the Nobel Prize–winning economist Douglass North went on to say that "throughout history, institutions have been devised by human beings to create order and reduce uncertainty in exchange."[7]

"Uncertainty in exchange" is of note if we are interested in intangible investment and what might be slowing it down. Investment is of course a form of exchange, and it is more prone to uncertainty than other forms of exchange because it happens over time: when people invest, they are incurring costs now in the hope of reaping benefits in the future. And *intangible* investment, as we will see, generates its own uncertainties.

We start, then, by examining the conditions or stages of exchange and then move to identifying which institutions support those conditions.

The Conditions or Stages of Exchange

What is needed to consummate a mutually beneficial exchange? Such an exchange may be monetary or nonmonetary. A partner may be one person or a coalition of many (for example, a firm buying from another firm). Are there some key elements of exchange, or is exchange so diffuse that it defies categorisation? We believe that there are four steps in exchange.

Step 1. Information: Find a Potential Partner with Whom Exchange Is Mutually Beneficial

Most analysis of exchange takes the condition of a beneficial exchange for granted: a buyer and a seller are already matched.[8] In the early stages of the COVID-19 crisis, for example, health authorities were desperate to find personal protective equipment (PPE), ventilators, and a vaccine. Fundamentally, this aligning or matching process is a problem of *information*: health agencies needed information on where to find PPE, who might be able to start producing ventilators, and what the formula for a vaccine might be.

What are the main features of information? First, information may be *dispersed* (buyers of PPE did not always know who the sellers were). There must be a way to unearth who is on either side of the market. Second, information may be uncertain and even *asymmetric*: health providers didn't know the quality of the PPE. Worse, if buyers thought that the only people in the market were poor-quality suppliers, then the market might drive out good suppliers who were unable to convey that information. Third, information may simply be *missing*. We did not know who might be producing ventilators, and in early 2020 it was unclear when a working vaccine would be available.

Step 2. Collective Action: Make Sure That All Those Who Benefit from the Exchange Contribute

Once a PPE supplier is found or a vaccine is discovered, a way must be found to make sure that everyone who will benefit from it pays for it. In a one-to-one exchange, this process is straightforward; but when the state is paying, the exchange is for collective provision. Some argued, for example, that the provision of PPE, or more broadly health services, to foreign visitors would deny the equipment to others. Thus, some collective-action problems occur when parties benefit from something for which they did not pay: for example, neighbours watching your fireworks display, or a chemical formula that is used by others who did not invest in its creation. Perhaps you can bargain with your neighbours or charge a knowledge licence fee to rival chemical companies. No matter the solution, an important element of solving collective-action problems is determining whether beneficiaries can be excluded or made to contribute. Other collective-action problems occur when goods need to be combined and an individual holds up the entire transaction. The building of a transport link across many parcels of land is one example.

Step 3. Commitment: Make Sure That a Partner Doesn't Renege on the Exchange

When an exchange is made over time, it will fail if the partners cannot commit to future performance. A payment for PPE to be delivered in three weeks needs to be based on the commitment that the PPE will be forthcoming. The development of a vaccine required the commitment of massive resources that companies might reasonably expect to recoup in the future.

Step 4. Minimise Haggling or Influence Costs: Don't Absorb Too Many Resources in the Process around Exchange

The process of exchange may involve what one might call "haggling" or "influence" costs. Paul Milgrom and John Roberts list the costs of bargaining as the costs of the bargaining activity itself, the costs of monitoring, the costs of enforcing, and the costs if there is failure to agree.[9] Some of these might be the costs that people incur to "influence" the decision, such as the cost of lobbyists and inducements. Some of these costs are thus part of the information part of transactions—for example, trying to gather data on whether the contract has been fulfilled. And some might be part of the collective-action problem—for example, excluding beneficiaries. But they seem sufficiently important to enumerate separately. In addition, Oliver Hart and John Moore suggest that exchange often involves "haggling costs."[10] Haggling costs include the psychological costs of the natural tension that many people feel in bargaining, the cost of disappointment, or feelings of aggrievement due to perceived unfairness in an exchange.

How Do Institutions Support the Four Aspects of Exchange?

To relate these four key features of exchange to institutions, let us turn to the work of anthropologists. According to the anthropologist Eleanor Leacock, the Innu (whom she referred to as the Montagnais), an Indigenous people in modern-day Quebec, had in the 1600s no concept of land ownership. Rather, land was a common resource available to everyone.[11] Hunters hunted wherever they liked and fed their families accordingly. Trade or exchange with outside parties, at least as conventionally understood today, was minimal.

By the 1700s, trade started to develop between tribes and external parties, such as seafarers. With this, Leacock argues, nonownership of land changed. The tribes started to allocate parcels of land to families, who were allowed exclusive hunting rights. Beaver traps were marked and designated for particular families. Similar patterns were found among the hunters in the forests of the Labrador Peninsula. Family hunting territories were divided up. In addition, hunting was banned in a central land area unless families faced a shortage in their own area, in which case they could access the communal land. Families rotated and hunted on different land areas each quarter. In the northwestern United States, ownership was more stable, and a system of inheritance emerged. By contrast, Native Americans in the southwestern plains of the United States had no property rights, with the land remaining a common resource for all. That arrangement changed only when European settlers arrived with cattle.

Douglass North describes the evolution of many societies in a similar way. They start off with exchange within families but little exchange with others. As exchange grows beyond a single village, it becomes more anonymous, and activities around exchange grow. These activities include the provision of security, financing, and redress for nonperformance, which suggests the development of some key institutions, or those "humanly designed constraints," that help the various dimensions of exchange.

Trust, Reputation, and Reciprocity

Before widespread trade, exchange was mostly within families and, perhaps, between tribes/villages close to each other. We can think of trust and reciprocity as an "institution" that helped early trade. Anthropologists have written extensively on how such rules are stable outcomes of a repeated game with a small number of known players. One shouldn't overromanticise, however. Trust and reciprocity do not mean that earlier societies were always kind and forgiving, or a counterpoint to the relentless chiselling of modern-day capitalist societies. The process of ensuring trust requires punishment of those who break that trust. And the more severe the punishment, other things being equal, the more likely trust is to be maintained. We may wish to return to a more trusting society, but such a society may well depend on very harsh penalties for those who abuse that trust. Further, as societies become larger and trade more, it is impossible to know all the parties to an exchange, so trust must be replaced with something else, such as reputation or a money-back guarantee.

Property Rights

What happens once the nature of exchange changes? Harold Demsetz considered the incentives faced by the hunters that the anthropologists described. He reasoned that if no hunter owns land and cannot control the hunting by others, then no individual hunter has any incentive to invest in increasing or maintaining the stock of animals. It is quite likely, therefore, that excessively intensive hunting takes place, imposing costs on other hunters and future generations (what economists call *externalities*, the effects of one person's actions on others). Before the fur trade developed, excessive hunting was a minor concern in very large areas of land with a sparse population of hunters. The interactions between hunters were minimal, and the land could support the relatively few hunters and replenish the stock of game quite naturally. Once the fur trade developed, however, the interactions between hunters become material as hunters demanded fur not only for themselves but also to trade with others.

Society needs a mechanism to deal with these interactions. One mechanism that goes a long way towards solving this problem is property rights. Once property rights are enshrined, individual hunters have an interest in the number of animals and in the future. They can, in principle, bargain with each other about the size of catches and the like. These arrangements are especially relevant in the fur trade, because beavers tend to live in particular areas rather than roam across wide areas; so, allocating a particular area to a particular hunter gives that hunter strong incentives to husband the hunting opportunities.

Why, then, did the Native Americans in the southwestern plains of the United States have no property rights before European settlement? Demsetz suggests two reasons. First, property rights developed only when European settlers arrived with cattle. Second, the animals of the southwestern plains are primarily grazing animals that do not confine themselves to the limited spaces that beavers do. Therefore, the value of assigning distinctive property rights to parcels of land was much less for those who hunted roaming animals.

Finally, Friedrich Hayek argued that the development of property rights is crucial if a market is to develop. These rights in turn help solve dispersed information problems. Hayek[12] saw a transaction not as the exchange of a good or service but rather as the exchange of the ownership rights regarding its use (the ability to resell it, for example, or to exclude others from using it). Thus, property rights are the key institution that allows a market to develop, which then solves the problem of dispersed information via the information content of market prices.[13]

Of course, property rights, whether individual (your house) or collective (shared property or patent pools), have to be secure and respected; we group this institutional feature under commitment below.

A Mechanism for Collective Decision-Making

Property rights can take a large number of forms. Land can be owned communally, privately, or by the state. As we have seen, the early hunters in the Labrador Peninsula instituted common land. Thus, exchange requires institutions that provide a mechanism for collective decision-making.

There are many possibilities. One is simply to have trust and reciprocity.[14] The polar opposite is to design a political system to regulate decisions by the state, such as various forms of voting. In the middle would be large firms with the right to use their capital as they choose. In other words, society must find a way to allocate *authority* around exchange.

Although collective decision-making or authority may help with collective-action problems, it might be very costly if much haggling and many influence activities (lobbying, bureaucracy, and so on) are involved, one part of what economists call *transactions costs*. If these costs are high, institutional design will have to economise on such costs.[15]

Contract Enforcement

Because property rights have to be secure and respected, contract enforcement is key. A particularly stark problem occurs when exchange takes place over time. As Daron Acemoglu, Simon Johnson, and James Robinson put it, "In any market situation where economic exchange takes place, and the *quid* is separated from the *pro quo*, issues of commitment will arise."[16] Commitment is a particular problem for governments, or more broadly for any authority. If the legal system permits, the private sector can commit by signing a legally binding agreement. But authorities make the law. By definition, they cannot sign an enforceable contract for the future. This lack of commitment is then a key problem requiring an institutional solution. The institutional solution is a set of political institutions that enable commitment. Acemoglu and colleagues argue that the English Civil War (1642–51) and the Glorious Revolution (1688–89) provided exactly this type of institutional change.

The Tudor monarchs, particularly Henry VIII, tried to build an absolutist monarchy that could arbitrarily confiscate property and raise taxes. The outcome of the civil war was the transfer of power from the monarch to Parliament, a change consolidated in the Glorious Revolution. Such an institutional change provided credible commitment that confiscation would no longer occur or would at least be lessened. Indeed, Acemoglu and colleagues further trace this change to the expansion of world trade and to the emergence of a new class of merchants whose economic interests were directly opposed to arbitrary appropriation by a king.[17]

Because of commitment, such political institutions are delicately poised, as the case of the transition from white to majority rule in Zimbabwe illustrates. The initial electoral system guaranteed white voters 20 percent of seats in the legislature despite the fact that whites comprised only around 3 percent of the population. But within five years that system was changed, and subsequent amendments to the constitution allowed for the redistribution of land, opening the door for the Mugabe government to redistribute land via both legal and extralegal methods. Political institutions, argue Daron Acemoglu and James Robinson, therefore have to navigate between needing a strong state to enforce contracts and provide collective goods and needing a strong society in case the state gets too strong—hence the title of their book, *The Narrow Corridor*.[18] Barry Weingast has advanced a similar view.[19]

All this suggests that institutions that help with commitment are the key to exchange over time. Contract enforcement and trust are obvious institutions that help with commitment. For governments, which cannot commit, institutions that solve collective-action problems and minimise influence/haggling costs are key.[20]

The Conditions for Exchange and Institutions That Support Those Conditions: A Summary

Table 3.1 summarises the conditions needed for exchange and the institutions that support those conditions. It shows the key conditions for exchange, in the first column, mapped against the classes of institutions in the first row. As set out in the second column, an institution that helps with trust/reciprocity/reputation ticks all the boxes. Such an institution helps exchange by helping with commitment, collective action, information, and haggling costs. In the third column, property rights, whether private or collective, help with collective action, as the early hunter case studies show, and with information, if they can help institute markets. In the fourth column, collective decision-making helps with collective-action problems and with dispersed information. For example, to the extent that it helps harness dispersed information, a voting system aggregates voters' wishes. Finally, contract enforcement should help predominantly with commitment. It may also help avert haggling costs if, for example, access to binding arbitration or justice in the event of disagreement is quick, low-cost, and fair.

The table makes clear a number of points. First, it stresses the importance of trust (reciprocity/reputation) as a cross-cutting social institution for improving exchange. Scholars have noted this importance over and over again, tracing, for example, the many economic arrangements that hope to maximise trust. Two good examples are family firms and trade between like members of an ethnic/religious group.

Second, the table raises an important question: What is a "good" institution? The gaps in the table show that with the exception of trust, institutions do not cover all parts of the exchange process. Consider private property rights. As we have

TABLE 3.1
Conditions Needed for Exchange and Types of Institutions That Support Them

	Type of institution that potentially supports those conditions			
Condition needed for exchange	Trust, reciprocity, reputation	Property rights (private, collective)	Collective-decision mechanisms (e.g., voting system, centralised or decentralised authority)	Contract enforcement
Commitment	✓			✓
Collective action	✓	✓	✓	
Information (dispersed, asymmetric, missing)	✓ (asymmetric)	✓ (dispersed)	✓ (dispersed)	
(Absence of) influence/ haggling costs	✓			✓

Note: The elements of the table show what we consider the main relations between the rows and columns.

seen, they might help improve incentives for hunters to husband animals or firms to invest in intellectual property. But, by themselves, they are no guarantee of low haggling costs. Any statement, then, that "more" (or more secure) private property rights is a "good" institution for growth is incomplete. Such rights will not provide an incentive for exchange if there is expensive haggling over, say, hunting areas or the right to licence knowledge from patents. Eric Posner and E. Glen Weyl point to a similar problem using the example of a railway line requiring one hundred adjacent parcels of privately owned land.[21] Private property will not help here because the owner of the one hundredth parcel can hold up the entire project, even though the other ninety-nine owners are willing to go ahead with it. In this case, they argue, private property is a good institution for information purposes (trade in land parcels will reveal values via prices) but a poor institution for collective-action purposes.[22]

The observation that institutions may not support all the conditions of exchange is also a key point made by Acemoglu, Johnson, and Robinson.[23] As they note, centralised authority such as parliamentary government might be a good way of solving the problems of collective action, but an agent with authority, especially government, may suffer from a commitment problem. As we have seen, a private person can sign a legally binding contract, but a government cannot, because it can always change the law. Furthermore, centralised power and authority by themselves do not guarantee the absence of lobbying and influence costs and may indeed provoke them.

Third, if there is a change in the underlying dimension of exchange, then the institutions that were previously suitable may no longer be so. Take trust as an example. Primitive economies had little contact and trade with others. But as they grew, the information and commitment conditions required to trade with outsiders became more and more important. Trust between locals was not enough—hence the need for new institutions, such as contract enforcement, to support those new conditions.

In the rest of this chapter we explain how the move to an intangible economy is an example of a change in the underlying conditions of exchange that requires new institutions. But first we illustrate that point with the promised example: the lighthouse.

What Got You Here Won't Get You There: Institutions and Technological Change

As we have seen, institutions help support some, but not all, conditions of exchange, which means they have to change as the underlying conditions change. So what counts as a "good" institution is not an eternal verity but can change over time as the economy changes. The history of lighthouses illustrates this point.[24]

The Lighthouse and the "Right" Institutions

Lighthouses have a special place in an economist's heart. One of the earliest lessons that first-year economics students are taught uses lighthouses as an easy-to-understand example of public goods. And they are taught it using the concept of exchange. The Economics 101 story goes something like this: In the old days, lighthouses provided a vital service of warning sailors of the presence of rocks. This service was valuable but nonexcludable in that anyone could use it, whether they contributed to the cost of running the lighthouse or not.[25] In short, lighthouses provide a classic example of the condition in which exchange requires the solution of a collective-action problem. The lighthouse provides a public good and so tends to be provided by governments, funded by taxation. Once upon a time, the story goes, there were inadequate institutions and too few lighthouses; then good institutions arose to fix the public goods problem, and lighthouses abounded.[26]

At first glance, the history of lighthouses bears out the Economics 101 story of a single act of institutional innovation. Consider the Lizard Lighthouse off Cornwall, in the southwest United Kingdom, which illuminates a dangerous rocky peninsula running a long way into the English Channel. Indeed, the stretch of coast is so dangerous that it is known as the "graveyard of the seas." Sir John Killigrew, a local landowner, obtained permission to build a lighthouse in 1619, but he could only ask for voluntary contributions. He got none, and his newly built lighthouse was demolished a few years after it was built. In 1751 a new lighthouse was built by a local landowner, which is the current lighthouse. The lighthouse used a coal-fired brazier, but it was considered ineffective as a lighthouse until new lights were installed in 1811 and 1874, by which time it was no longer privately owned.[27] The institution of private property, so the story goes, held back exchange (in this case, the provision of a lighthouse) for literally two centuries, until the right institution, public ownership, developed.

In broad scope the explanation of inappropriate institutions is accurate. But the details help us understand just what went wrong. There are two dimensions to the provision of lighthouse services that have to be supported if exchange is to take place. First, the supply of light is a supply of *information* to mariners. This is an enduring feature of lighthouses; the light has to be reliable, recognisable, and trusted, just like any other successful information good. Second, a lighthouse presents a potential collective-action problem if it cannot exclude its use by ships that pass by and don't pay. However, excludability as a dimension of exchange is not as "natural" a feature of this market as the Economics 101 lecture implies. In fact, it is determined by the specific location of the lighthouse and the technologies used. Regarding technologies, as David van Zandt points out, if premodern ships had had radios and mobile payment systems, it would have been possible to have a system whereby passing ships would radio lighthouses and, upon payment of a fee, the lighthouse keeper would fire up the light.[28]

Ancient mariners with cell phones may seem far-fetched, but the actual development of lighthouses shows how technical change modified the way lighthouses worked and affected the institutions needed to maintain them. Although the information feature was enduring, the collective-action feature (as with technical change) became more important.

In 1566 the maritime charity Trinity House was granted an early form of patent on its lighthouses. That is, in return for a licence payment to the government, it could build a lighthouse and keep any fees after paying the licence. But even though Trinity House had the state-granted monopoly, there was also private provision of lighthouses because successive kings did not recognise those exclusive rights.[29] Public and private lighthouses coexisted up to the 1830s. But if excludability was a problem, how did the private lighthouses survive? The Eddystone Lighthouse, for example, was indeed built privately, far offshore, in 1699. Why were lighthouses then taken into public ownership? And why did France and then the United States have an entirely publicly owned system?

The reason is that excludability, and thus the appropriate institution, changed because the technology changed. The technical change was the invention of proper lighting. In the early 1800s, lighthouses were lit with candles or oil lamps using mirrors that typically absorbed about half the light they reflected, and their range was limited to around five to eight miles. The breakthrough came in 1819 when the Frenchman Augustin Fresnel invented a series of prisms that concentrated the light rays into a single beam. In addition to increasing the range to thirty miles, Fresnel's apparatus could rotate and so, with varying speed, could send out flashing light signatures whose length depended on the distance from the coast. Fresnel also helped navigation by giving each lighthouse a different signature. Starting in 1825, the French built a network of fifty-one lighthouses (from thirteen originally), funded by the Ministry of Public Works using the new technology. This programme was completed in 1854.

Matters in the United Kingdom were very different. In 1836 there were fifty-six lighthouses, fourteen of which were private.

But none of them had the new dioptric technology, despite the United Kingdom's sending a representative to France in 1821 and seeing a demonstration of the technology in 1822. By 1854, the French had a new-technology lighthouse every 12.3 miles of shore, whereas the United Kingdom had a lighthouse every 14 miles of shore. Half of those lighthouses had outdated reflectors. By 1851, the United States, after a tax-funded building program, had twice as many lighthouses as the United Kingdom. Almost all of them used the Fresnel lens.

The key point here is that institutions, including public and private ownership, have to adapt to the technical change that alters the importance of the underlying dimensions of exchange. A lighthouse must distinguish between harbour lights, for which excludability is *not* a problem, and landfall/seacoast lights, for which excludability is a massive problem. Before the invention of the Fresnel lens, lighting technology was so poor that effectively the only seacoast lights were harbour lights. They could charge for their services because the only ships that passed were on their way to the harbour and so the lighthouse was funded out of harbour fees. Indeed, local pilots promoted lighthouse building to help them navigate. Thus, private lighthouses could fund themselves from local charges. For example, although the Eddystone Lighthouse was a long way offshore, almost all of the ships that passed it were on their way to Plymouth harbours. Lights intended for general coastal navigation, such as the Lizard Light, faced a much more severe excludability problem. Therefore, they could not support themselves from local charges.[30]

When the Fresnel lens was invented, seacoast lights became a more effective possibility. It was only with the new technology that excludability became a dimension of exchange and so needed a new institution. And, indeed, seacoast lighthouses then had to be publicly funded out of general tax revenues.[31]

The institution appropriate to the old technology regime, local funding, was not appropriate to the new one, which needed collective action to institute national funding. For the new technology to be adopted, those institutional arrangements had to change. Britain, which was slow to change, invested in fewer lighthouses.

Properties of Institutions

The lighthouse example highlights four interesting properties of institutions that are important to the argument of the rest of this book. Institutions are *specific* to particular economic circumstances in the same way that the ideal institutions for maintaining lighthouses changed along with lighthouse technology. They are subject to *inertia,* in that they tend to persist even after those circumstances have changed, like Britain's lighthouse institutions. They are inherently *unpredictable,* in that it is not always obvious which set of rules and norms will work best, especially when we are dealing with new technologies or new ways of doing business. And they are subject to *politics*: coalitions of people with a vested interest in preserving suboptimal institutions can often prevail.

Specificity

Some institutions that economists study are very broad. Research on the origins of modern economic growth often focuses on macro-institutions such as "limited government,"[32] "a culture of innovation,"[33] or the "improving mindset."[34] These institutions are important across different cultures and across wide stretches of time. The strength and enforceability of property rights, for example, are relevant to how much investment took place in medieval European water mills, in fields in the nineteenth-century American West, and in houses in present-day Latin America.[35] In general, the research suggests that property rights and the ability to enforce them increase investment. Medieval lords were less likely to go to the expense of building a mill in domains where they feared expropriation; Western ranchers invested more in their land when the invention of barbed wire allowed them to cheaply fence in their land; and people today are less likely to invest in their own homes if the legal system of their countries makes it hard for them to legally own them or prove their ownership.

But institutions are fractal. Macro-institutions are generally composed of smaller, more specific institutions, which in turn are composed of their own institutions, and so on. The more detailed we get, the more qualitative variety we see, and the more contingent institutions are on one another and on the wider context in which they exist. Richard Nelson made this point forcefully in 1994, when he pointed out that new technologies often have their own institutional requirements.[36] For example, the deployment of radio relied on institutions to regulate spectrum and content; the rise of the motorcar depended on institutions that governed everything from road safety to fuel supply to land use; the commercialisation of electricity was based on institutions ranging from how electricians were trained and exchanged knowledge to technical standards for the production and transmission of electrical power. This old idea has been given a new lease on life in tech-policy debates that focus on the concept of *tech-governance fit*, the idea that certain forms of government are particularly well suited to certain general-purpose technologies.

Looking at institutions at the wrong granularity can lead to mistaken diagnoses about what is wrong in an economy. As

Elinor Ostrom observed, "The institutional analyst faces a major challenge in identifying the appropriate level of analysis relevant to addressing a particular puzzle."[37] This warning suggests that we should be open to the possibility that when the mode of production in the economy changes, its institutional needs do too. The Quebec Innu and lighthouses are cases in point.

Inertia

Institutions also exhibit inertia. They can persist past their sell-by date, compromising economic performance. The classic example is the QWERTY keyboard layout, which was originally devised to keep frequently used keys apart so as to reduce jamming in mechanical typewriters. Some expertspoint out that you can type faster on different keyboard layouts.[38] So, if we ditched QWERTY, we would be able to type faster and a common activity would become marginally faster and easier. But even though typewriters are now just curios and the jamming of the keys a distant memory, QWERTY persists because users learn to type using it and because consumers expect it. Technologists call things like the QWERTY layout *skeuomorphs*: design features that persist even though they reflect a technical constraint or feature that is now redundant, like the rivets on jeans or the floppy disk "Save" icon on a computer. If something as trivial and as obviously arbitrary as the layout of a keyboard can become stuck, how much more must this be true of deeply embedded, culturally cherished norms and rules?

Economist Avner Greif developed a theory of when institutions change and when they do not, pointing to several reasons why institutions persist.[39] These include the difficulty of coordinating (the collective-action problem), people's lack of attention to the changing environment, and the fact that people and society cleave to habits and routines. The idea is a familiar one in British culture, in that critics such as Thorstein Veblen and Corelli Barnett have sought to attribute various aspects of the United Kingdom's relative economic decline to the persistence of outmoded institutions, from systems of elite education and technical training to the structure of capital markets and corporate governance. In some cases, careful scholarship casts doubt on these claims. For example, David Edgerton's histories of postwar Britain point out that the country's institutions were much friendlier to technology and industry than pundits casually suppose.[40] There is a risk of observing a bad outcome and assuming that a given institution is outmoded and therefore must be the cause.

Nor is it true that bad institutions are insuperable obstacles to economic growth. The story of the Industrial Revolution in Britain is a story of businesses and inventors circumventing and repurposing outmoded institutions to take advantage of new commercial opportunities, from passing acts of Parliament, to chartering companies, to building railways, to raising finance from local notables rather than financial markets. Where there is a big new economic opportunity but institutions are struggling to keep up, a kind of bricolage is often possible. But it is more costly than good institutions; we should not forget that British economic growth in the glory days of the Industrial Revolution (the nineteenth century) was around 0.3 percent per year—low compared with the United States and Germany, which were in a position to learn from Britain's gambles and put better institutions in place from the start. In short, when we survey the institutional landscape at a time of economic change, we should not be surprised to encounter hangovers, skeuomorphs, and relics.

Unpredictability

When information is absent or missing, exchange will have unpredictable consequences. Richard Nelson made the point that institutions are the product of evolution, not design. Individual policies or rules may be designed, but as soon as you combine rules, laws, and norms into a functioning institution, they take on emergent properties that are hard to predict. Thus, the creation of new institutions is a faltering process that is hard to get right.

The evolution of the modern venture capital industry provides a good example. A functional venture capital sector and the norms and practices that go with it is an example of an institution, and it is one that has clearly shaped the economic development of Silicon Valley and, by extension, the world.[41] From an economic point of view, venture capital is about providing risk capital to young firms that have a good chance of becoming very valuable in a short amount of time. In certain places and at certain times—for example, Northern California and Massachusetts in the second half of the twentieth century—that broad investment strategy ought to have been a slam dunk because many of the required institutions already existed. Instead, what became the norm for venture capital in Silicon Valley took time to develop: forming partnerships, in which limited partners provided the capital; performing very detailed due diligence; taking minority equity stakes and board seats; banking on a few "home runs"; and providing incentives to partners. The precursor to modern venture capital funds, Boston-based American Research and Development, was a listed company (which created continual financial problems) and had not yet mastered the art of cutting bad investments loose. It took the failure of ARD, along with more than a decade of experimentation, for the modern model to be devised and adopted. It is simply hard, ex ante, to know what a good institution looks like.

This difficulty is compounded if we take into account the effects of institutional inertia and specificity. If institutions are hard to craft well, tend to persist, and specific to technologies, then the risk of legacy institutions increases.

Consider the Wright Brothers' patent war, a sad episode in the history of intellectual property. In 1906, at the dawn of the era of aviation, the Wright Brothers were granted a patent on the method they had devised to control the flight of an aeroplane. The breadth of this patent was very broad, covering not just the Wright Brothers' wing-warping technique but also any form of flight control.[42] This patent allowed Wright Aviation to sue any competitor using ailerons for prohibitively large licensing fees, which discouraged investment in the nascent aviation industry, especially in the United States. (And, as it turned out, wing warping was a very poor technology that was superseded by the ailerons that are used today.[43]) The problem became acute when the US government was unable to procure any US-built aircraft suitable to deploy when it entered World War I. US government intervention forced Wright Aviation and its competitors to form the Manufacturers' Aircraft Association, allowing low-cost use of each other's patents.

The broad institutional context here is American intellectual property law. But the specific decision by the Patent Office to approve the Wrights' unusually broad patent effectively created a different set of institutions within the aviation industry—a sort of institutional microclimate—that had very bad economic effects. In 1906, aviation was an exciting niche with no clear dominant technology; even if the long-term impacts of the decision to grant a broad patent could have been calculated, it is not clear that a patent examiner would have been aware of their importance. But the institutional dynamic that the decision created persisted for over a decade, requiring the extreme raison d'état of a world war to motivate the government to intervene and change it.[44]

Institutions are complex, and their effects, which are often complicated and analysis resistant, are not usually obvious to those involved in designing them. Thus, we should not be surprised that governments and others charged with designing the rules and practices that form the basis of new institutions underinvest in what is already a difficult task, and that sometimes the mistakes and compromises get preserved to the detriment of the future.

Politics

Bad institutions do not persist only because of specificity, unpredictability, and inertia. They can also persist because of vested interests.

The idea of a small group of people metaphorically holding the public ransom is a mainstay of political rhetoric. Political scientist Mançur Olson provided a framework to explain why and when we might expect this to happen.[45] Changing an institution or preserving a failing one requires political action; taking such action has costs, both financial and social. One such cost is that of coordinating the action—say, organising a strike or forming a cartel and keeping it secret. Where an institution benefits a small number of people but imposes smaller costs on a larger group, the small group will find that its costs of coordination are lower and the benefits for individual members are higher. Therefore, we would expect cliques and cabals to be better at conspiring and combining than big, diffuse groups are, even if the aggregate interest of the big group is larger. Silent majorities are silent for a reason.

Olson also observed that, throughout history, small groups have a particular advantage when the matter at stake is not obvious, as in the case of income tax rates and income tax exemptions. Income tax rates, which are usually progressive, take a larger percentage of rich people's income, but income tax exemptions are typically much more generous for richer groups. A rich minority might want to lobby to cut income taxes on very high salaries, Olson argued, but the issue is so salient that this kind of carve-up is likely to be widely understood and difficult to pull off. But lobbying for an obscure deduction or loophole can be done more subtly, even if the net effect—to reduce the tax paid by the rich and increase the burden on everyone else—is the same.

What's more, those who benefit from existing institutions are likely to continue supporting them. The economic historian Bas van Bavel elaborates on this idea in *The Invisible Hand*, arguing that "holders of economic power consolidate their economic and later political domination and acquire formal, legal power as well, which they use to sustain the market institutions that benefit them or develop new institutions that consolidate their dominant position in markets."[46] Van Bavel provides a number of vivid case studies of economies that grew richer but failed to develop the institutions they needed to operate effectively at a higher economic level; as a result, they stagnated or declined. These include Abbasid Iraq, northern Italy in the late Middle Ages, and the Netherlands after its seventeenth-century golden age. In each case, van Bavel argues, the incentives on those who had the power to shape institutions were not conducive to productive investment or to the further growth of the economy.

Lagging institutions are a key part of China's decline. Many people are surprised to learn that China was the richest nation in the world in 1000 CE. Whilst the country as a whole likely fell behind other countries in 1300, the leading regions of China were as rich as or richer than the leading European nations until the eighteenth century. Scholars have attributed China's economic success to more centralised and autocratic institutions in Asia, but whether these institutions are overly powerful (and appropriate) or excessively weak (and cannot provide public goods, for example, by enforcing property rights to prevent piracy) is disputed.[47]

The lesson here is that changing outmoded institutions is hard political work because of the power of vested interests, and that it is even harder when the problems are not obvious.

These four characteristics of institutions—their *specificity*, their *inertia*, their *unpredictability*, and their *politics*—can combine under some circumstances to cause problems when the economy experiences technological change. The specificity of institutions means that the institutions that helped promote equitable and sustained growth in yesterday's technological landscape may not work as well today. Their inertia means that these outmoded institutions often persist after they have ceased to be useful. Their unpredictability means that well-intentioned efforts to shape institutions to deal with new technologies may miss the mark, especially in the early days of those new technologies. And the politics of institutions are such that small groups with vested interests often prove very effective at defending institutions that are, on balance, socially harmful.

The Institutional Demands of an Intangible Economy

Our discussion of the four characteristics of institutions brings us back to the shift to an intangibles-intensive economy outlined in chapter 1. As we have seen, from hunter-gatherers to lighthouse builders, institutions need to change with changing economic circumstances. Technical change in the provision of light turned the underlying need for a lighthouse from an information problem into a collective-action problem that needed a new institution. In the same way, the unusual economic properties of intangible capital—spillovers, synergies, sunk costs, and scale—and an economy increasingly dependent on it have changed the underlying conditions of exchange and generated new institutional requirements.

Because intangible assets have *spillovers*, solving the collective-action problem becomes more important. The spillovers create new demands on institutions relating to property rights. If the benefits of husbanding beavers mean that those beavers move to an adjacent hunting ground, then individual hunters will invest insufficiently in animal husbandry. For the same reason, we would expect profit-maximising businesses to invest less in intangibles if their benefits spill over to others.

An important role of institutions is to mitigate this effect. Sometimes this mitigation happens through intellectual property rights, such as patents or copyrights, which create an artificial legal restriction on spillovers: a private property right. Sometimes it happens through direct public subsidy, as when governments provide funding or tax credits for business research: a public property right. Other mechanisms are more complex. For example, academic research depends not only on public subsidy but also on a complex set of norms, rules, and nonmonetary incentives ranging from peer review and citation practices to H-indexes and Nobel Prizes. Often, civil society rather than government is the source of institutions that manage intangible spillovers, as when local chambers of commerce or industry groups develop standards or run apprenticeships or training schemes. Thus, an economy that becomes more intangible will put strain on the institutions, such as property rights, that aim to retain activity even with spillovers.

What of *synergies* between intangibles? Intangibles need to be combined for synergies to be realised.[48] But what needs to be combined with what? Synergies place demands on *information* in the economy. In general, the act of matching or combining requires a *platform* for them to be combined and a *mechanism* for attracting potential partner intangibles to that platform. A corporate science lab might be a platform and its takeover of other firms the mechanism for bringing other intangibles onto the platform. Another platform might be a city and the places and institutions the mechanism that inspire people to meet and exchange ideas. Still other platforms might be search engines and entertainment providers.

The emergence of platforms, which help with synergies and spillovers, increases the economic importance of cities, and by implication an intangibles-rich economy relies more on the institutions that govern how cities are built and managed—in particular, the land-use and planning systems. Note, too, that if the combination of intangible assets is important, so potentially are influence and haggling costs. These costs manifest themselves in litigation and thickets around patents, but more constructively the social norms and trust around patent pools and open-source software help to manage these costs and resolve collective-action issues.

The *sunkenness* of intangible investments creates additional demands on *commitment* and the institutions of business finance. Most external business finance takes the form of debt, which especially for smaller businesses involves a claim on the firm's assets and significant institutional lock-in. A move to a world in which more firms have mainly intangible assets will require institutional innovation in business finance. To a certain extent, sunkenness is a consequence of inadequate property rights. For

TABLE 3.2
Exchange and Types of Institutions

Condition needed for exchange	Type of institution that potentially supports those conditions: Trust, reciprocity, reputation	Property rights (private, collective)	Collective-decision mechanisms (e.g., voting system, centralised or decentralised authority)	Contract enforcement	Property of intangibles needing condition of exchange
Commitment	✓			✓	Sunkenness
Collective action	✓	✓	✓		Spillovers
Information (dispersed, asymmetric, missing)	✓ (asymmetric)	✓ (dispersed)	✓ (dispersed)		Synergies
(Absence of) influence/ haggling costs	✓			✓	Scale

example, if there is trade in patents, knowledge investment can be recovered.

Finally, the *scalability* of intangible investments turns the economy into more of a winner-takes-all structure, which boosts the incentive to lobby and expend effort on influence activities to create regulatory regimes that favour the winner.

The final column of table 3.2 builds on table 3.1 to set out the way in which each property of intangibles requires more of the different conditions of exchange and so stresses different institutional types. Table 3.2 shows that institutions that help with some, but not all, dimensions of exchange matter in the intangible economy. For example, if spillovers are likely to occur, then collective action is more of a problem. But creating more private property rights to help collective action might not generate intellectual property (IP) investment if the haggling costs to combine IP are too high. Imperfect collective decision-making mechanisms, such as a nonfunctioning planning system that restricts cities and lowers synergies and spillovers, will be costly to an intangible economy. Public support for intangible investment may help with spillovers but not with synergies if there is insufficient variety of investment.

Why a Slowdown?

In the following chapters, we examine how present-day economic institutions do a poor job of supporting intangible investment. But there is one general question that is worth addressing now. If our current institutions are intangible-unfriendly, why have flows of intangible capital developed in the way they have, increasing steadily for several decades, to around 12–15 percent of GDP per year, before stagnating?

There are two plausible explanations. The first is that current institutions may work well enough to support intangible investment in some subsector of the economy but not a wider transition. Consider, for example, the importance of equity finance, which we discuss at greater length in chapter 5. One underlying problem is that most of the world's financial institutions are set up to provide debt finance, which, owing to the sunkenness of intangible capital, is poorly suited to intangibles-rich firms. In fact, a small but important set of equity finance institutions has arisen, in the form of the venture capital sector, to finance a few sectors of the economy where intangible investment is unusually important, mostly software and biotech. But for the vast majority of businesses, the institutional bias of finance is still towards debt.

The second explanation is that in some cases, the growing stock of intangible capital makes existing institutions less effective at promoting intangible investment. One example is intellectual property rules, which we discuss in chapter 4. Intellectual property rules help mitigate the problem of spillovers with intangible assets, but as intangibles become more important, the costs of patent thickets increase and the incentives for rights holders to lobby governments to change the rules in rent-seeking ways increase.

Summary

Institutions, the humanly devised rules of interaction, help with particular dimensions of exchange, such as commitment, collective action, and information. But those dimensions change in importance over time, and so institutions have to change too. Thus, with the rise in intangibles, the various components of exchange have had to change, along with the institutions that help those particular components. An intangible economy needs institutions that help economise on haggling costs and help solve collective-action and information problems caused by spillovers and synergies and commitment problems owing to sunk costs.

In the rest of the book we explore these problems, and their possible solutions, further. A city is a nexus of public and private ownership rights and collective decision-making where closeness helps with spillovers and synergies, but collective-action problems of congestion and crowding abound—likewise for science policy that tries to solve collective-action problems but needs information and resistance to influence activities. Competition and monetary policy try to help with the collective-action problems of sound currency and competitive markets from which all individuals benefit, but none so much that it is worth their spending resources to individually enforce.

PART II

Fixing Our Changed Economy

4

"The Progress of Science and Useful Arts"

REFORMING PUBLIC INVESTMENT AND INTELLECTUAL PROPERTY

Governments spend billions of dollars a year to mitigate the problem of intangible spillover, funding research and education or protecting intellectual property (IP). But the systems for doing so are often haphazard or dysfunctional, even though the demands placed on them grow each year. Fixing them involves reconciling two paradoxes and overcoming significant political hurdles.

A significant chunk of government responsibility involves fixing one particular problem associated with intangible capital: the fact that its benefits spill over. If you've attended a publicly financed school or university; if you've paid for a book, a video game, or a piece of music; if you've used any of the countless technologies, from mobile phones to steroids, that owe their invention to publicly funded research, then you have interacted with government in its guise as the Spillover Police.

The idea that governments have a role in addressing spillovers is mainstream. From a theoretical point of view, it has been well established among economists for over half a century,[1] and among policy makers for even longer than that. Large publicly funded research programmes and national systems of public education, for example, became commonplace among rich countries in the first half of the twentieth century, and IP laws have an even longer heritage.

Governments, along with nongovernmental bodies such as universities, fund or subsidise education and training, R&D, and artistic and creative content for the benefit of firms and citizens. They also invest in intangibles for their own benefit, and some of these intangibles have wide and important spillovers. (Two examples are the US Armories' development of manufacturing systems based on interchangeable parts in the nineteenth century and the development of semiconductors for use in ballistic missiles.) Governments also manage systems of intellectual property rights (IPRs), including patents, copyrights, and trademarks.

Governments and Spillovers

If spillovers worked in a straightforward way, we would have two clear methods to increase intangible investment and improve productivity and growth. Specifically, we would need to strengthen and clarify property rights such as patents and copyrights. We would also need to increase public investment in R&D, education, and other intangibles. Unfortunately, this is not easy to do. Two big paradoxes make increasing intangible investment and strengthening IPRs difficult and even counterproductive. In addition, there are significant institutional barriers to putting policies in place to overcome these problems.

The First Paradox: The iPhone and the Wheelie Suitcase—Quantity versus Quality

If you follow debates on technology policy, two origin stories crop up with remarkable regularity: the iPhone and the wheelie suitcase. The stories behind their development illustrate both the process of innovation and, by implication, the state's role in it.

The iPhone story, popularised by Mariana Mazzucato's influential book *The Entrepreneurial State*,[2] goes as follows. You think of the iPhone as a private-sector triumph, but it is nothing of the sort. In fact, all its component parts, from its touchscreen display to the architecture of its chipsets to the protocols used to encode the web pages and music files you can download, had their origins in significant amounts of government investment. No state, no iPhone: this is a vivid articulation of the idea that intangible investments have spillovers and without public funding will be underprovided. According to David Willetts, a former UK science minister and Conservative politician, this account was influential in convincing many on the right that innovation should not be reduced to a private-sector story.[3]

The wheelie suitcase is a different type of story. Robert Plath, a pilot, thought of attaching a pair of wheels to his suitcase; in doing so, he changed luggage forever. The point here is that such an obviously useful and now-ubiquitous invention is a simple combination of two existing products. "The Rollaboard," in the words of the science writer Matt Ridley, "feels as if it could have been invented much earlier."[4] Those who deploy the wheelie suitcase example usually use it to draw attention to a different aspect of innovation: the fact that the specific combination of ideas really matters. Sometimes they link this idea to a call for more radical and diverse thinking, sometimes to a call for greater entrepreneurship or more extensive markets.

We can also use the wheelie suitcase to tell a story about the synergies of intangibles. By finding the right combination of two existing technologies, Plath created a new and valuable technology. If all innovations were like the Rollaboard, what would really matter is *not* total investment in R&D but rather *the very specific combinations* we can make out of them. This view of innovation reflects an old debate among economists. During the 1950s and 1960s, while neoclassical and Keynesian economists took part in a vast transatlantic debate on the nature of capital, a heterodox economist of the Austrian school named Ludwig Lachmann proposed his own theory of how capital worked.[5] He claimed that assets are essentially heterogeneous and that any attempt to add them together to determine a stock of capital is fundamentally wrongheaded. What mattered instead was how firms and entrepreneurs chose to combine capital, and the key economic problem was the lack of knowledge ("unknown unknowns") of these combinations (a theme of the Austrian school economists from Ludwig von Mises to Friedrich Hayek, Lachmann, and Israel Kirzner). Followers in the Austrian school argued that policy should focus less on maximising investment and more on encouraging entrepreneurs to identify these valuable, novel combinations of capital.[6]

The heterogeneity and lack of knowledge of combinations of capital remain a problem for economists today. Our systems of measuring GDP and productivity are based on the idea that capital can usefully be measured and added up based on its cost or its market value, which can be tricky with heterogeneous capital. How do you add up an iPad and a Boeing airplane? In addition, intangible capital is *more* heterogeneous than tangible capital. Many tangible assets, from vehicles to machine tools, are mass-produced, and they can be bought and sold in secondary markets. This is less true for intangible assets, particularly those relating to innovation. The large synergies they exhibit when they are combined in the right way means that an intangibles-rich economy would behave more like the economy Lachmann and his followers described than a mostly tangible economy would. Perhaps, therefore, what really matters today is getting the right intangibles and combining them in the right way.

We can frame these goals in terms of "quantity" versus "quality." Solving the spillover problem through public subsidy addresses the *quantity* problem of a lack of intangible investment. But if it's true that intangible capital is often heterogeneous and that making the right combinations of investment really matters, then the problem we face is one of *quality*.

The institutions that help exchange can be in conflict when we are trying to solve the quality problem. We fix the collective-action problem of spillovers by delegating R&D funding to a centralised authority. But if an intangible project needs combinations/synergies, then it also needs information that a centralised authority may not be able to provide. Likewise, that centralised authority might provoke influence activities, such as scientists trying to get their favourite project selected. Also, commitment may be a problem. Some critics note that once a government backs a project, it continues to support it for political reasons even if it is failing, perhaps even preventing new and better projects from coming into the market. Matters would improve if the government could commit to not taking such actions, but this is a difficult goal to accomplish.

Quantity versus Quality?

Policy makers have traditionally tried to achieve both quantity *and* quality. Governments fund public R&D in universities and government labs to increase the quantity of R&D, give tax breaks to entrepreneurs, and subsidise risk capital in the hope of encouraging more clever combinations of ideas. However, a problem arises if these two goals end up in conflict, particularly if policies to increase the quantity of intangible investment by subsidising it end up systematically reducing its quality. In that case, we might expect to see diminishing returns to public investment in certain types of intangibles, along with evidence that the wrong intangibles are being produced.

There is at least circumstantial evidence for both of these problems in two important fields of public intangible investment: technological and scientific research, and postsecondary education and training. In both cases, most governments spend large amounts of money subsidising or directly providing the intangibles in question. Additionally, there is a widespread belief that the overall, undifferentiated investment in capital is economically important. Governments closely track how much their countries spend on R&D as a percentage of GDP and often have targets to increase it. They also monitor the number of young people in tertiary education. What's more, when it comes to education, there is evidence that in the past, those who believed that quality trumped quantity were wrong. Claudia Goldin and Lawrence Katz's landmark work *The Race between Education and Technology* begins by describing how the United States in the nineteenth and early twentieth centuries invested heavily in school-age education compared with European countries and reaped big productivity benefits as a result, even as European observers wondered what the point was of teaching future farmhands and labourers to read and write.[7]

In both cases, there is evidence that the "quantity" approach may be causing problems today. A growing body of literature suggests that the productivity of scientific and technological research is slowing down. We are not talking here about complex causal links such as the relationship between R&D and GDP growth, but rather about the more straightforward relationship between investment in R&D and discoveries.[8] Alongside this quantitative evidence of a slowdown are widespread anecdotal reports of how public funding systems make it harder to do breakthrough research.[9]

We see similar evidence regarding postsecondary education. The salary premium that university graduates enjoy over nongraduates appears to be steadily shrinking, and more graduates end up in jobs that do not require a college degree. As a review of postsecondary education carried out by the British government in 2018 notes, "34 per cent of graduates in England and Northern Ireland are in non-graduate jobs, more than all the other countries in Europe except for Ireland and the Czech Republic."[10] And the idea that many university degrees do not adequately prepare individuals for future work is widely espoused by politicians, business leaders, and opinion formers. This idea goes hand in hand with the belief that the education system in countries such as the United States and the United Kingdom does a poor job of providing specific technical skills, which in turn is a big problem for employers.

Three specific mechanisms seem to be driving these problems: the fact that the rules for allocating public investment are inherently imperfect, the difficulty of updating rules as technology changes, and the public funding systems' vulnerability to capture by special interests.

Flawed Rules for Allocating Public Investment

The first mechanism is the perverse effect of targets and rules. Governments are creatures of law. When they enact an R&D tax break, fund academic research, or subsidise a university education, they must do so through rules that are simple enough for government officials to apply at scale. Thus, there is almost always a discrepancy between the intention of the rule and the precise rule itself. So, for example, a government's *intention* may be to fund the most promising scientific research projects that offer the biggest benefits for society. But the societal benefits of research are very hard to measure ex ante, so in practice a government measures other things, such as the quality of the researchers' grant applications, the researchers' publication record, metrics about the institution they work for, and a host of other variables that approximate "expected societal benefits" but are at best an imperfect proxy.

In the mid-1970s, the psychologist Donald Campbell and the economist Charles Goodhart came up with eponymous laws to the effect that quantified incentive systems always lead to perverse outcomes.[11] That is, targeting a chosen measure will end up corrupting that measure. Campbell's law and Goodhart's law certainly seem to come into play in the field of public research funding. The so-called *metric tide*, through which researchers and research funding in rich countries become subject to ever more sophisticated performance management and appraisal processes, is widely viewed as a mixed blessing at best. Although it has eliminated some egregiously inefficient practices and academic fiefdoms, it has also discouraged much breakthrough work and caused large amounts of time to be spent on project proposals and compliance.

Modifying Rules as Technology Progresses

In addition to being imperfect, the rules for subsidising intangibles are sometimes downright perverse, either because they are based on outdated models of how investment takes place or because they overlook some important type of investment. Let's consider two examples: the growing importance of software tools and data in research, and what is called the replication crisis.

It is widely agreed that the explosion of computing power in recent decades has increased the returns to data-intensive research.[12] Much research involves the creation and analysis of new data sets, along with the development of new tools to do so. Consider, for example, OpenSAFELY, a data platform that allows medical researchers to study data from British patients' National Health Service electronic health records securely and pseudonymously, and that enables urgent COVID-19-related research using very large data sets.[13] Ben Goldacre, one of the project's leaders, has frequently written about the difficulty of persuading traditional research funding bodies to finance the development of these kinds of data sets and tools, and of having them recognised as legitimate research outputs alongside traditional academic publication. Research funders are beginning to change their attitudes, but it is a slow process, and it is constrained by the bureaucratic nature of funders.

Another widely recognised issue in science is the *replication crisis*,[14] in which a whole range of research findings that were thought to be reliable turn out to be uncertain: when researchers try to replicate the experiments on which the findings are based, they are unable to obtain the same results, suggesting the original findings were at best the result of luck and at worst of fraud. So, for example, the psychological phenomenon of *priming*—the idea that showing a person a series of words or images about, say, old people will cause them, subconsciously, to act in an "elderly" way—was shown to be either nonexistent or much weaker than psychologists had thought. The replication crisis has given rise to systematic attempts to see if time-honoured findings are actually replicable.[15] Such replication attempts are often funded by philanthropists, such as John Arnold. Replication attempts could be an extremely valuable undertaking, greatly enhancing humanity's knowledge base. But again, traditional research funders have been reluctant to underwrite it, and academic institutions have not seen replication as a high-status activity for researchers.

Some commentators[16] have argued that science funders should put far more of their money into building new data sets and tools, and into replication. But funding organisations change slowly and often have weak incentives to respond to technological changes in how research is done, making these kinds of shifts harder to accomplish.

Capture by Special Interests

Institutional capture and conflict of interests also play a role. Some academic researchers may be less interested than government funding agencies in generating useful spillovers from their work. Universities typically have a strong interest in receiving fees in return for educating students but much weaker incentives to ensure that students actually learn things that will be useful in later life. Governments sometimes try to solve these problems with more rules and metrics, which can help—but then we are back to Campbell's law and Goodhart's law.

The Second Paradox: Blackberries and "Blurred Lines"—the Dilemma over IP

The other way that governments try to mitigate the problem of intangible spillovers is through IPRs, in particular patents and copyrights. Here again there is a dilemma.

The basic idea behind IPRs is straightforward. If competitors can copy ideas quickly and at no cost, then there is less financial incentive for a company to take the time and effort to invent them in the first place. Put another way, the government overcomes the spillover problem by granting inventors a temporary monopoly over the intangible asset they have created, banning others from taking advantage of the spillover.

But there is a well-documented literature of problems with patents and copyrights. Take the case of the Blackberry, the most popular smartphone in the days before the invention of the iPhone. In 2000, Blackberry's owners, RIM, and other mobile phone manufacturers were sued by NTP, a small company whose main activities were owning a set of wireless patents and suing mobile phone companies for infringing on them. NTP's case was questionable at best, but after six years of costly litigation RIM ended up paying $612.5 million to settle the action. This case is a classic example of *patent trolling*—the use of patents to extort money from innovators, with few positive effects on the incentive to invest in innovation in the first place. Researchers James Bessen and Michael Meurer[17] estimated that the costs of patent litigation represented 14 percent of total R&D costs in the late 1990s, a truly remarkable waste. It is certainly true that war-by-patent has become an integral part of the smartphone industry. The economists Michele Boldrin and David Levine described how Microsoft and Apple used thickets of patents to hinder Google's entry into the smartphone market, arguing that the motivation for Google's $12.5 billion acquisition of Motorola Mobility in 2011 was to acquire its patent portfolio—not to use the patented innovations directly but rather to use them as the basis for countersuits against Apple and Microsoft.[18]

For a different perspective, consider the 2013 pop song "Blurred Lines," by Robin Thicke and Pharrell Williams.

"Blurred Lines" was controversial not just for its lyrics and video, which were widely criticised as misogynistic, but also on IP grounds. Two years after the song's release, a California jury found Thicke and Williams guilty of copying Marvin Gaye's 1977 song "Got to Give It Up" and awarded $7.4 million in damages for copyright infringement. What was unusual about this case is that there seems to have been little doubt that "Blurred Lines" was to some extent a pastiche or homage to Gaye's song, but written in such a way that Williams was confident it would not be ruled as plagiarism. (Thicke claimed to be so buzzed on Vicodin and alcohol that he could barely remember writing the song.) The jury—as juries sometimes do—had effectively moved the goalposts of musicians' understanding of music copyright law, making it in effect significantly stricter and more uncertain. In the words of Justin Tranter, a prolific songwriter, "[Recent high-profile plagiarism cases are] definitely making people second guess a lot in sessions. Like, 'Oh fuck, does this maybe sound a bit like that?' . . . It is crazy, and I've seen labels now hiring musicologists for every single song they're going to release."[19]

These stories highlight several major problems with IPRs. First, they encourage firms to spend time and money on zero-sum legal chicanery, such as patent trolling and hiring forensic musicologists, rather than on positive-sum innovation. Second, they create what legal scholar Michael Heller[20] called *gridlock*, in which old ideas act as a block to the extent that innovation depends on mixing different ideas together, either by creating nasty surprises like the Gaye estate's claims against "Blurred Lines" or by simply creating a soup of permissions that are too arduous to negotiate. This soup would likely defeat a latter-day Public Enemy trying to record songs made of dozens of samples.

Opponents of IP also contend that the benefits of patents are overstated. Boldrin and Levine argue that if patents did not exist, then first-mover advantage could provide a sufficient reward for firms that invest in innovation. For example, they observe that it took a year for Apple's competitors to create a product similar to the iPhone, during which time Apple enjoyed exclusive control over the market for the new generation of smartphones. They also note that one of the original motivations for patents—specifically, that it made an innovation "patent" in the sense of public, so that others could learn from it—is no longer effective, because most patents are written so as not to provide true disclosure regarding how the underlying technology works.

That said, the extreme case of getting rid of IPRs altogether is at best unproven. Economists such as Zorina Khan, who has written extensively on the history of the patent system, argue that patents make an essential contribution to the American economy.[21] A review of the research literature by Bronwyn Hall, Christian Helmers, Mark Rogers, and Vania Sena makes the point that firms use complex combinations of patents, other IPRs, trade secrecy, and other rights to protect their innovations, and that would-be patent abolitionists may be making the Chesterton's Fence mistake of getting rid of something that works in ways they don't fully understand.[22] And it seems clear that certain activities where the cost of copying is cheap—such as drug discovery or publishing—would be radically changed, probably for the worse, if there were no IPRs. The economist Alex Tabarrok summarised these trade-offs in the Tabarrok curve (figure 4.1), plotting innovation on the *y* axis against patent strength on the *x* axis. The curve is an inverse U shape: With no patents at all, innovation is relatively low. With super-strong patents, it is even lower. But between those two points,

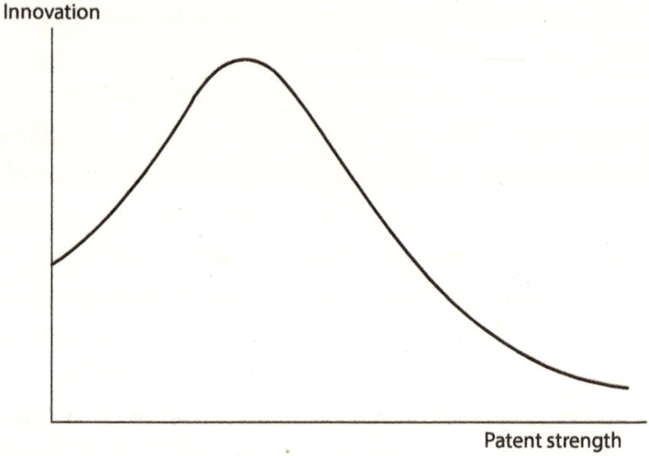

FIGURE 4.1: The Tabarrok Curve. *Source*: Tabarrok 2013.

the curve rises: there is a happy medium between no IPRs and draconian ones.

We believe that what's really going on here is similar to the dilemma we presented above in our discussion of publicly funded intangible investment. The basic shape of the curve is driven by a trade-off between the spillovers of intangibles and the synergies. If spillovers are abundant and big, then strong IPRs are helpful. A good example is the publishing industry. Without copyright laws, it would be trivially easy to copy the latest Hunger Games or Harry Potter novel the day after it is released and sell it royalty-free. (File sharing already results in vast numbers of copies being given away free.) The rewards from writing a best seller would diminish. But if synergies between intangibles are the dominant effect, then very restrictive IP rules are a big hindrance. This world is more like Boldrin and Levine's description of the smartphone industry, or Ridley's of wheelie suitcases, where any new product requires using a very large number of historical innovations. In this world, would-be innovators will be forced to spend vast amounts of money paying off claims by owners of other relevant innovations, or they may just not bother.

We can extend this discussion to training and education as well as to intangibles related to innovation. The equivalent of IP protection for training is rules that tie workers to a firm that has funded their training. These rules may take the form of noncompete clauses, employer loan forgiveness, or prohibitions on untrained workers, such as occupational licencing. The negative effects of these systems have been extensively documented. On occupational licencing, the economist Morris Kleiner, for example, has documented higher prices but no higher quality in US states with more restrictions on dentists and mortgage brokers.[23]

What's more, IP rules run the same three risks that systems for providing public intangible investment do. Goodhart's law manifests itself when innovators focus on gaming IP rules rather than innovating. The challenges that early hip-hop artists faced from music rights holders are an example of how an IP regime that is basically fit for purpose can become much less effective when technology changes (in this case, not the physical technology of sampling but rather the "aesthetic technology" of the musical style itself). And, of course, everyone agrees that the field of IP is rife with lobbying and special interests. (In one of the authors' time advising on innovation policy, the most affable and skillful—and presumably the most expensive—lobbyists he had the pleasure of being lobbied by were invariably acting for IPR holders.)

IPRs and Centralisation

In summary, the debates around the public funding of intangibles and the extent of IPRs are grounded in two phenomena: the spillovers of intangibles (and how governments can mitigate their discouraging effect on intangible investment) and the synergies of intangibles (and how governments can create the conditions where as many synergies happen as possible). If you believe intangible capital is quite homogeneous and that spillover effects are very strong, then you should favour stronger IP rights and greater public subsidy of intangibles. This is the quantity theory of intangible subsidy. If you believe that intangible capital is very heterogeneous and that the benefits of getting precisely the right combination are very high, then you should favour a milder IP regime and a system that encourages entrepreneurial experiment even at the expense of the total amount of intangible investment. This is the quality theory.

Designing a Better System

This idea of a trade-off between compensating for spillovers and promoting synergies helps make sense of many common policy proposals for reform of our systems of IP and intangible subsidy. For example, the agenda set out in Edmund Phelps's *Mass Flourishing* and Matt Ridley's *How Innovation Works* is predicated on the idea that the synergy problem is big and the spillover problem is relatively unimportant.[24] Therefore, we should cut IP protection and public sector R&D (both of which lead to distortions) and promote entrepreneurship (which gives us more chances to identify the really valuable synergies). A central argument of Mariana Mazzucato's *The Entrepreneurial State* is that government funding for R&D and other types of innovation investment is predicated on the idea that the spillover problem matters most.[25] Accordingly, we need a lot of innovation investment in order to have a chance of big, valuable breakthroughs.

Another important idea in *The Entrepreneurial State* is that of "mission-oriented" investment, whereby governments focus public R&D in particular areas such as green technology or health care.[26] Such investment attempts to solve the quality problem of public subsidy. Good-enough government planning, the argument goes, can focus publicly funded research in areas where it will be most valuable. Quality theorists such as Ridley would dispute this argument, pointing out that the problem of quality is not just about picking socially beneficial goals but also about allowing for a wide range of entrepreneurial experiment, because finding the winning combination of intangible investments is too complex for just one big organisation to get it right.

We see a similar dichotomy in the debate on higher education funding. In the United Kingdom and many other rich countries, government policy has for a long time been based on the idea that more university graduates are, in general, a good thing and that the intangible investment their education represents is worth subsidising. The rationale for subsidy is partly one of spillovers and partly the belief that young people are capital constrained. The fifty-year expansion of universities around the world is a manifestation of the quantity theory of intangibles. There is of course a widespread critique of this expansion; we see it in Peter Thiel's rationale for setting up the Thiel Fellowships to fund smart kids not to attend university, and in the United Kingdom's 2018 review of postsecondary education. This critique holds that a lot of university education isn't worthwhile for students, employers, or society. Liberal arts degrees are too generic, and the nature of the university funding system provides very weak incentives for universities and for students to teach and study genuinely worthwhile things. What we need instead, according to the critique, is less but better education: more hard science degrees and more high-quality apprenticeships and technical training programmes (in which there is a high degree of synergy between the skills that students learn and the assets of businesses seeking to employ them). This type of education is of course the quality theory in action.

Many common proposals for reform are responses to the three problems that beset IP regimes or public funding: the problem of imperfect rules, the risk of rent seeking, and the difficulty of making sure the systems adapt to technological change. Proposals for more discretionary funding agencies, along the lines of the blue-sky US Defense Advanced Research Projects Agency (DARPA), abound. The United Kingdom announced its own version in 2019, while in the United States something similar but larger was proposed in the Endless Frontiers Act, which was introduced into Congress in 2020.[27] These plans, which give the funding staff greater discretion to pick radical projects, can be considered attempts to escape the tyranny of increasingly metricised and bureaucratic research funding systems, which are sometimes accused of being captured by academic interests.

Similarly, the proposals for improving the patent system set out by Boldrin and Levine also attempt to make the rules better suited to the specifics of innovation—for example, by calling for more interaction among antitrust, trade, and research and patent policies; by adjusting patent length in different sectors; and by taking economic as well as technical evidence into account when choosing whether to grant patents. The proposals for pharma patent and regulatory reform set out by Tyler Cowen and Ben Southwood include measures to ensure that the system reflects developments in how drugs are discovered and tested, such as the changing role of computer models; the role of surrogate end points in approvals; and the role of physician-led experimentation in discovering new uses for existing and traditional drugs.[28]

A similar case can be made for extending the list of intangibles that governments subsidise. Funding education and scientific research has been widely considered a legitimate government activity since the early years of the twentieth century. Other intangibles that have spillovers are less accepted. Consider open-source software. Nadia Eghbal's *Roads and Bridges* drew attention to the dependence of most technological projects on free software that is designed and maintained on a voluntary basis.[29] We are beginning to see attempts to share the costs of this labour—for example, the "sponsors" initiative launched in 2019 by the code repository Github to persuade large businesses to contribute to open-source costs. A logical next step would be to use public research funding to support open-source software costs. The Open Data movement, which wants governments to produce and publish more data on important issues, is growing, but it is still fairly new. Ben Goldacre, a medical researcher and science writer, has argued that research funders should get better at funding data tools as well as research leading to publications.[30] Dan Davies has observed that public service broadcasters often play an unrecognised role in providing training for the wider radio and television industry, but this role is weakened if the broadcasters are restricted to providing highbrow content that commercial channels don't offer.[31]

Recommendations

We can piece these recommendations together into a somewhat coherent programme that would probably be recognisable to most economic policy makers across the developed world.

First, we should cautiously weaken IP rights, rolling back patents in areas where their remit has grown—for example, by ending patents on software and straightforward business processes, reducing patent lengths in selected industries, requiring genuine disclosure of what makes underlying technologies work, and introducing prizes or patent buyouts for certain socially desirable inventions, such as antibiotics.[32] When the world was racing to develop a COVID-19 vaccination, the economist Joshua Gans suggested using a prize for a COVID-19 vaccine to solve the commitment problem—namely, that the successful development of a COVID-19 vaccine runs the risk of having governments take control of the vaccine for less than the market price, a question that ended up being hotly debated in 2021.[33] A precommitment to purchase such an important innovation may be optimal from the government's point of view because a vaccine would not only save lives but also save the rest of the economy; but the government has to find a way of committing to rewarding the vaccine company for its sunk costs.

That said, it's important not to apply the experience of vaccine development to government innovation policy generally. A prize works if the innovation is easy to specify: for example, Charles Lindbergh won the Orteig Prize for flying nonstop from New York to Paris, and the winners of the $10 million Ansari X Prize for carrying three people one hundred kilometres above the Earth's surface won twice within two weeks. The requirement for winning a prize for a vaccine may be relatively easy to specify (for example, a particular effectiveness rate), but not all innovations are so easily pinned down. Indeed, the precommitment to buy delivered COVID-19 vaccines, not a just a prize, was necessary because the innovation required *both* the formula and a successful manufacturing process.

Second, we should increase public funding for other types of intangibles alongside basic research and education, including more investment in well-designed vocational training (including training provided directly by state-owned businesses such as national broadcasters or national arts organisations), more investment in big open-data and open-source software projects, and more industrial development (for example, by funding R&D tax credits or public research centres such as the United Kingdom's Catapult Centres).

Finally, to cope with the metric tide and the capture of research funding by disciplinary interests, we should experiment with giving certain public funders of R&D more discretion to back radical and challenging projects, contingent on our ability to recruit excellent people into these roles.

Two Political Problems

None of these recommendations are particularly controversial, and most governments at least pay lip service to them. A left-leaning government might put more emphasis on government-set challenges, like the Green New Deal, and a right-leaning government might focus more on DARPA-style research and entrepreneurship. But the differences between Alexandria Ocasio-Cortez or John McDonnell, on the one hand, and Peter Thiel or Dominic Cummings, on the other, are smaller than the similarities. This would not have been the case a decade ago. But working out the approximate policy mix is not the most difficult challenge here. Executing these policies, and doing so effectively and at scale, requires a government to confront some important political questions and to challenge some vested interests.

There are two specific problems. The first problem is the tension between increasing the system's capability and protecting against lobbying and rent seeking. The second problem is obtaining political licence for what will likely involve transferring resources and status to unpopular elites.

Regarding the first problem: it is clear that public subsidy regimes and the problems of IP are in tension with one another. On the one hand, we want these regimes to be more resistant to outside influence. On the other hand, we want them to be more attuned to specific technological needs and technological change, and less subject to the tyranny of inevitably imperfect rules. This tension presents a challenge because the classic method for resisting the kind of lobbying that we are worried about entails organisations binding themselves with inflexible rules. Economists Paul Milgrom and John Roberts published an important paper in 1988 describing how organisations could resist influence activities by putting rules in place to constrain their discretion, like Odysseus lashing himself to his mast.[34] A classic example is central bank independence. For decades, governments had varied interest rates in response to short-term political pressures, even though this variability reduced economic growth in the medium term; putting rate setting in the hands of an independent central bank with a simple rule for setting rates took away the temptation and protected it from lobbying. And indeed, we see this tactic in various government institutions that deal with intangible investment. In the United Kingdom, the government proclaims its adherence to the Haldane Principle, whereby research funding choices are made by subject matter experts, not by politicians. The United Kingdom's Intellectual Property Office is an arm's-length body with a more devolved and technocratic remit than a typical government department.

But this approach has some big shortcomings. Rules-based, devolved bodies are prone to the Goodhart's law trap that encourages gaming rather than high-quality intangible investment. Once a government has devolved a mandate to make it harder to interfere with it, it is ipso facto harder to alter the mandate if technology means the rules need to change. And political independence can be a brittle strategy. If the rules are watertight, they can indeed make lobbying harder. But if there is wiggle room in the rules or the system, then an apolitical organisation can be more vulnerable to external pressure than the government itself, because by definition an apolitical organisation has less political capital.

Governments also resist lobbying and influencing activities by committing their own political capital to a particular issue and position. When a government makes something a priority and dedicates resources to it—money, analytical capacity, decision-makers' bandwidth and time, the willingness to be unpopular, the ability to build political coalitions in support—it can usually resist considerable amounts of influencing and lobbying. Casual empiricism tells us that when something is a political priority for a government, it can brush off wealthy and committed lobby groups quite effectively. Brexit may well be a case in point.

All of this means that government can shift the Tabarrok curve in its favour, achieving the benefits of policies that solve the spillover problem while preserving as many synergies as possible. This requires an investment in state capacity when it comes to funding R&D, education, software, data, and other intangibles. State capacity is partly a matter of resourcing: hiring technically skilled staff, building analytical capability, and using these capabilities to invest in intangibles and administer well-run IP regimes. But it is also a matter of committing political capital. These functions need political support to protect them from lobbying and capture, and to support their claims for public funds.

This brings us to the second political challenge: legitimacy. If governments are to invest more of taxpayers' money in intangibles, make real investments in state capacity, and spend more of their political capital to protect the system from undue influence, then they need to find a way to balance the books politically. Unfortunately, none of these investments are easy to defend in an age of populism and status inequality. The organisations that produce and administer intangible investments are often run by what might be unkindly called *metropolitan elites*. This group includes scientists, university academics, patent attorneys, and technocrats, who often work in big, thriving cities. This is not the demographic or geographic constituency most political parties are eager to please; indeed, in recent years many political parties around the world have become successful by baiting these groups performatively. Moreover, the issues at stake are not for the most part the issues of heartfelt popular appeals or bread-and-butter politics. Hospitals, national defence, poverty, and injustice tug at voters' emotions; patent policy, not so much.

There are a few possible solutions. One option that is available to a minority of governments is to present intangible investment as a response to external threats. Political scientist Mark Zachary Taylor has noted that countries that faced a strong external threat balance (angry or hostile neighbours, relatively few internal civil tensions) tend to have the strongest track record of innovation (a function of investing in intangibles, such as R&D).[35] Taylor's list of "rapid innovators" includes Japan, Israel, Taiwan, Korea, Singapore, and Finland, most of which combine internal cohesion with clear foreign threats. Taylor argued that invoking external threats helped override opposition to investment in innovation; it is certainly true that these countries are recognised as having strong and capable institutions for encouraging R&D, from Israel's Innovation Authority to Finland's TEKES (their funding agency for innovation), Taiwan's

ITRI (Industrial Technology Research Institute), and Japan's MITI/METI (Ministry of International Trade and Industry). But their success is not just a function of abundant state investment. These countries also seem to have created the conditions for a lot of successful entrepreneurship, and they delivered on quality as well as quantity of intangibles. Bob Johnstone eloquently sets out the importance of Japanese technology entrepreneurship in his book *We Were Burning*.[36] Several of these countries also perform very well on various global education league tables, which we also associate with doing well at intangible investment. Unfortunately, most countries cannot choose to adopt this approach. Countries that are fortunate not to have nearby angry neighbours, or are unfortunate in that they lack internal cohesion, have to try something else.

One possible approach is to buy political capital elsewhere and then use it to increase state capacity for intangible investment. In late 2019, it was reported that Dominic Cummings, the UK government's chief strategic adviser and one of the architects of Brexit, used "Get Brexit done, then ARPA" as his WhatsApp byline. Whatever its pros and cons, Brexit—combined with the UK 2019 general election, which the ruling Conservatives fought on a low-detail platform of "Getting Brexit Done"—delivered a big increase in power to the government (including the biggest parliamentary majority since 2005), giving Cummings the authority to set up a blue-sky funding agency modelled on DARPA. Cummings's blog posts suggest that, for him, the point of Brexit is to smash the system and to create space to build state capacity, particularly in areas such as research funding.

Another option is for politicians to craft narratives to make intangible investment more politically resonant. One small but significant example of a government investing in public intangibles was the Open Data movement in the United Kingdom in the early 2010s. The UK government made a significant push to make a wide range of previously closed data sets freely available; it backed up this push by funding the establishment of the Open Data Institute, an independent, publicly funded body that materially increased state capacity in the field of open data (providing, for example, guidance and technical support on how to make data open). Its founders were Tim Berners-Lee, inventor of the World Wide Web, and Nigel Shadbolt, a computer scientist. The movement would have made much less headway if it had not received political support, in particular from Francis Maude, a senior UK government minister. Part of this support was linked to the creation of a useful, simplifying political narrative: the idea that open data would allow "armies of armchair auditors" to police government spending and effectiveness, an idea that had considerable political legitimacy with small-state Conservatives, especially at a time of public spending cuts. The armchair auditors' story was somewhere between an oversimplification and outright mis-selling, but viewed pragmatically, it played a useful role in winning political buy-in for what would otherwise have sounded to many Conservative politicians like an eccentric boondoggle. Finding emotive and ideologically correct ways of justifying good policy is an important part of what politicians and policy entrepreneurs do, especially in government.

Summary

Public-sector support for innovation faces a host of trade-offs. Spillovers from ideas give rise to a collective-action problem, suggesting the need for centralised coordination. But if ideas also need to be combined, then centralisation might stop the process of decentralised combinations that a market-coordinated system brings. In addition, centralised action might provoke wasteful influence activities and centralised authorities that might not be able to commit to leaving private investors to sink costs. Economic and political reforms will help this process, specifically a little less IP protection and more competition and political capital.

5

Financial Architecture

FINANCE AND MONETARY POLICY IN AN INTANGIBLES-RICH ECONOMY

An intangible economy makes borrowing harder and riskier. It also lowers the natural interest rate and so squeezes monetary policy. We need reform that allows pension funds and insurers to fund innovative companies and that allows fiscal policy to provide commitment to stabilising the economy with less space for monetary policy.

What do Charles Dickens, John Maynard Keynes, and Occupy Wall Street have in common? They all believe that bankers and financiers do a poor job of providing for the needs of the so-called real economy. This view is so common that some might even call it a cliché. But if we look at recent data on business investment and business finance, we see that something new is going on. In recent years, business investment has been gradually changing in ways that make established forms of business finance increasingly unsuitable.

These changes are causing a host of problems. They seem to be responsible for a slowdown in business investment as a first-order effect. The second-order implications are, we believe, even more troubling. The difficulty of financing modern business investment appears to be limiting equality of opportunity, reducing innovation, encouraging potentially unsound forms of financial innovation, and increasing risk in the banking system. The net result is a lower-growth economy that is more prone to financial crises.

We think of advanced economies as sophisticated and clever places, but at an individual level the opposite is often true. A hunter-gatherer in the State of Nature needs to be smart, savvy, and constantly alert, but modern life is full of rules and systems that allow people to carry out important tasks thoughtlessly, carelessly, and even stupidly—and everything will still work. As Alfred North Whitehead said, "Civilization advances by extending the number of important operations which we can perform without thinking of them."[1] The system is clever, so you don't have to be.

This is certainly true of our financial system. To its critics, the world of high finance seems too clever by half. Consider the titles of popular books on finance. A catastrophic hedge fund blew up "when genius failed."[2] The people who turned an energy company into a fraudulent derivatives operation were "the smartest guys in the room."[3] But many of the most powerful features of the financial system are in fact devices that make genius unnecessary. Debt finance turns complex business judgments into simple ones ("Is this debtor able to repay me?"). Company accounts provide a simplified, standardised, and reasonably honest way for outsiders to scrutinise the financial health of a business. Simple investment strategies such as index funds and value investing allow laypeople to achieve a return on investment that often outperforms that of highly paid fund managers. Shareholder value management, the management fad of running businesses to maximise returns to stockholders, for better or for worse simplifies the complex business of corporate governance. Inflation targeting provides clear and simple rules to judge the success of central banks. Unfortunately, these useful simplifying features do not work well when it comes to financing intangible-intensive businesses.

In this chapter we look at a range of features of finance and monetary policy, examining how they break down in an intangibles-rich economy, the problems they cause, the barriers to change, and some possible solutions.

Debt Finance: The Tyranny of Collateral

For the majority of businesses, external finance means debt finance—normally a loan from a bank.[4] A number of reasons explain the proliferation of debt finance. Most countries' tax systems favour debt over equity, allowing debt interest payments, but not the cost of equity, to be treated as a tax-deductible expense. In recent decades, the incentives for company managers to optimise their capital structure have sharpened. The shareholder-value movement, the rise of activist investors, and the growth of leveraged buyout funds make it harder for managers to ignore the economic advantages of debt finance. The institutions and norms of debt finance are more abundant than those of equity finance. Banks offer loans, employ loan officers, and use a range of tools to assess creditworthiness; businesses apply for loans. When it comes to equity finance, things are very different. The largest companies can access public equity markets. A tiny subset of the most ambitious small firms can access venture capital (VC). But for the most part, businesses are not used to seeking external equity, nor do institutions exist to provide it to most businesses.

Perhaps the biggest advantage of debt finance is its simplicity. As writer and investment analyst Dan Davies[5] pointed out, an equity investor needs to consider all sorts of things when deciding to finance a business: "How much could this be worth in a really good outcome?"; "What further projects might grow out of this one?"; "What effect will the sharing of the upside and downside have on the way the thing is managed?"; and "Am I selling my shares too cheap?" For a debt investment, all you need to think about is "Do I think this guy is good for the money?," and all the borrower needs to think about is "Can I pay this back?" Debt finance is useful because it reduces the cognitive load on both the lender and the borrower.[6]

Intangibles, Debt, and Collateral

Debt finance creates a fundamental problem for an intangibles-intensive firm. It involves the creditor taking a charge on the debtor's assets, to be invoked if the debtor cannot meet its financial obligations. But intangible assets are more likely to be sunk costs—worth little or nothing in the event the debtor business fails. A firm with a greater proportion of intangible assets is likely to be a less attractive prospect for a lender, all else being equal.

Stephen Cecchetti and Kim Schoenholtz make this point forcefully: "The financing of intangible investment requires overcoming the 'tyranny of collateral.'"[7] They also point out that US firms in the intangible-intensive software sector have debt that is about 10 percent of book equity, while firms in the tangible-intensive restaurant sector have a debt-to-book value of almost 95 percent.

It would, of course, be wrong to say that intangibles-intensive firms and even intangible assets themselves can never be financed with debt. Large-scale commercial lenders do not always or exclusively lend against collateral. They also use loan covenants related to earnings.[8] The economists Chen Lian and Yueran Ma[9] document that amongst US nonfinancial listed firms, 80 percent of debt is based predominantly on cash-flow-related covenants. The most common types of covenants in place were a cap on the level of debt to earnings and a cap on interest payments to earnings (interest coverage).

But the privilege of borrowing against cash flow rather than collateral tends to be available only to larger, more established firms. The smaller firms in Lian and Ma's sample still borrow predominantly on a collateral basis; 61 percent of lending was asset based. Furthermore, these studies investigated listed firms, which are typically larger firms to begin with. For small and medium-sized firms, the story is different. In 2015, the Bank of England conducted a survey of major UK banks' lending to UK small and medium businesses with revenues less than £500 million (excluding real estate). This survey found that over 90 percent of lending was secured against some sort of collateral. Over 60 percent of exposures were collateralised by property and/or debentures, including charges over plant, equipment, and vehicles.

These lending practices create problems for businesses reliant on intangible assets and with few tangible ones. Giovanni Dell'Ariccia, Dalida Kadyrzhanova, Camelia Minoiu, and Lev Ratnovski examined the composition of commercial bank lending in the United States using comprehensive data from 1977 to 2010, a period over which the ratio of intangible to tangible capital in their sample of US firms rose from below 40 percent to just over 100 percent.[10] They found that the fraction of total bank loans going to commercial and industrial (C&I) lending fell significantly in the period (in 1977, C&I loans were 22 percent of US commercial bank balance sheets, falling to 15 percent in 2010), while real estate lending boomed (increasing from around 35 percent of bank balance sheets to 75 percent). Tellingly, they show that business lending fell the most in areas where intangible assets have grown. The implication is that the move to the intangible economy has contributed to the substantial change in commercial bank balance sheets towards real estate loans.

Other recent research seems to support this conclusion. One study showed that Japanese firms with more intangible capital are more likely to choose equity finance than debt finance.[11] A US study observed that intangibles supported 25 percent less debt finance than tangible assets, and that the debt they did support tended to be unsecured or convertible debt rather than secured loans.[12] These data support the idea that there is a growing gap between the financial demands of intangibles-intensive firms and the ability of capital markets and financial institutions to meet these demands. It may also be that regulation aimed at increasing the stability of the financial system has the unintended consequence of making the intangible investment problem worse: a study of the creation of the Single Supervisory Mechanism (SSM) for euro-area banks found that firms borrowing from SSM-supervised banks reduced their intangible investments and increased their tangible investments and cash holdings.[13]

Institutional sources of equity finance are not always useful in filling the gap, particularly for smaller firms that are not publicly listed. The UK experience is instructive here. As the Bank of England points out,[14] UK pension funds and insurance companies allocate only around 3 percent of assets to unlisted equities, which is where most VC funding is located. As the US evidence suggests, this could hold back the creation of domestic VC. In addition, the returns from VC investment, although risky, are substantial (18% returns after fees for average VC investment

1970–2016 compared with 11% for average returns to the MSCI world index).[15]

There are a number of reasons why funds and insurance companies are so reluctant to invest. First, quite understandably, such institutions do not want to expose themselves to risk. Second, and related to the first reason, monitoring such investments requires expertise and effort and the UK pension funds are, relative to those in other rich countries, highly fragmented, with few large pension funds.[16] Third, there are rules that cap pension fund spending on fees, further limiting the employment of additional expertise that investment in intangible-heavy businesses will need. Relatedly, as the Bank of England's Alex Brazier has pointed out, 8 percent of the £1.4 trillion assets in UK investment funds are held in "open-ended" funds[17]—that is, funds that owners can redeem each day by selling their assets if they want to. This system is ill suited to providing unlisted, less liquid, capital (and in any case is an illusion, because the value of the fund sinks if many owners rush to redeem). Regulations, such as Solvency II, impose similar restrictions on institutions such as insurers.

A Slowdown?

Does this problem of debt finance help explain the slowdown in intangible investment we saw in chapter 2? If the tyranny of collateral existed before the financial crisis, then it must have worsened postcrisis. And, indeed, the idea that it has worsened is fairly plausible. After the financial crisis there was a pullback in lending, and banks, whether by regulation or intention, became more cautious. These changes, coupled with the limited capacity of the existing system, might have led to a notable decrease in lending for intangibles. So, either credit costs for intangibles have worsened since 2007, or the frictions associated with raising a given dollar of investment have increased.

Evidence that something did happen comes from a pair of studies by the International Monetary Fund (IMF). JaeBin Ahn, Romain Duval, and Can Sever compared intangible investment by firms before and after the financial crisis.[18] They found that firms that were large borrowers in the run-up to the crisis reduced their intangible investment after the crisis by much more than those that were smaller precrisis borrowers. Interestingly, their results hold for the ratio of intangible to tangible investment. That is, it was not the case that *all* investment fell for the more highly leveraged firms. Rather, the effect was on investment in intangibles. So, it looks like intangible investment got harder after the financial crisis.

Equity Finance: Accounting, Value Investing, and Diversification

Very few firms have publicly traded shares, but those that do are generally large and their behaviour disproportionately important to the economy as a whole. When it comes to equity investment, a number of rules and norms have simplified what would otherwise be the difficult process of working out the likely value of a complex firm and deciding whether to buy its stock. The discipline of financial accounting, the standards and principles that underpin it, and the regulators and professions that administer the system together mean that generalist investors can learn a lot about a wide variety of businesses from the comfort of their computers or phones.

Also of interest in this context is one of the many time-honoured strategies that equity investors have used to make their lives simpler: the strategy of value investing, pioneered by Benjamin Graham, who was Warren Buffett's mentor. In its simplest form, value investing involves buying "value" stocks—those whose shares are worth less than their accounts would suggest—and selling their opposites, so-called "glamour" stocks. An important study by Josef Lakonishok, Andrei Shleifer, and Robert Vishny showed that between 1968 and 1989, for example, a strategy of mechanistically buying value stocks and selling glamour stocks would have earned a healthy return of 6.3 percent per year.[19] This insight formed a major part of some of the most cited papers in financial economics, helped Eugene Fama win a Nobel Prize, and informed the strategies of innumerable investment funds. Lakonishok and colleagues' paper also provided an explanation of why value investing worked: The average investor was bad at distinguishing between fundamental business problems and transitory problems—in particular, assuming incorrectly that short-term misfortunes are actually long-term weaknesses. By going long on value stocks, investors could enlist the power of *mean reversion*.

Mean reversion is a mighty force in many domains of life, perhaps well illustrated by the *Times* columnist Daniel Finkelstein in his description of English Premier League football.[20] The iron rule is that a club doing well one season almost always does badly the next season: for every extra point a team added to its total in one season, it will lose 0.22 points in the next. When Leicester City won the league in 2015–16, it gathered forty more points than in 2014–15, something no other Premier League club had ever done. The following season, however, it underperformed by thirty-seven points. In the business world, mean reversion is the tendency of every business to gravitate over time towards average performance: most of today's stars will be average performers in the future, as will most of today's dogs.

But in an age of intangible capital, it turns out that both company accounts and value investing strategies are much less useful. The work of the economist Baruch Lev has been vital here. In his book *The End of Accounting*, coauthored with Feng Gu, Lev shows that financial accounts had become progressively less informative about the market value of public companies, because their value depended increasingly on investments in intangibles.[21] Accounting rules typically did not allow most intangibles to be included in financial accounts, and even if they did, the intangibles' value was often not close to their cost because of the importance of synergies between intangibles.

In 2019, Lev, in collaboration with Anup Srivastava, noted that value investing as a strategy had not delivered historically good returns since 2007 and in fact had also underperformed in the 1990s. They provided two explanations. First, the accounting metrics used to identify glamour and value stocks no longer worked well, because many more businesses owned intangible assets that were not reflected in their balance sheets. Second, mean reversion, the wind in the sails of the value strategy, had slowed down. The rule that many disfavoured companies would do well and many market darlings would underperform has gotten much weaker, especially since just before the financial crisis. One explanation is the growing importance of intangibles. In Lev and Srivastava's words, "Escaping the low-valuation group [i.e., value stocks] requires massive investment in intangibles and acquisitions, and often a radical restructuring of business models, which most value firms can't afford. . . . Glamour firms, in contrast, operate intangibles-based business models which enable longevity and high profitability. Shorting these enterprises is a losing proposition." Thanks to the growing importance of intangibles, mean reversion has been replaced by the

Matthew effect ("For whoever has will be given more, and they will have an abundance").[22]

We might also expect the Matthew effect to have an impact on bank lending. Bank lending is, after all, a high-volume, low-effort process. Banks cannot afford to perform detailed due diligence on every small business that asks for a loan and are more likely to rely on very rough heuristics that are perhaps even simpler than those used by mechanical value investors. This practice doesn't matter much in a world of high mean reversion: if the worst cohort businesses have a decent chance of getting better, then you can afford to be wrong occasionally if you have a large portfolio of business loans. But in a world where good businesses stay good and bad ones stay bad, poor due diligence is more costly, giving banks another reason to reduce their business lending.

Shareholder Value Management in an Age of Spillovers and Synergies

Another element of complexity in financial capitalism is corporate governance. Managing a company involves a whole set of complex trade-offs and value judgments. And if that company is publicly held, then its owners—its shareholders—will be a different set of people from the managers who are actually making the decisions. This situation leads to a number of well-studied problems. How should managers trade off different goals: long-term profits versus short-term profits, the goals of the business versus the needs of society, profit versus the environment, shareholders versus other stakeholders? How can shareholders align managers' incentives with their own incentives?

Among this confusion a new idea was born. *Value-based management* holds that managers should run their business to maximise the value of its shares, that boards should be independent from managers (no more joint chair-CEOs), and that managers should receive more of their pay in forms that rise and fall with their employer's stock price, like options, or actual equity. The job of protecting workers' rights, the environment, and the community is assumed to lie elsewhere—for example, with unions or governments. The Friedman Doctrine, named after a 1970 essay by Milton Friedman that argues "the business of business is business" rather than serving the needs of stakeholders, began growing in popularity in the 1980s and now represents the mainstream position on corporate governance, especially in the United States and Britain. The epitome of value-based management is activist hedge funds, which buy into the stocks of companies with unimpressive share price performance and try to force management to improve it.

Value-based management is another example of a financial innovation that cuts down on cognitive load. It replaces a messy, embedded, judgment-based system with a simpler set of rules and a more clearly divided set of responsibilities. It is an innovation that harnesses a powerful force: if managers own stock or options, then shareholders can rely on the managers' self-interest to motivate them to improve company performance: the interests of the principal and agent are better aligned.

Of course, value-based management has many critics. Their criticisms hinge on two issues. The first is spillovers. Because the decisions that a business makes resound across the whole economy, shouldn't a business think twice about closing the only factory in a small town, polluting a river, or marketing a morally questionable product? The second is short-termism. If stock markets are irrational and shareholders uninformed, mightn't the pursuit of shareholder value lead to foolish shortcuts and important but complex projects foregone? Detailed research suggests that many of these concerns are overblown (Alex Edmans's *Grow the Pie* provides a good overview of the evidence), but the debate continues to rage. These two issues become more significant in an economy dominated by intangible assets.

Consider spillovers. As we have seen, intangible assets often generate positive effects beyond the firm investing in them. Thus we might expect businesses to invest less in them than is good for the economy as a whole. A particularly salient example is R&D. Alon Brav, Wei Jiang, and Song Ma looked at what happened to business R&D at firms that were targeted by hedge funds,[23] an event that usually causes them to focus more on delivering shareholder value. They found an interesting result: R&D expenditure at these firms fell, but each dollar of R&D produced more patents, and those patents were more heavily cited, implying they were of better quality. This is good news from the business's point of view: it is investing less but getting better returns on that investment. The R&D projects being cut are, on average, those that bring little benefit to the firm. But there may well be a hidden economic cost if someone else would have ended up exploiting these spillovers.[24]

Something similar seems to be happening to traditional corporate research programmes. Once upon a time, company R&D labs produced seminal inventions, from the semiconductor and the graphical user interface to nylon and Kevlar. Many of these inventions were based on what we might call upstream research, not the implementation of research that was largely done elsewhere. But over the past four decades, the amount of upstream research done by corporate labs has declined sharply, and storied institutions like AT&T's Bell Labs and the DuPont Central Research Department have been closed down.[25]

To understand what was going on, economists Ashish Arora, Sharon Belenzon, and Lia Sheer studied publications by US companies and patents between 1980 and 2015.[26] By looking at how often one firm's research was cited in patents by another firm, they were able to estimate the size of knowledge spillovers and how these were changing over time. They showed that the significant fall in corporate research over the past few decades went hand in hand with an *increase* in spillovers. In an age of fast, free digital communication, cheap air travel, and open innovation, it has become easier to adapt other businesses' ideas, and businesses respond by doing less original research. They quote a former Bell Labs researcher: "Xerography was invented by Carlson in 1937, but it was only commercialized by Xerox in 1950. . . . In the few years surrounding commercialization, Xerox was able to invent and patent a whole range of related techniques. [. . . By contrast] when Bednorz and Mueller announced their discovery of high-temperature superconductivity at the IBM Zurich lab in 1987, it took only a few weeks for groups at University of Houston, University of Alabama, Bell Labs, and other places to make important further discoveries."[27]

Now let's turn to the other purported problem of value-based management: short-termism. Companies managed for shareholder value, so the argument goes, will overlook attractive but complex projects that are hard to explain to ignorant traders with short attention spans. Instead, they will settle for simple but suboptimal plans: cut costs, eke out the current product line, return cash to shareholders. Again, to some extent the critics' argument is overblown; the study by Brav, Jiang, and Ma discussed earlier found that activist investors were associated with long-term increases, not just temporary bumps, in the value of the companies they bought into.[28] Alex Edmans looked at what happened when financial institutions accumulated largeish positions, or *blocks*, in a company's stock. Companies with blockholders turned out to be more willing to invest in R&D—probably, Edmans concluded, because an investor with a large position found it worthwhile to scrutinise complex investment plans with short-term costs, whereas dispersed investors were more likely to challenge the plans.[29]

In sum, we have a set of financial instruments and institutions that suit a world with low information load and low spillovers: bank debt, value investing, and simple governance rules. These are becoming less and less suitable for an intangibles-rich economy. Before considering reforms, we turn to monetary policy.

Monetary Policy Making

Another simplifying institution on which the business finance system relies is the way central banks seek to affect investment through monetary policy. In most modern economies, monetary policy works via inflation targeting by an independent central bank and banking regulation.

The institution of an operationally independent central bank is an application of the need for institutions that provide the commitment that we saw in chapter 3. The temptation of running the economy hot before elections might be too much for some governments, and so delegating policy, by asking sober central bankers to hit an inflation target, makes sense. Inflation targeting also fits with our theme in this chapter in that it's policy with a low information load; a clear target is easy for most people to understand. As John Kay and Mervyn King argue, an easily understandable objective is particularly important in conditions of "radical uncertainty" where the economy is plagued by many "unknown unknowns."[30] Indeed, they presciently cited a pandemic as such an unknown before the COVID-19 crisis.

The problem is that just as finance has become harder in an intangible world, so has simple inflation targeting. Before explaining why this is so, let's see why it matters. Consider two remarkable facts. First, policy rates (that is, the interest rates set by Central Banks) are currently near zero in most developed countries. Since 2009, policy rates in the United States, the United Kingdom, and Continental Europe have averaged 0.54 percent, 0.48 percent, and 0.36 percent, respectively (data to April 2021). Second, the economists Jason Furman and Lawrence Summers have documented that in the United States, the average policy interest-rate reduction in the nine recessions before the COVID-19 pandemic was 6.3 percentage points. In the United Kingdom, the cut was 5.5 percentage points in the five pre-COVID-19 recessions. Since in practice it has proved hard to cut interest rates much below zero, economies currently have only a fraction of the room to respond to future recessions by cutting interest rates compared with past responses.

Inflation targeting has three broad elements. First, the central bank sets interest rates relative to their *natural* or *neutral* level, a long-run level at which inflation is stable. Second, such changes in interest rates affect demand, changing consumption, investment, and net exports via the exchange rate. Third, demand affects inflation. As we will see, the transition to the intangible economy affects all three of these elements, and the increased stress on the institution that is monetary policy loads more responsibility for stabilisation policy onto the shoulders of the fiscal authorities.

The Interest Rate and Demand: Investment

When a central bank lowers or raises the interest rate, it affects demand via consumption, investment, and net exports. Here we concentrate on the most volatile element, business investment.[31] Rates affect business investment via three channels: the cost of capital channel, the bank lending channel, and the broad credit channel.[32]

The *cost of capital channel* directly affects the attractiveness of the marginal investment project that a business is considering. Higher interest rates mean that future cash flows are worth less and, all things being equal, investment projects are less worthwhile. They also affect exchange rates and asset values. Via the *bank lending channel,* monetary policy affects banks' balance sheets, which in turn affects their appetite for lending. For example, a rise in interest rates may reduce the value of a bank's assets, which in turn may bring the bank closer to regulatory capital adequacy ratios and in so doing restrict its ability to engage in further lending without first raising new capital. Through the *broad credit channel,* monetary policy affects firms' balance sheets (higher rates would cause a deterioration, for example), which in turn affects their attractiveness to creditors.

Suppose lenders in general face problems getting information from borrowers, in particular the likelihood of a successful project or default on the loan. As a result, they demand a premium for lending and impose conditions on their loans. The oldest and best-known condition is a collateral requirement, usually a tangible asset such as a building (real estate). But as we have seen, lenders will also lend on the basis of a firm's earnings (revenues minus costs). The two most popular of these loan covenants cap lending at a maximum of a firm's earnings or cap interest payments at a certain percentage of a firm's earnings (interest coverage ratio); usually both are applied simultaneously to the same loan. Such covenants are intended to help prevent bankruptcy in the first place, but they also give the lender, in the event of bankruptcy, a stronger legal claim on the value of the restructured firm.[33]

Thus, as interest rates rise, the cost of capital channel comes in: the marginal investment project is cancelled. The other channels then amplify the fall in investment. Asset prices and firm cash flows fall and interest payments rise. More generally, the broad credit channel is a source of amplification when the economy goes into recession and demand falls. During downturns, when firms most need to borrow, their collateral and prospects have declined, making it harder to borrow.

The Effects of Interest Rates on Demand in an Intangibles-Rich Economy

So far, so good. Under these circumstances, central bankers can exert a reasonable degree of control over business investment by simply raising or lowering the interest rate. But for a firm with abundant intangible assets, these mechanisms become less predictable. Because intangible capital is less easy to pledge as collateral with creditors, and because young intangibles-based firms often have few or no earnings, the intangibles-rich firms may become disconnected from debt markets and traditional banks. Instead, investments could be funded more through retained earnings and equity. For these firms, there is reduced potency of monetary policy via the broad credit channel in an intangibles-rich economy. For others, the effect might be stronger in an intangibles-rich economy. If screening intangibles-based firms is more difficult for lenders, then those firms that do try to borrow to make intangible investments may face more stringent conditions on their borrowing and hence might be more sensitive to changes in borrowing costs. Furthermore, through their very intangible nature they may find it more difficult to meet the terms placed on their debt—for example, through lack of collateral—and so be more likely to be close to and constrained by the limits on those terms. So this side of monetary policy becomes more unpredictable.

Demand and Inflation

Changes in consumption, investment, and net exports shift what economists call the *demand side* of the economy. But the effect on inflation also depends on the supply side. The *supply side* is generally represented by the Phillips curve, which shows that inflation comes from two sources. First, if you pump up the economy too far above capacity, inflation starts rising (known as the *unemployment/inflation trade-off*). Second, if a government loses credibility and everybody expects inflation to be much higher, then they push for higher wages. As a result, prices increase and the economy spirals into a self-confirming inflationary crisis.

How well does this framework fit the facts? In the 1950s and 1960s, the supply side of the economy was expanding very rapidly with postwar reconstruction. The concomitant increase in demand therefore caused very little inflation. Matters changed dramatically in the 1970s, when very high inflation combined with an economy that was operating far below capacity (that is, unemployment was very high). Economists at the time, accustomed to observing the economy only through the lens of shifting demand, took a while to understand that events like oil shocks had likely changed supply and prices.

In the past decade, a new challenge has arisen: persistently low inflation. No matter the state of demand, inflation has been stubbornly low—most notably in Japan, where inflation has been very low for two decades. One way of interpreting this persistently low inflation is that the Phillips curve has become "flatter." Indeed, this claim was central to the change in monetary policy framework announced by the US Federal Reserve in August 2020.[34] A flatter Phillips curve means that for any particular rise in demand above capacity (or falling demand below capacity), the responsiveness of inflation has decreased greatly. The good news for monetary policy makers, then, is that inflation stays relatively close to the target no matter how far away the economy is from its capacity. But the bad news is that inflation can stay stubbornly away from its target, which might well mean that inflation expectations can remain very low. This reasoning might explain the persistently low inflation in Japan.

Economists have a variety of stories as to why the Phillips curve has become flatter. The essential question is the extent to which firms adjust their prices as they come up against rising costs, perhaps due to capacity constraints. A car company, for example, is likely to raise the price if unexpected demand rations its ability to shift cars off its production line.

One story is that globalisation has made the notion of domestic capacity constraints much less meaningful. Firms can switch production abroad or source shortage items more readily. Another is that the logic of capacity constraints is much less appealing in an intangibles-intensive economy. For instance, a software company that experiences a rise in demand can supply more software via the internet at zero extra cost. The notion that its "capacity" is somehow restricted doesn't seem to apply. Maybe, then, the movement towards a more intangible economy can help explain the flattening of the Phillips curve.[35]

The Interest Rate and the "Neutral" Interest Rate

Whilst central banks can change interest rates, they are ultimately limited by the natural forces that affect interest rates in the economy in general.[36] The neutral real interest rate, usually abbreviated as R* (pronounced "R star"), is the rate that would prevail when the economy is in long-run equilibrium; that is,

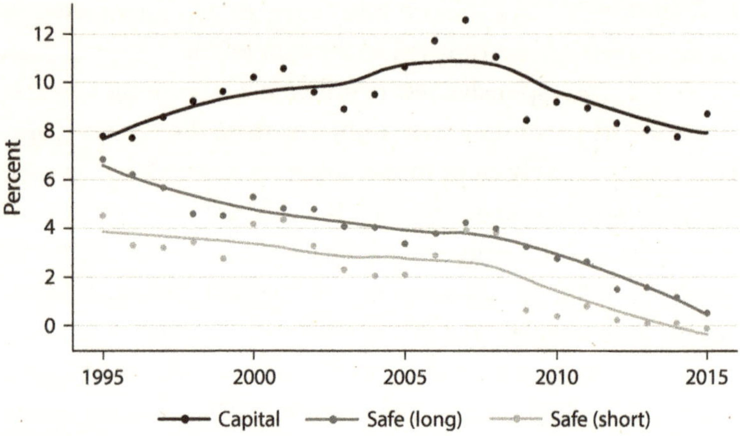

FIGURE 5.1: Yields on Safe Assets and Capital, 1995–2015. *Note*: Lines are exchange-rate-adjusted nominal GDP weighted averages of countries: Austria, Czech Republic, Germany, Denmark, Finland, France, Italy, Netherlands, Sweden, the United Kingdom, and the United States. Yield on capital is the ex post yield on the market-sector-invested capital stock, excluding residential assets. Safe rates are nominal sovereign bond yields. The solid lines are smoothed representations of the data points (dots). *Source*: Haskel 2020a.

when the savings that savers are willing to supply equals the investment that firms are willing to undertake. The neutral rate can fall if more people are eager to save, as the population ages, for example, and people need to save for retirement. This higher supply of savings lowers the price of borrowing—in this case, the real interest rate. If savers are seeking a safe asset, then the result is a lower safe interest rate or a lower yield on safe assets.

Figure 5.1 shows two types of yields for advanced economies (weighted averages across a sample of countries). The two lower lines are the yields on short and long government securities, specifically three- and ten-year government bonds, which we will call a "safe rate." As the figure shows, these safe rates fell consistently over the period 1995–2015 by about 4 percentage points. The figure also shows an average rate of return for the business sector, which, interestingly, rose but then fell back to where it was. So, returns on safe assets have been falling, whilst those on business investment remained about the same, which means the "spread" between the two is rising. Other measures such as the spread between bank deposit and lending rates, corporate bond spreads, and equity risk premiums also increased over this period.[37]

What explains *both* the fall in the safe rate and the rise in the spread between the safe rate and the risky rate? The rise in the wedge strongly suggests an increase in the required risk compensation between safe lending to governments and riskier lending to firms.

The economist Kevin Daly argues that both effects share a common factor—namely, the increased involvement in the global economy of risk-averse savers in China who are both saving more and demanding more risk-free assets.[38] But it also seems reasonable that at least part of the rise in the risk premium was driven by the trend towards intangible investment. If intangible assets are harder to use as collateral, then a shortage of collateral will drive risk spreads higher. Or, over and above collateral, intangibles may just be generally riskier to invest in; spillovers create a risk that a free-riding third party may reap the returns generated by an intangible investment.

Figure 5.2 sets out a simple test of this view. If the trend towards intangibles is raising risk spreads, then there should be a positive correlation between spreads and intangible intensity. As the figure shows, this is indeed the case. Those countries and years with more intangibles have higher spreads.

What does this imply for inflation-targeting central banks? The returns on safe assets have fallen and the spread between safe and risky assets has increased, putting downward pressure on the safe R*. The safe rate of interest that keeps lenders and borrowers in balance has fallen. But if R* has fallen, then central banks are boxed in. If they want to support the economy,

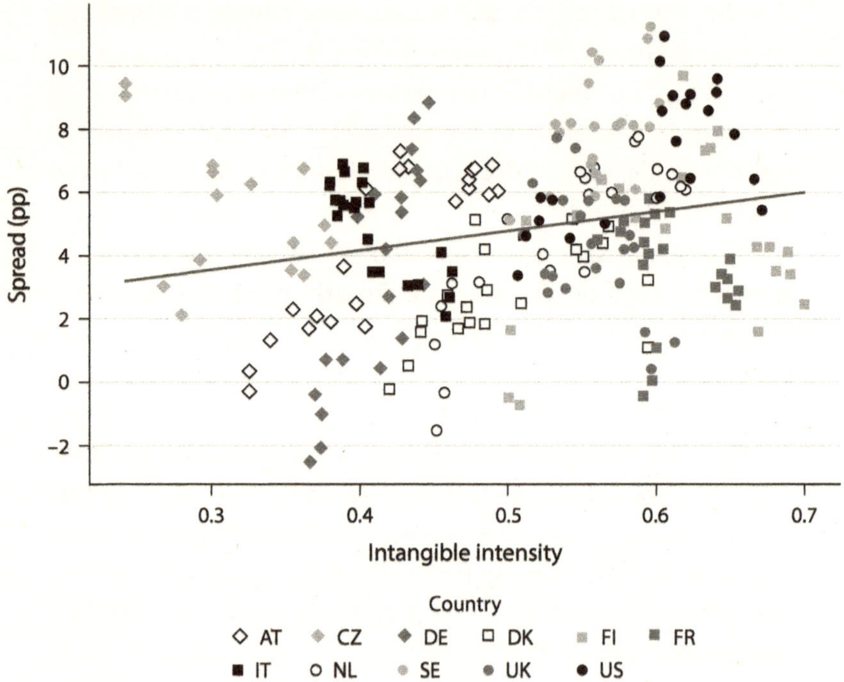

FIGURE 5.2: Intangible Intensity and the Return on Capital Spread. *Note*: Chart plots the spread between the return on capital and long-run safe rates from 1995 to 2015. Returns on capital are adjusted for tax rate differences. The safe rate is the nominal return on ten-year sovereign bonds. Because of the significant variance in sovereign yields in the euro area, the German ten-year was used across the euro area in each year. Intangible intensity is the ratio of intangible investment to total investment. Countries included are Austria, Czechoslovakia, Denmark, Finland, France, Germany, Italy, the Netherlands, Sweden, the United Kingdom, and the United States. Spain was excluded, as an outlier. *Source*: Haskel 2020a.

they must cut their rates, over time at least, in line with R*. If they hold interest rates still whilst R* falls, they are implicitly tightening policy. Thus we end up in a position where central banks have to keep interest rates very low just to keep up with the very low R*. The decline in R* makes inflation targeting, via the tried-and-tested mechanism of interest rate changes, much harder during economic downturns. Monetary authorities will simply have less room to lower rates when an adverse shock hits.[39]

Workarounds for Intangible Finance

Institutions, even very durable ones, are not set in stone. If it is true that the business finance system is doing a poor job of matching investment capital to intangible-intensive firms, then we would expect to see some signs of new institutions arising and new strategies being implemented to meet these needs, however imperfectly. As it happens, a number of workarounds have been developed, including IP-backed debt, VC, and business owners' homes as collateral. Have they solved the problem?

IP-Backed Debt

Some workarounds are useful, but only for a small number of firms or assets. Consider the rise of *IP-backed debt.*[40] A small but increasing amount of debt is now secured against intellectual property (IP) rights such as patents or music rights. Patent offices in countries including the United Kingdom and Singapore have been working with lenders to help develop these forms of debt. However, it seems unlikely that existing forms of IP-backed debt will offer a real solution to the tyranny of collateral. Most intangibles do not generate IP rights, and even when they do, the markets for them are often shallow and illiquid.[41]

Venture Capital

The second innovation is the steady expansion of *venture capital.* It is no coincidence that the sectors in which VC has been most active and successful (software, computing, internet services, and biotech) are heavily dependent on intangible assets.

Several features of VC are a response to the nature of intangible assets. VC is equity rather than debt finance, which avoids the tyranny of collateral. VC often proceeds in stages, allowing information and synergies in an intangible-intensive project to be revealed. The business model of VC funds is predicated on successful companies achieving runaway growth, which is facilitated by the scalability of intangibles. Because VC is concentrated, privately owned equity, VC funds can closely scrutinise management's plans while reducing the risk that the benefits of their intangibles spill over to competitors. In addition, good venture capitalists pride themselves on being well networked, at least in part to facilitate the partnerships, deals, and acquisitions that make the most of the synergies that arise between intangibles. Indeed, investment from top-tier venture capitalists is desirable to some extent because their investment is an imprimatur that opens doors to new partnerships in industries where partnerships often mean the difference between success and failure. For all these reasons, VC is an excellent external financing option for intangible-intensive businesses that can get it.

Unfortunately, as Josh Lerner and Ramana Nanda have observed, VC seems not to be scalable to other industries besides software and related technologies (energy, for example).[42] Perhaps most businesses are poorly suited to VC finance because they don't offer the explosive growth that the economics of a VC fund demands to justify its costs. At the same time, the availability and desirability of VC finance probably marginally weaken the average quality of banks' loan books to the extent that some minority of VC-backed businesses might in a previous age have been able to access bank finance.

The hunger for capital from intangible-intensive firms that are unable to attract VC finance and have too little collateral to interest bank lenders has also given rise to new financing options. The past decade—the period when most business investment took the form of intangible assets—has seen the development of a wide range of so-called alternative finance products aimed at smaller firms reluctant to take on bank debt.[43] Some of these arrangements involve lending against things other than financial assets, such as invoice discounting. Others involve lightly regulated equity (such as equity crowdfunding) or unsecured bonds (such as minibonds). And still others involve using cryptocurrencies to finance new businesses or new organisational structures like special purpose acquisition companies. Some of these products look like unimpeachably valuable financial innovations, connecting willing providers of capital to willing firms. Others look more questionable. Some critics have claimed that some consumer bonds and crowdfunding issues offer bad risk–return trade-offs to investors too naive to know better. In addition, some crowdfunding leverages investors' goodwill towards a particular type of business to provide capital at a submarket rate. It is no coincidence that some subsectors with ferociously passionate customers, such as microbreweries and CrossFit gyms, are disproportionate users of crowdfunding.

Perhaps the best interpretation of the Cambrian explosion of alternative finance is that the acute need for intangible-friendly capital is creating space for poorly designed financial innovations to arise—and storing up future pain for investors as more of these schemes fail.

Business Owners' Homes as Collateral

Perhaps the most common workaround for financing intangible-intensive businesses is less of an innovation than an adaptation: falling back on business owners' homes as collateral. Banks in the

United States and the United Kingdom have long used liens on directors' houses as security on business loans. As Dan Davies put it, "Historically, a very high proportion of business lending in the British market has been mortgage-lending-in-disguise. The business loan is usually secured, and usually additionally secured by a charge over the owner's house."[44]

As Giovanni Dell'Ariccia and colleagues have shown, when the amount of intangible capital owned by businesses in a particular locality increased, the growth rate of commercial loans by local banks fell and the growth rate of real estate loans increased.[45] More recent research at a more micro level has confirmed these correlations. Saleem Bahaj, Angus Foulis, Gabor Pinter, and Jonathan Haskel find that intangible investment in UK firms rises with an increase in the house value of the firm's directors.[46] This correlation is in line with the hypothesis that the more intangible-intensive firms may have to rely more on outside tangible assets to overcome lending frictions.[47]

Consequences of Inadequate Financial Institutions and Proposals for Reform

The fact that so many of the handy simplifications and processes that our financial system relies on no longer work well has several likely consequences. First, if it is harder for many businesses to obtain external finance for intangible assets, we would expect to see less intangible investment in the economy as a whole, and especially on the part of particular businesses—specifically, small and new firms (other than the small minority able to access VC) and laggard firms in industries with strong, intangibles-rich leaders. It does appear that the VC model has not been able to expand outside its usual lending. And the persistent effects from the financial crisis suggest that it has become more difficult to get bank lending for intangibles, although the precise avenue is hard to pin down.

Second, if banks become less willing to lend money to smaller firms, we would expect their balance sheets to increasingly consist of real estate loans, partly because they are less willing to undertake business lending to companies without tangible collateral and partly because they are more likely to look for liens on domestic property when they do make business loans. Thus, banks become more exposed to the property market. We have seen the rise in real-estate-backed lending as a proportion of US bank assets. In the United Kingdom, the stress tests of the Financial Policy Committee, the regulatory body in change of bank stability, suggest that a 1 percent change in residential property prices raises UK retail banks' impairment by £0.5 billion. For comparison, a 1 percent change in GDP (i.e., the whole economy, not just housing) impairs retail banks by much less, £0.1 billion.[48]

The third problem presented by the difficulty of financing intangibles-rich businesses relates to the supply of entrepreneurs. A world in which would-be entrepreneurs increasingly need to own a home to use as collateral to raise business finance is concerning because of the potential effects on access to finance. As Dan Davies points out, not all potential business founders own a home.[49] If a lack of home ownership becomes a greater barrier to starting one's own business, then the talent pool of entrepreneurs will shrink and new business information might be impaired. This argument is similar to the "Lost Einsteins" argument—that productivity is held back when potential inventors lack the early encouragement to pursue careers that make the most of their talents.[50]

Finally, it becomes harder to use interest rate changes to set monetary policy, at least in the face of adverse shocks. The result is an increased sense of fragility in the economy, because policy is less able to help the economy.

Proposals

The first challenge to address is how to create a better financial architecture to enable firms to invest in intangible assets. This requires a thoroughgoing change to the incentives and regulations we put on business finance.

One important measure is to end the asymmetric tax treatment of debt and equity. Businesses in almost all countries can treat debt interest payment, but not equity finance, as a business expense for the purposes of determining their tax liability. In *Capitalism without Capital* we advocated ending this advantage—for example, by allowing an equity tax credit, proposed in *Tax by Design* or in *Bridging the Gap in the Financing of Intangibles to Support Productivity*.[51] The longer this bias continues, the more costly it becomes.

The second step is to alter financial regulations to make it easier for investment managers to back intangibles-rich firms, especially ones whose securities are less liquid. It is worth focussing on the pension and insurance companies, as we discussed above, because they have massive amounts of assets under their control. Getting them to invest more in intangibles-based firms turned out to make a big difference in the United States. The economists Sam Kortum and Josh Lerner documented a dramatic rise in VC funding in the United States in the late 1970s/early 1980s, laying the foundations for another leap in the late 1990s, which they show was also associated with more patenting.[52] They also show that this initial change was driven by a change in regulations in 1979 that allowed pension managers of US funds to invest some funds in high-risk assets, including venture capital.

The problem of low pension / insurance investment is an example of the kind of collective-action problem that we set out as requiring institutional reform in chapter 3. The need for each individual fund to have more information could be solved by establishing a collective fund (or funds) that invested in illiquid equities that would spread risk and also achieve economies of scale to enable the kind of monitoring of companies that investment in illiquid assets requires. This collective action would lower the costs and risks and potentially raise investment in the type of VC funding that the intangible economy requires. Examples of these types of proposals are the Investment Association's proposed long-term asset fund[53] and the British Business Bank's proposal for a pooled investment vehicle.[54] At the time of writing, in the United Kingdom, the Bank of England, the Treasury, and the Financial Conduct Authority have convened an industry working group to facilitate investment in productive finance, including through the creation of a Long-Term Asset Fund that would likely require regulatory changes (another collective-action problem).[55]

Wouldn't such encouragement be risky, however? Once again, there is a collective-action problem. Remember that current investment is in open-ended funds. This is of course risky in that one person can successfully immediately redeem his or her savings, but all persons cannot. The resulting dash for liquid assets would force the fund to have a fire sale of its assets. Thus, it is not clear that moving to more illiquid investment is riskier. Further, restrictions on equity investment that force firms into more debt risk more and deeper crises.[56]

The third proposal is for investment managers themselves. Many investment managers have for some time been moving towards investing on environmental, social, and corporate governance (ESG) principles—that is to say, taking into account the wider effects of the companies in which they invest, not just their financial returns. Often the focus is on negative externalities: shunning tobacco companies that harm their customers' health or coal businesses that damage the environment, for example. Investment managers and asset owners should start thinking more about positive spillovers as part of their ESG mandates, particularly the positive spillovers from intangible investments. A business that invests heavily in, say, R&D or training may reap a reward in terms of its future earnings, which will eventually be reflected in its stock price. But if that R&D or training has positive spillovers (which it almost certainly will), it is creating a social benefit too, just as surely as a notorious polluter creates a social disbenefit by harming the environment. Funds with an ESG mandate should put a premium on firms that invest heavily in R&D, in design, and in training and other assets with positive spillovers, and asset owners who care about the future of the world should seek out funds with such a mandate.

Turning to monetary policy, the problems of the low room for monetary policy means an increased role for fiscal policy. But fiscal policy is not perfect either. It can lag. Or it can be held up. Or it is unpopular. There are at least three alternatives.

The first is to give more power to the monetary authorities. Governments can, as they have done since the financial crisis in the United Kingdom, for example, guarantee central banks' quantitative easing (QE) programmes—that is, back their purchases of government bonds or commercial debt. Alternatively, central banks might implement "dual rates" that allow commercial banks to fund themselves cheaply from the central bank. (The European Central Bank is currently using dual rates, along with negative interest rates.) And indeed, JaeBin Ahn, Romain Duval, and Can Sever's study showed that intangible investment fell by less in countries where monetary policy makers cut interest rates to offset negative shocks.[57] But such policies raise substantial questions about central bank independence. Passing money to commercial banks is nakedly fiscal policy, in that it guarantees the loss of a sum of public money in favour of a private entity and so might just as well be done by the government and not by an independent central bank.[58] It would be better to devote energy to improving the conduct of fiscal policy directly.

The second alternative is to either make fiscal policy independent or strengthen the role of independent auditors of fiscal policy. Two independent agencies with considerable clout are the UK Office of Budget Responsibility and the US Congressional Budget Office. They are examples of institutional arrangements for finding commitment. One possibility is to give such a role to the central bank if its policy space becomes exhausted, whereby the central bank could become an independent voice on the quantum of fiscal policy required in a recession.

A third possibility is to make fiscal policy more "automatic." This type of policy is discussed by IMF economists Olivier Blanchard, Giovanni Dell'Ariccia, and Paolo Mauro and by James Smith at the Resolution Foundation.[59] One automatic fiscal policy is a progressive tax system. With such a system, earners receive an automatic tax cut when the economy contracts and incomes fall or when the economy expands and incomes rise. Of course, this automatic stabiliser is even stronger if the tax system is extremely progressive. This type of policy also entails making social insurance programmes more generous so that when the economy falls, more income insurance is provided. The net effects of this policy on the deficit depend on the flexibility or inflexibility of government spending. For example, if government spending hardly falls during a recession, or indeed rises because of the increased provision of social benefit, this type of automatic stabiliser can be expensive and therefore politically difficult.

Despite the political difficulties, this type of automatic stabiliser could be extremely beneficial in the European context. To give a specific example, as the economists Jim Feyrer and Bruce Sacerdote point out, the US federal income tax (17 percent of US GDP) is extremely progressive.[60] Europe has no comparable equivalent. The United States therefore provides an important automatic stabiliser mechanism. As Feyrer and Sacerdote document, for every $100 of adverse shock, US states get a $25 federal tax cut. Despite reforms since these calculations, there are comparatively smaller fiscal policy transfers between nations in the euro area. This lack of fiscal transfers ends up causing considerable tension and political difficulty. Such arguments normally come to the fore during crises, which is precisely when they can be even more destabilising.

Another type of automatic stabiliser is a programme of interventions targeted at particularly affected areas of the economy that would come into operation in periods of recession and be withdrawn when the economy recovers. These interventions might include, for example, temporary tax policies for low-income households or investment tax credits. Blanchard, Dell'Ariccia, and Mauro suggests that these policies might be triggered when a certain threshold is crossed—perhaps that of GDP, hours, or unemployment.[61] These programmes have the considerable advantage of being targeted at the most needy and responsive groups in society.[62] In particular, they might be targeted regionally, thus helping with the levelling-up agenda around reducing regional inequality.

The political context for these types of automatic stabilisers, we think, changed significantly over the course of the COVID-19 pandemic. The political acceptability of financial support, especially support targeted at areas that were disproportionately affected by the pandemic, seemed to be much more widespread than was previously the case. Perhaps, then, now is the time to achieve political agreement regarding a series of automatic stabiliser rules that target those most affected by a recession. The commitment of targeted support would lower risk and uncertainty all around and so quite possibly prevent low expectations from becoming self-fulfilling as the economy slows down.

Finally, we might ask how these calculations change in a world with very high public debt (98 percent of GDP in the United Kingdom in 2020). The standard approach is to start by noting that the debt-to-GDP ratio will rise if the primary deficit is very high and/or if interest rates rise relative to growth, with the second effect depending on the starting point of the debt/GDP level. (If the starting point of the debt/GDP level is very high, then a rise in interest rates has a bigger effect on the rise in debt/GDP levels.)[63] But the reverse is true: as Jason Furman and Lawrence Summers note, at high levels of debt, a rising growth rate relative to GDP will have an even bigger effect on reducing debt/GDP than if debt is small, making the need to raise growth even more urgent.[64]

Summary

The characteristics of intangibles make financing an intangibles-rich economy much harder. The sunkenness of much intangible investment makes it more difficult to offer it as collateral to conventional banks. Thus, firms seeking to invest must either rely on their own cash reserves or pledge their houses in order to get finance. This situation is not going to give us an adequate level of investment in intangibles. The financial instruments we need to help us are not those suited to the tangible economy. Rather, we need more equity and less debt and more learning and understanding of the economy and firms than before.

A more intangibles-rich economy makes setting monetary policy much harder. More intangibles raise risk in the economy and lower the neutral safe rate of interest, which boxes in central banks, forcing them to keep interest rates low. This restricts their ability to offset adverse shocks to the economy via interest rate changes, adding to our feelings of fragility.

Reforms to intangible financing, such as ending the bias of the tax system, are urgently needed. So are reforms that allow pension funds and insurance companies to invest in intangibles-based companies, in a way that may even reduce risk and raise returns. Also needed is an improvement in the automatic nature of fiscal policy to help when monetary policy gets stuck. Automatic stabilisers would involve targeted payments to the most vulnerable groups, as well as a more progressive tax system. The COVID-19 pandemic has raised the political acceptability of these types of proposals, and now is a good time to adopt them.

6

Making Cities Work Better

The growth of intangibles increases the importance of some aspects of life that are very tangible indeed: physical proximity, where you live and work, and urban real estate. Unfortunately, the institutions that govern these things—from how we use land in thriving cities, to how we help left-behind places, to how we work remotely—aren't up to the challenges that an intangibles-based economy places on cities and towns. What's more, these institutions are entrenched, and improving them will require not only technocratic fixes but also ideological, distributional, and cultural change.

Once upon a time, the country's leading cities were thriving and expanding. They were doing so well that some people worried that the rest of the country was being left behind. Critics said that cities were too rich, too smug, and too fond of self-dealing. Then a virulent epidemic came along, making cities suddenly seem less safe and less appealing. At this point, a revolutionary writer picked up his pen and described a better world in which metropolitan elites were more humble and cities less mighty.

You would be forgiven for thinking that the writer in question is a modern chronicler of the Rust Belt, left-behind towns, of rural "somewheres" increasingly fed up with metropolitan elites and dreaming of a post-COVID future in which cities are humbler. But in fact the author was Thomas Jefferson, writing over two centuries ago in response to the yellow fever epidemic of 1793, which had ravaged Philadelphia, then the capital of the United States.[1] Jefferson had long thought that cities were morally and politically suspect: "I view great cities," he wrote to Benjamin Rush, "as pestilential to the morals, the health and the liberties of man."[2] His critique was also an economic one: "They nourish some of the elegant arts; but the useful ones can thrive elsewhere, and less perfection in the others with more health virtue & freedom would be my choice." Jefferson believed an agrarian society was a healthy one, both metaphorically and literally, and he cited as evidence the havoc that yellow fever had wreaked in big cities.[3]

For the most part, Jefferson lost his battle against cities, and over the past two centuries the populations of America and most other rich countries shifted from the countryside to the city. Agriculture as a share of national output has dwindled to almost zero. And, in the past few decades, the prosperity of cities has been on the rise again, following something of a decline in the postwar decades as rich urbanites moved to the suburbs, pulled by cars and pushed by crime. In an intangibles-rich economy, businesses and workers are attracted to cities, where they can exploit synergies and gain from spillovers. But although cities are economically more productive than ever, they are not delivering for all their inhabitants. The wage premium that less skilled workers get for moving to cities has evaporated. The price of real estate in cities rises and rises, and concerns about gentrification grow.

In addition, there is a growing gap between thriving cities and the rest of the country, particularly between cities and "towns," a term that in British political discourse has come to mean poorer, usually postindustrial conurbations with fewer than two hundred thousand inhabitants. Inhabitants of towns tend to be older, whiter, less educated than city dwellers, more alienated from the establishment, and keener on populist politics. The resulting political agenda would not seem too out of place in the mouth of Thomas Jefferson: a feeling that the "triumph of city," to use economist Edward Glaeser's phrase, has gone too far and that a rebalancing is needed.

And then along came COVID-19, creating a new dynamic as large numbers of office workers around the world found themselves forced to work from home, in some cases for months. In the United Kingdom, 45 percent of people surveyed were working from home in the winter of 2020, and 40 percent in March 2021, compared with perhaps 5 percent in pre-pandemic times.[4] Videoconferencing went from a novelty to a mainstay of working life. This new normal raised the question: Might some people never return to the office? If they don't return, might that solve some of the economic problems of rich-but-crowded cities and of left-behind places?

In this chapter, we look at the institutions that govern where people work and live in the context of the intangibles-rich economy. We begin by looking at the importance of cities and whether COVID-19 has changed that for good (spoiler: probably not). We then look at the problems facing thriving cities and left-behind places, and the kinds of institutional change necessary to fix them. Finally, we ask how to make the most of the changes some workers have seen as a result of COVID-19-enforced remote working.

The Rise of Intangibles and the Rise of Cities

The economic rise of certain cities in the past thirty years has been remarkable. During this "great divergence," to borrow a phrase coined by the economist Enrico Moretti, the most dynamic places have pulled ahead of the least dynamic places in many ways, most notably in building a cluster of educated workers.

We would expect this outcome in a world where intangible capital is becoming more important. When the economists Gilles Duranton and Diego Puga analysed "agglomeration effects"—the link between city size and economic growth—they identified three causes, which they called matching effects, learning effects, and shared facilities.[5] Being in a big city makes it easier to *match* employees to jobs, customers to services, and partners (business, social, or romantic) with one another. It also makes it easier to *learn* from other workers and other firms. And it allows people to *share* costly resources. The matching and the learning functions become even more important in an economy with more abundant synergies and spillovers. The economist Edward Glaeser describes the rise of cities since 1990 as driven by "human-capital intensive services."[6] We would add that these services are also intangible-capital intensive. Successful cities have also traditionally generated work for less-skilled workers, in sectors such as hospitality and food service. For a long time, these jobs also enjoyed a wage premium; the benefits from intangible-intensive businesses in cities to some extent trickled down.

Cities have grown, even though better transport and technology, from cheap flights to ubiquitous electronic communication, have made it easier to exploit the spillovers of intangibles such as R&D from a distance. For example, the economist

Matt Clancy points out that average distance between the inventors listed on a patent doubled between 1975 and 2015.[7] It seems that the strength of local knowledge spillovers has gotten weaker since economists first measured it quantitatively in 1993.[8] But even while technology makes it easier to collaborate remotely, there are forces operating in the opposite direction, making cities even more attractive and productive. For starters, cities seem to be especially good at generating unusual combinations of technologies as measured by novel combinations of terms in patents—synergies at work.[9] Even if spillovers are working better at a distance than they used to, they still mostly happen face-to-face; and as intangibles grow as a share of the capital stock, that advantage becomes more and more important.

But the forward march of the world's megacities had begun to falter well before COVID-19 forced office workers to work from their homes. In particular, rising housing costs are increasingly eating up the productivity benefits of big cities.[10] As a result, the higher productivity that firms enjoy from being in thriving cities is less likely to translate into higher profits or higher disposable income for workers, because housing costs increase to consume the difference. It is worth stressing that this constraint is not a *natural* limit. The world's superstar cities, from London to San Francisco to Shanghai, have a lot of space and could be much denser. Rather, it's a function of poor institutions, specifically outdated rules for planning and land use, that were devised not to maximise agglomeration effects but rather to prevent new development in cities by moving people to new exurban settlements. Such land-use practices are arguably less costly in a world of fewer intangibles.

The economist William Fischel was one of the first to point out the political consequences of homeowners' particular economic interests. In *The Homevoter Hypothesis* he describes how homeowners, which he calls homevoters, are like investors who want the company they own to do well: homevoters have a financial interest in the success of their communities.[11] The institutions that hold our cities back enjoy the support of a diverse coalition of the rich and the poor. Those lucky enough to own their own houses or apartments block new development because it could reduce the price of their own home, either by causing congestion and disruption or simply by reducing its scarcity value. Poorer city dwellers block new developments because they often involve replacing cheaper, older housing with newer, less affordable stock ("luxury apartments"), displacing poorer residents and disrupting existing communities, without increasing housing supply enough to lower prices—in short, gentrification. Rich and poor alike tend to be sceptical that national governments will provide sufficient new infrastructure and services to meet the needs of an increased population, even though in theory a larger population should be able to afford to pay for it.[12]

But the problems of thriving cities in an intangibles-rich economy pale in comparison with those of smaller towns and declining cities with little intangible capital. Part of the problem is that dysfunctional cities are unpleasant places in which to live and work. Just as thriving cities impose positive externalities on residents, declining cities impose negative ones. Crime and poor services make people less willing to live there, while every business that leaves reduces the spillovers of being in the city for businesses that remain. These effects become more apparent the more businesses are dependent on being surrounded by other businesses generating spillovers.

In the United Kingdom, many smaller cities face an additional problem: they lack good transport infrastructure, meaning they function like much smaller cities than they actually are. The economist Tom Forth has written extensively on this topic.[13] It is hard to match a worker to a new job if commuting across the city takes two hours because there is no metro line, and it is difficult to learn from other firms if travelling to meetings is time prohibitive. The result is a vicious cycle: the central government (which controls these decisions in the United Kingdom) is unwilling to invest in transport in cities it sees as declining, and the cities continue to decline because they cannot take advantage of agglomeration effects because of their poor internal transport links.

Smaller cities have another problem in an age in which synergies are more and more important. Paul Krugman remarked that in places like Rochester, New York, one highly productive industry often begat another over time.[14] In Rochester, John Jacob Bausch founded an optician's shop in 1853 that became Bausch & Lomb (inventor of Ray-Bans). This expertise in lens crafting then spilled over to Eastman Kodak, founded in 1888, and then to Xerox, founded in 1906 (though its development of xerography did not happen until after World War II). This succession of very productive businesses made Rochester a rich place for a long time. But eventually its luck ran out. Xerox declined, and a new local hero did not emerge to fill the gap. As Krugman points out, we can expect some cities to decline as a result of bad luck—and this sort of bad luck happens more often in small cities, which may have only a small number of highly productive firms, than it does in big cities, which in effect place many bets. Krugman likened this situation to "gambler's ruin": a card player with a small kitty is less able to ride out bad luck than one with deep pockets. We would expect this problem to be even more troublesome in an economy in which spillovers and synergies are more important.

In addition, we must consider the Matthew effect: thriving, growing cities do better and grow more, while cities that are poor in intangibles do worse and worse. Smallness tends to be a disadvantage, though some smaller cities or towns can defy the power of agglomeration if they have lots of intangibles—for example, in the United Kingdom, university towns such as Cambridge (population 125,000), or towns with a big, productive local firm, such as Rolls-Royce in Derby (population 255,000). But if the spillovers from a big employer are what is making a place rich, then the place is vulnerable to gambler's ruin. Not every town can have a world-leading university.

One consequence of the growing divide between places is political dysfunction. In his book *The New Geography of Jobs*, Enrico Moretti reports disengagement with the political process, but shortly after his book's publication, a wave of political entrepreneurs around the world provided disengaged voters with something that appealed to them: populism, often combined with promises of bringing back a social and economic world that had been lost.[15]

We might hope that technology will rescue us from this double bind of rich-but-strangled cities and decaying, disaffected towns and that the COVID-19 home-working revolution might accelerate this change. In 1968, computer scientist Douglas Engelbart demonstrated videoconferencing and simultaneous collaborative document editing.[16] Three decades later, the journalist Frances Cairncross coined the term "the death of distance" to describe a world in which these technologies would free the economy from the vulgar constraints of place.[17] At the beginning of 2020, place remained at least as important as ever: to the extent that people invoked the death of distance, they did so as an example of the naive optimism of yesteryear, alongside flying cars, the paperless office, and the end of history.

COVID-19 offered a new hope for remote working. With nearly half of all workers forced to stay at home in many countries, firms were faced with a compulsory experiment. Many workers and some employers found that remote working was not as bad as they thought. Few people missed their commute,

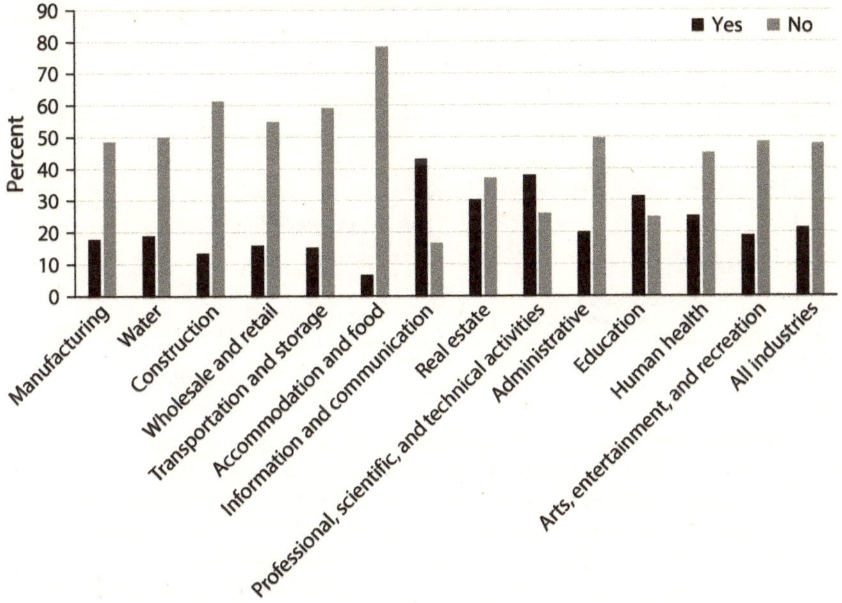

FIGURE 6.1: Percentage Intending to Use Increased Home Working as a Permanent Business Model. *Note*: Average of waves 14 (September 21–October 4, 2020), 16 (October 19–November 1, 2020), 18 (November 16–29, 2020), 20 (December 14–23, 2020), 22 (January 11–24, 2021), and 24 (February 8–21, 2021). Note that "Other Services" has been removed from the sample. Question: "Does your business intend to use increased home-working as a permanent business model going forward?" Data are employment-weighted. *Source*: ONS Business Insights and Conditions Survey data, reported in Haskel (2021).

people learned to use videoconferencing and collaboration software, and many businesses that would have never considered a wholesale move to remote working found that it was possible to do business without everyone in the office.

But the experience of home working suggests that while remote working will increase after COVID-19 lockdowns end, the office is not dead yet. A large survey of UK businesses conducted by the Office for National Statistics showed that only a minority of firms were looking to increase home working on a permanent basis (figure 6.1). Moreover, the survey found only

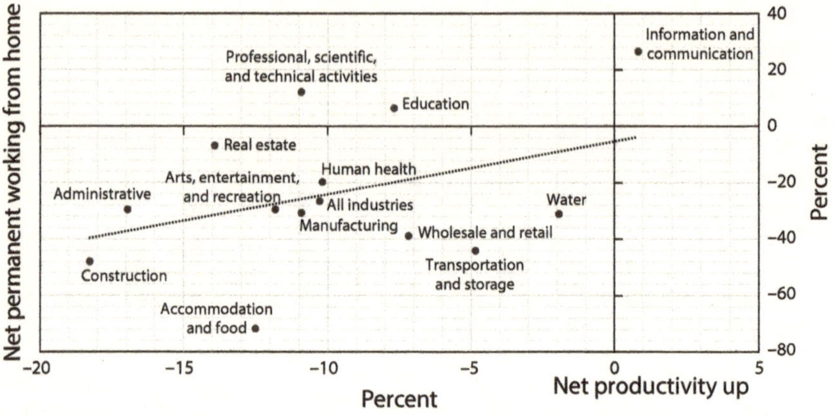

FIGURE 6.2: Net Percentage Expecting Increased Home Working as Permanent versus Net Percentage Reporting Increased Productivity from Home Working. *Note*: Average of waves 14 (September 21–October 4, 2020), 16 (October 19–November 1, 2020), 18 (November 16–29, 2020), 20 (December 14–23, 2020), 22 (January 11–24, 2021) and 24 (February 8–21, 2021). Note that "Other Services" has been removed from the sample. Question: "How has the increase in home-working affected the productivity of your workforce?" Data are employment-weighted. *Source*: ONS Business Insights and Conditions Survey reported in Haskel (2021).

one sector where firms thought that productivity had increased rather than decreased from home working: the information and communication sector (figure 6.2). Unsurprisingly, this sector had the largest percentage of firms that said they intended to increase home working. The sectors with the second- and third-highest shares of firms saying they would increase home working (professional, scientific, and technical activities, and education) reported that net productivity had fallen as a result of home working.

All this suggests that home working will increase as a result of COVID-19 and that, at the margin, this increase will help to both mitigate the pressure on the busiest cities and potentially increase the attraction of living in quieter places. But this will be an evolution, not a revolution, and the underlying importance of cities and clusters will not go away.

Technocrats versus Politicians

It seems, then, that remote working will not make cities obsolete or solve the problems of congestion and housing shortages. Let's now turn to two ways of addressing rising demand for city living: the technocrat's solution and the politician's solution.

The technocrat takes a deep breath and starts with the facts on the ground. Economic growth will happen in cities if we let them grow, but towns are a losing bet. So, let's change planning rules to allow towns to grow. The holy grail of technocrats in UK public policy is to shrink or even get rid of greenbelts, the 1.6 million hectares of protected, undeveloped land around cities and towns first established under the 1947 Town and Country Planning Act to discourage sprawl and ribbon development. They would point to the large amounts of greenbelt land close to a London Underground station, much of which is not bucolic countryside but rather unattractive scrub or unprepossessing intensively farmed fields. Paul Cheshire and Boyana Buyuklieva estimate that 46,867 hectares of buildable land are within 800 metres of a light-rail station that is forty-five minutes or less away from a city centre, and 29,722 of those hectares are located within greenbelts. That is enough land to raise the housing stock by 7 to 8.8 percent, about the number of houses built in all of England in the past fifteen years.[18] Technocrats would also point to the very restrictive planning rules that keep highly productive places such as Oxford and Cambridge small, limiting the spillovers and the economic benefits of all the R&D funded by the taxpayers there. Their American counterparts would point to problems of restrictive city zoning laws, of codes mandating excessive parking requirements or low density for new developments. In both countries, they would point to the power of NIMBYs (citizens who oppose house building, the abbreviation taken from their supposed refrain, "not in my back yard") in planning and zoning decisions.

Their vision is centrally driven relaxation of planning laws so that more housing can be built in thriving cities. The corollary is that cheaper, more abundant housing will allow more people to move from poorer places to richer ones and allow them to keep more of the extra wages they make from the shift. An extreme version of this vision was set forth in the 2008 policy paper *Cities Unlimited*, which earned a certain notoriety in the British media.[19] Thanks partly to some lurid reporting, *Cities Unlimited* was taken to be an argument that postindustrial cities such as Middlesbrough and Sunderland should effectively be closed down, and that the population should move to massive expansions of intangibles-rich places such as Oxford and Cambridge. A nonobvious detail of such proposals is that if more low-skilled people can afford to move to big cities because housing becomes less expensive, then the average population that stays behind in towns will be higher skilled on average than is the case now, when migration is a worthwhile option only for the most highly skilled. Perhaps most technocrats would not go quite as far as *Cities Unlimited* proposes, but we can see many less extreme versions of these policies in practice: the UK central government's housing plans, such as the 2020 proposals to shift planning powers from local government to development corporations, and measures in certain US states to shift zoning powers from city governments to state governments, which, it is thought, will be less likely to give in to local NIMBYism.

Such proposals horrify politicians with their impracticality. NIMBYism is common. Richer voters who own houses don't like to see their neighbourhoods spoiled by excessive development—and because their houses are often their most valuable assets, and perhaps even their retirement plans, they do not want to take risks with it. Poorer voters who rent don't like to see gentrification change their neighbourhoods beyond recognition, especially when it threatens to price them out of the market. Stopping development and blocking planning applications is the bread and butter of local politics. The strategy of managed decline for poorer cities is even crazier. In most countries, politicians are expected to deliver for the geographical constituency that elected them; saying "You'll be better off if you move to the city" is not acceptable. Voters demand a vision of how declining places will turn around and return to their former glory, and if you can't offer them one, they'll vote for someone who will.

Technocrats and politicians might agree that the possibility of the death of distance is no help at all. Technocrats will point out that it hasn't happened yet, and there is no sign that it will. Politicians will say that there's no sign that people want it (and, in the aftermath of COVID-19, will continue to make threats about how remote working will lead to all sorts of bad economic consequences, from the offshoring of jobs to the collapse of local economies). The net result is an unhappy compromise, with halfhearted attempts at planning reform and half-baked attempts to help left-behind places.

Planning-reform proposals typically end up being watered down in the process of delivery. An example is a recent proposal in the United Kingdom for Community Land Auctions, an economically unimpeachable idea for releasing more land for housing development while allowing local government to capture part of the planning gain. This proposal was defeated by a mixture of lobbying and political scepticism. Or consider the UK government's local housing deals, which have been bogged down in years of haggling between central and local government, with the result that very little housing has been built. In addition, the complexity of the system creates perverse incentives on construction firms, shifting their focus from house building to land speculation and lobbying to obtain building consents. At the same time, the political imperative to "do something" about lagging places leads to an abundance of rhetoric but few concrete plans.

Better Institutions with Smarter Politics

The problem with most existing solutions is that they either solve for the political problem without reference to the economic realities or solve for the economic problem without reference to what is politically realistic. But there is a better way. It is based on putting in place new institutions that work economically but also work with the grain of politics. Let's consider how to help not only growing cities but also left-behind places.

Building Homes

The biggest problem that cities face is the difficulty of building more homes. Demand to live and work in cities is going up, but supply is going up much more slowly, causing rents to rise. Housing prices are rising too; indeed, they are rising faster than rents because of low interest rates, but rents are our real concern. This high demand means that anyone who owns a property that is not very dense (say, a two-story, semidetached house) could in theory make a large, even life-changing windfall gain by selling it to someone to develop into more dense housing (say, a four-story multitenant unit). Some people may not feel that the windfall is big enough to justify the hassle of selling and moving, but given that we are talking about gains in the six figures of pounds or dollars, some certainly will.

Of course, in most cities, those who attempt to sell their own plot for redevelopment find the redevelopment blocked by local laws. These restrictions are sticky because it is in no one's interest for their neighbour to develop their house into apartments, which causes disruption and potentially reduces the value of the other houses in the neighbourhood. Changing these rules is almost impossible because they are set at the city level or local authority level. There are simply too many voters to get on board, and in any case most voters will not be homeowners. Economists would recognise this situation as a coordination failure: many individual owners have a strong incentive to redevelop their plot, but they do not want their neighbours to do so unilaterally, and they cannot coordinate to change the rules to allow them all to do so.

As John Myers of London YIMBY ("Yes, In My Back-Yard") points out,[20] political scientists have given considerable thought to this type of problem. Elinor Ostrom studied how communities managed so-called common pool resources, such as fishing grounds and grazing lands. She looked at how bottom-up management of these resources often worked better than top-down control by governments—so long as good institutions and norms existed to allow people to manage the resources.[21] Urban space and the shared city environment is a modern-day example of a common pool resource.

This is where two interesting proposals, called *street votes* and *block-wide zoning*, come in. Street votes is a proposal being advanced by London YIMBY; block-wide zoning was first suggested by US urban scholar Robert Ellickson in the 1990s.[22] These proposals involve radically devolving the approval for planning and zoning decisions to small, local areas. Rather than being made at the level of a city or a local authority, planning decisions would be made by the owners of properties on each street or each city block. Residents could, if they agreed, build up to an agreed limit, perhaps four or five stories, along the lines of mansion blocks seen in many nineteenth-century cities. The beauty of devolving power is that it makes it easier for people to coordinate to do more development. It may well be that many streets or blocks choose not to develop; after all, for some people, staying in their existing homes may be worth more than the possibility of a large windfall gain. But the law of averages suggests that *some* will, resulting in an increase in housing space that residents have actually chosen.

London YIMBY[23] has proposed a number of protections that could help avoid unpopular outcomes. For example, a vote could be triggered only if a certain number of locals proposed and supported one. A supermajority of two-thirds of local homeowners, and/or a supermajority of people who have owned property in an area for more than five years, could be required. The goal is to find areas where residents genuinely want the increased amenities and land values that come with higher density, not to force density onto those that do not want it. A related idea, "community boundary extension," would allow small communities such as villages to reduce the size of their surrounding greenbelts to allow more development and to share the gains.

These proposals have two striking features. First, they align incentives in a way that many planning-reform ideas do not. Households that vote for more housing—which provides a large societal benefit in an age of big agglomeration effects—gain financially. Streets or blocks that vote against development do not reap this reward. Second, the proposals increase rather than decrease local power and capacity.

There are signs that these proposals are gaining in popularity. Robert Ellickson proposed a form of street votes in 1998, when awareness of NIMBYism was beginning to rise. Robert Nelson, an American zoning expert, proposed something similar in 1999. More recently, the United Kingdom's Royal Town Planning Institute lent support to this sort of "microdemocracy" in a 2020 position paper. A high-profile UK government commission on the built environment recommended trials of street votes and block votes.[24]

Bumping planning decisions up to state or national governments in order to avoid resistance at the city level is appealing from a theoretical point of view. A bigger government should in theory be able to resolve the coordination problem. But in practice, it is likely to fall prey to lobbying, leading to the sort of deadlock and half measures that have characterised previous attempts at housing reform in the United Kingdom. This discussion serves to illustrate some of the principles we saw in chapter 3. Property rights, in this case for local homeowners, help with collective-action problems. Centralised decision-making might help with spillovers, but it provokes wasteful influence activities.

Building Infrastructure

The other problem that thriving cities face is infrastructure and services, particularly transport. Poor-quality transport and congestion make cities effectively smaller than their populations would suggest. And if residents do not believe that transport capacity will increase with population, they are more likely to resist new development.

Technocrats have their own solutions to offer. The most straightforward is to borrow to build new public transport and pay for it over time with the tax revenues from the increased economic activity in the now-more-bustling city. More ambitiously, city leaders can introduce congestion charging or charge for parking where it is currently free. In both cases, motorists pay for a shared resource that they could previously consume ad libitum, and provide a source of revenues that can be spent on improving roads and public transport. Edward Glaeser's recent article, "Urbanization and Its Discontents," makes the general point that city institutions (from transport and traffic management, to policing, to schools) are lagging behind the challenges that cities face and causing ever-larger economic problems.[25] In the United Kingdom, some surprising voices have supported road-user charging in recent years, including the RAC Foundation,[26] a motoring charity, and at least one right-leaning think tank.[27]

The challenge here is not just choosing the optimal policy but rather—as with NIMBYism—overcoming politics and special interests. Drivers dislike being charged, and they are better at mobilising resistance than a larger group that might benefit from less congestion or better mass transit in the medium term. Police unions resist accountability or community policing methods; teachers' unions resist new curriculums.

One part of the solution involves political choice. Politicians can to some extent overcome vested interests if they commit political capital to ignoring them or mobilise countervailing coalitions that would not arise spontaneously. Indeed, this is a big part of what politicians do and what politics is. So, for example, the British government elected in 2019 has suggested that it will accelerate investments in mass transit in larger English cities outside London, where its lack had probably been reducing agglomeration benefits. It remains to be seen whether the government will make good on this promise, but it certainly seems that it has decided to commit more political capital to the issue than previous governments did. Equally, the 2020 Black Lives Matter protests in the United States, which have cast light on the power of police unions and the extensive legal protections that some police forces enjoy, may have the effect of mobilising enough opposition to have them reduced. As the case for improving city institutions strengthens, politicians may be more willing to spend political capital on it.

As with planning, good policy design can help make the politics easier. Donald Shoup, an economist who has spent two decades studying the malign effects of free parking and minimum parking requirements on American cities (in Los Angeles County, parking spaces are 14 percent of the county's incorporated land area and 1.4 times larger than the area of the roadway system), has argued that one way to make the case for charging for parking is to ensure that the revenues are spent locally.[28] Street trusts would give a share of road-user charges to the specific streets that people drive down. These solutions echo Elinor Ostrom's solutions for managing common pool resources by assigning rights and empowering communities to deal with them. They offer an appealing way for urban leaders to solve an institutional problem that is holding big cities back.[29]

Left-Behind Places

In thriving cities there are too many well-meaning technocratic solutions that don't work politically. Left-behind places face the opposite problem. Well-meaning politicians (and some not-so-well-meaning ones) are quick to make promises to restore past greatness, but these promises are usually divorced from economic reality.

The election of Donald Trump in 2016 owed something to his popularity in once-prosperous manufacturing towns and his promise to restore American manufacturing. Similarly, following the 2019 British general election, in which the Conservatives won many traditionally Labour seats in struggling northern and Midlands towns, parts of the UK Right showed a renewed desire that might be summarised as "make towns great again." David Skelton, a Conservative pundit, argued for "the creation of prosperity hubs to renew post-industrial towns as engines of innovation" and "the reindustrialization of forgotten towns," calling for local tax breaks, investment in skills, the relocation of government departments, and local applied R&D funding.[30] The postliberal think tank Onward called for the government to use "science, research & development, and skills spending to tempt world-class companies in emerging sectors such as renewable energy and advanced manufacturing to cluster in [the Conservatives'] new heartlands," which involves "break[ing] free of the traditional conservative economic playbook of trickle-down growth and bring[ing] purpose back to towns."[31]

These types of policies are not necessarily bad. But in a world of agglomerations, smaller, poorer cities and towns start at a big disadvantage. To catch up, they must swim against a strong current. And no clear policy toolkit has been proven to work. Politicians who promise to help towns rarely appreciate the level of sustained investment and political commitment required. Nor do they appreciate that the policies they call for—broadly defined industrial policy, local tax breaks, and investment in skills—do not have a clear track record of helping smaller, poorer places.

This is not to say that nothing can be done for towns. But a more nuanced approach is required, one that recognises the difference between different types of left-behind cities and allows for experimentation where necessary.

With the right specific investments, some struggling places can benefit from the effects of agglomeration. As we've seen, some of the United Kingdom's midsize cities—for example, Birmingham, Leeds, and Manchester—are far less productive than their size suggests they ought to be, because a combination of traffic congestion and poor public transport renders them functionally smaller than they really are. Public R&D investment in these cities is much lower than one would expect, given the levels of business R&D, because of distortions in the way the UK government allocates funding. In these cities, a relatively straightforward programme of investment could help.

Similarly, some struggling towns are within commuting distance of thriving cities but are poorly connected to them. Research by the Centre for Cities, a UK think tank,[32] suggests that many towns can benefit from better transport links between towns and cities. Other economists point out that some very poor towns are already quite well connected to cities and that agglomeration effects are massively weakened at commuting times of more than half an hour. But at least some British towns that politicians frequently cite as places in need of economic assistance are within existing city regions (Wigan and Oldham in the Manchester City Region, for instance) and ought to benefit from better cities policy. We should make sure the transport links are in place to make these benefits a reality.

These options won't work for every city. For towns that are too small to have agglomeration effects and don't invest much in intangibles at the moment, policy makers must consider other options. One possibility is to focus on making towns better places to live rather than promising them a productivity miracle that policy makers do not know how to deliver. As William Kerr and Frédéric Robert-Nicoud point out, some people who move from one town to another do so for remarkably prosaic reasons: "William Shockley, who shared a Nobel Prize in Physics for his work on semiconductors and transistors, moved to the San Francisco area to be near his ailing mother. Later, the spinoffs from his firm Shockley Semiconductors included Intel and AMD. Similarly . . . Bill Gates and Paul Allen move[d] Microsoft from Albuquerque to Seattle, their hometown. . . . [P]roximity to family won out."[33] These examples point to the importance of providing strong public goods and family-friendly amenities such as low crime levels, parks, and a hospital for regular routine births.

To the extent that we want to encourage productivity growth in towns, and in the absence of a clear model that works, we need to take a more tentative and experimental approach, as in the Basque Country.

What Local Areas Have Prospered in an Intangible Economy?

The Basque Country in Spain has achieved significant prosperity and growth in part through the efforts of the sixty-year-old Mondragon Corporation, a workers' federation and business group that owns banks, stores, and manufacturing businesses and employs more than seventy thousand people. The Mondragon Corporation's cooperative organisation has made it a poster child for the Left, though it was founded by a Catholic priest and is, in many ways, a red-blooded capitalist undertaking that competes vigorously in various enterprises, including supermarkets, well beyond the Basque Country. Its success is striking for its emphasis on intangibles. It invests heavily in technical training and R&D, even running its own schools and worker-development centres. Mondragon's overarching structure seems to encourage the internalisation of these investments' spillovers and to mirror some of the agglomeration effects that big cities enjoy.

The Mondragon model has developed over six decades, and the Basque Country has been one of the more productive and prosperous parts of Spain since the late nineteenth century. The Basque Country's experience suggests some tactics for other government policy makers to copy. In particular, if there are big synergies between intangibles, then a policy of gradually supporting these intangible investments with public funding can lead to productivity growth.

Another possibility is *community wealth building*, which encourages local economic development through local government procurement and local public or community institutions, such as community banks, cooperatives, and housing associations. Community wealth building also involves "buying local" for many services, such as maintenance of social housing. In the United Kingdom, it is sometimes known as the Preston model, after the northern town that adopted it and became an example for democratic socialist economic policies. In the United States, it is associated with the role played by the Democracy Collaborative in Cleveland, Ohio. Its supporters often advocate it on ethical and distributional grounds, claiming that it increases wages, reduces inequality, and prevents profiteering. Its critics often focus on its protectionist qualities: surely buying local wastes money and destroys value if there are better, cheaper suppliers elsewhere.

We have no strong empirical view on whether or when community wealth building works. But it is interesting to think about why it might work from a productivity point of view. One notable aspect of the Preston model is the way it encourages investment in intangibles. The clearest example is training—for example, by using public-sector contracts to provide apprenticeships and technical skills. The Centre for Local Economic Strategies, a think tank focused on community wealth building,[34] provides other examples, including a UK local authority that reorganised its social care provision to a more effective model (an intangible investment in organisational development). Perhaps community-owned organisations can help encourage complementary investments in intangibles that create value. From an intangible point of view, the local aspect matters, because people can coordinate effectively at the local level to solve the synergy problem of intangibles.

These models deserve more evaluation and experimentation as a way of helping poorer places become more productive. At the same time, because there is not a consistent or reliable recipe for success, it is important for politicians to be realistic in their expectations for local growth.

Speeding the Death of Distance

We observed earlier that the rise in remote working occasioned by COVID-19 would not make the problems of place go away, but it may help address them at the margin. Shifting some employees to remote working will not reverse the Triumph of the City, but it will weaken it and offer an opportunity for some left-behind places to catch up, if they can formulate an attractive offer for remote workers. But making working from home work well raises its own institutional questions, which we will look at now.

The idea that changes in technology take a long time to be implemented is exemplified by the electrification of industry that happened decades after the invention of the original technologies; business practices and factory design had to catch up with the transformational new possibilities. According to Amara's law, the impacts of new technologies are overestimated in the short run but underestimated in the long run.

Similarly, the "death of distance" would likely be a considerable game changer, challenging the dominance of cities and perhaps having deeper cultural effects on commuting and associations in the workplace. At the time of writing, we are in the midst of a massive unanticipated experiment in one such profound change, namely working from home (WFH). Not everyone can work from home, but an estimated 47 percent of the UK workforce was working remotely in the summer of 2020 as a result of the COVID-19 pandemic. What will the effects of WFH be on an economy increasingly reliant on intangibles?

Working from Home versus Working at Work

At least some employees rather enjoy working from home.[35] In doing so, they avoid commuting, deal with caretaking responsibilities, minimise distractions from coworkers, maintain social distancing, and perhaps even enjoy more free time. On the employer side, many firms whose employees are working from home are asking themselves, What's the point of paying sky-high rents solely for the privilege of an empty office, surrounded by other empty offices?

Working at work does have quite a bit of value, though. First, you may well be learning a lot from your coworkers. On-the-job training is especially valuable for younger workers at the start of their careers. Second, working from home exposes employees to a particular kind of risk. When an employee works from home, it is typically harder for the employer to monitor performance. How can the reliable employees convince the employer that they have been working hard and not relaxing on the beach? They could offer to sign a performance-based contract. But that would be complicated, intrusive, and perhaps impossible; a simpler solution requiring less cognitive load is simply to come to the office. By requiring employees to come into work, the employer ensures that employees are not watching TV or going to the beach when they should be working. Famously, Marissa Mayer started her tenure as CEO of Yahoo! in 2013 by *banning* working from home, reversing an earlier move to more home working and requiring employees to come into the office or quit the company, and in the summer of 2021 Tom Cook, the CEO of Apple, announced that he wanted his home-working staff back in the office in the autumn.

Perhaps it is not surprising that the productivity effects of working from home are decidedly mixed, according to a survey by Isabel Sawhill and Katherine Guyot.[36] In one experiment at a large Chinese travel agency, call centre employees were randomly assigned to work from home. Those working from home increased their performance by 13 percent, partly due to more calls per minute but mostly because they simply took fewer breaks and fewer days off. After the experiment ended, however, the workers who remained at home were less likely to be promoted.[37] In a different study, of a knowledge-intensive IT services consulting company, working from home during COVID reduced productivity.[38] These examples show how much productivity varies across jobs in different sectors. A job that is more or less a single task, like answering a phone, can likely be done just as productively at home, whereas a job that is a bundle of tasks, including interacting with others, may not be as productive done at home.

One clear lesson from the 2020 experiment is that WFH requires tools, skills, and norms. Some of this became obvious in the first weeks of lockdown. Staff needed a computer and a broadband connection in order to do anything; they needed software (remember the global argument in the spring of 2020 over whether Zoom was safe enough to use for millions of business meetings across the world?); and they needed a chair, a flat surface, and a place to work (revealing inequalities in people's living conditions that had not been obvious when everyone was in an office).

But other things are harder to work out. How does a business exchange information effectively among staff who are working remotely? How do you replicate the casual conversations in the office kitchen or at the water cooler? How much of the training that junior staff members get requires them to be physically around experienced workers? If staff returns to the office only a few days a week, as some businesses are doing, how can that be made to work, and what rules and norms are needed? A small number of businesses that are used to remote working have already developed such norms, but these standards are not widely known, and in any case are often tailored to the specific activities of a certain business (in particular, software development, where workflows and outputs are relatively easy to represent and share remotely). But most sectors and industries are at the beginning of a long process of discovery.

Once upon a time, what we think of as traditional workplaces like factories and offices were novel. Businesses didn't know how to run them effectively, and workers didn't know how to behave in them. But norms and rules for doing so soon developed, along with a host of practical innovations from the time clock to the assembly line and from the office chair to the workplace canteen or cafeteria. The years to come will require the same kind of institutional innovation among remote workers—or, if that does not happen, a disappointed return to a world where 95 percent of work happens in the office.

All of this will need more intangible investment by firms into processes such as monitoring workers and screening new hires. And it will likely raise the returns to "soft skills," such as trust and reliability. The economist David Deming has documented how the value of social and other noncognitive skills has risen in labour markets in the past forty years. Indeed, the value of cognitive skills, such as IQ tests, over and above education has, if anything, fallen since the turn of the century.[39] The move to remote working will make soft skills even more important.

Summary

Cities have become more important as the economy has become more intangible. As the importance of spillovers and synergies has risen, people have moved into cities, not away from them. But homevoters can potentially put a lock on further development. Devolving more power to local areas should improve amenities more effectively. But the basic attraction of cities is the matching possibilities they offer. Distance has not yet died sufficiently to offset that powerful clustering force.

7

Reducing Dysfunctional Competition

Worried that competition between firms is lessening, many economists and policy makers have called for a return to the more aggressive competition policies of the 1960s and 1970s and for the breakup or nationalisation of large business, such as tech platforms. We believe this is the wrong approach, because the change in interfirm competition is driven not by policy change but rather by the increasing importance of intangibles. And there is a neglected aspect of competition: the frequently wasteful rat race competition between individuals. Mitigating this rat race should be more of a priority for educators and governments.

We are living, we are told, in an age of monopolies. The days when Standard Oil or U.S. Steel commanded the economy and ran it to their liking may be long gone. But unlock your smartphone and, critics argue, the glowing icons you see represent a group of monopolists every bit as powerful and entrenched. And the problem is not just with trillion-dollar technology platforms. A growing gap between the most profitable and productive firms and the laggards can be seen in most countries and sectors, and it troubles many economists and policy makers.

For the past decade, there has been a growing groundswell of opinion about the institutional fix needed to deal with the problem of decreasing competition among firms. At its heart are two ideas. The first is that competition policy has been heading in the wrong direction for four decades, and the problems are now coming home to roost. The second is that tech companies present a new and especially dangerous threat to competitive markets.

The most proposed remedy to the perceived failure of competition policy is a return to the antitrust principles of the 1960s and 1970s, in particular a greater willingness to intervene when firms enjoy very large market shares. Proponents of this view sometimes describe themselves as neo-Brandeisians, after Louis Brandeis, a trust-busting Supreme Court judge of the early twentieth century. Their critics refer to their movement, with its back-to-the-future vibe, as "hipster antitrust."

The view that antitrust is failing us, especially in the digital arena, enjoys broad support. The 2019 investigation of the US House Judiciary Committee into digital markets is a prominent example.[1] It calls for more vigorous antitrust enforcement that includes breakups of dominant platforms, data portability requirements, and prohibitions on the abuse of dominant bargaining power. President Biden has appointed Lina Khan, a legal scholar who advised the investigation, as chair of the Federal Trade Commission. The United Kingdom conducted its own special review of digital competition in 2019, led by US economist Jason Furman. The European Union shares this concern regarding digital competition, as exemplified by the Digital Markets Act, which is particularly concerned with large internet platforms and seeks to regulate and limit their market-shaping ability. Speaking in October 2020, the EU commissioner Margrethe Vestager described digital platforms as "gatekeepers, with enormous power over our lives. They can influence our safety—whether dangerous products and harmful content can spread widely, or whether they're quickly removed. They can affect our opportunities—whether markets respond to our needs, or whether they just work in the interests of the platforms themselves. They even have the power to guide our political debates, and to protect—or undermine—our democracy."[2]

In this chapter, we argue that a different type of institutional reform is needed in a world where intangibles drive economic performance. Our argument has several parts. First, the apparent decline of competition among firms cannot be properly understood without taking into account the growing importance of intangibles. When the effects of intangibles are considered, some apparent symptoms of growing market power, such as rising markups and greater concentration at a national level in some markets, turn out to be illusory; others are real, but they owe as much to the changing nature of capital as they do to changes in the philosophical basis of regulation. Second, intangibles-rich businesses create different challenges for regulators, requiring them to be more expert, an argument that many advocates of hipster antitrust would support. Finally, whilst antitrust has typically concentrated on falling competition between firms, we think it important to consider rising competition between workers: competition for schools, jobs, and status. We argue that this competition among workers owes much to the growing importance of intangibles. In particular, it increases the risk of zero-sum competition among workers, escalating the risk of malinvestment in unnecessary degrees and meaningless credentials. Our institutions currently have very little immunity to this trend, and fixing it is a priority.

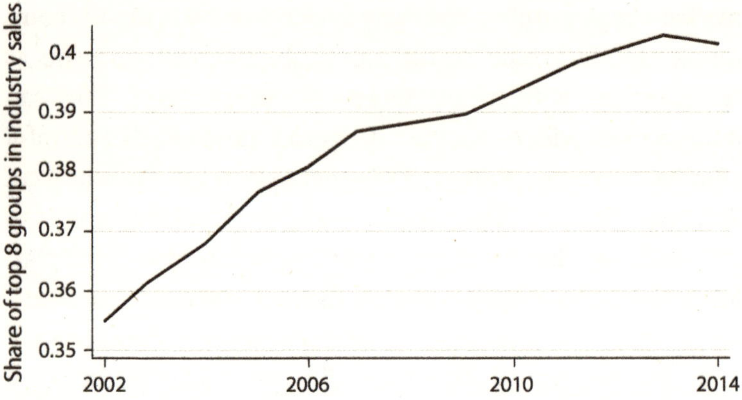

FIGURE 7.1: Top Eight Industry Concentration since 2002: Share of Top Eight Firms in Industry Sales in Thirteen Developed Countries. *Note*: The countries are Belgium, Denmark, Finland, France, Germany, Greece, Italy, Japan, Portugal, Spain, Sweden, the United Kingdom, and the United States. Included industries cover two-digit manufacturing and nonfinancial market services. Concentration is measured by the share of the top eight business groups in the sales of each industry in each country. The figure shows changes in the (unweighted) mean concentration across country-industry pairs. *Source*: Bajgar, Criscuolo, and Timmis 2020.

The Received Wisdom on Declining Competition

Let's first review the standard argument regarding the problem of interfirm competition, which is most clearly set out in the important research of the economist Thomas Philippon. Figure 7.1 shows cross-country evidence since 2002. *Concentration* (the share of the top firms) is a standard measure used by competition authorities throughout the world. If there are a small number of competing firms in a market, most economists start to worry. This situation is often associated with less competition over prices and variety of goods and weaker incentives to innovate.

A related phenomenon is the rise in what economists call the *markup*, the difference between the marginal cost of producing a product and how much that product sells for. Influential research by Jan De Loecker and Jan Eeckhout[3] suggests that markups have been steadily rising since 1980 in the United States and in Europe (see figure 1.5, which summarises this trend for the world). This is another red flag for economists: in competitive markets, we would not expect markups to keep rising because consumers would vote with their feet and shift to buying from competitors with lower prices.

What are the other symptoms of a lack of competition? A number of economists have argued that there has been a rise in the share of profits in the economy, particularly in the United States. Also, as we saw in figure 1.4, influential research by a team at the Organisation for Economic Co-operation and Development (OECD), led by Chiara Criscuolo, has found a steady rise since 2001 between the leading firms in the industry and the laggards.[4]

To many economists, enduring leader/laggard gaps looks like another symbol of competition gone wrong. After all, the genius of competition is that only firms with the best product will do well in the marketplace. But the best product is subject to continual change, what the economist Joseph Schumpeter called *creative destruction*: "This process of creative destruction is the essential fact about capitalism."[5] In a well-functioning market we would expect to see laggard firms either exiting the market or replacing the leading firms as their products get better.

For some, another troubling aspect of competition in the modern economy is the overwhelmingly conglomerate nature of some of our new firms. Amazon started as a bookseller. It now produces movies and sells web hosting; Google has moved from a search engine to online advertising to an email service to driverless cars. This increasingly conglomerate nature of the economy reminds many of the industrial structure of the

1960s, when large conglomerates dominated many industries. That story did not end well: conglomerates were sluggish and unproductive, and most ended up being broken up by market forces.

In sum, many people see increased concentration, increased insulation of the leaders from the laggards, and the trend towards conglomerates as indications of a lack of competition. And, they argue, lack of competition takes the economy to many bad places: low innovation, poor management and employment practices, rent seeking, and dissatisfied consumers with nowhere else to go.

The Effect of Intangibles on Competition between Firms

We believe the rise in intangibles offers an alternative explanation for what has happened to competition.

Consider first the rise in concentration. Here, it is important to consider the difference between concentration in national markets and concentration in local markets. For many goods, national concentration matters a lot less than local concentration. Imagine two different countries. In the first, there are no supermarket chains, and every town has a single, independent supermarket; in the second, there are two supermarket chains, and every town has one store owned by each chain. In the first country, each independent supermarket can act like a local monopolist because few people will travel to the next town for their weekly shopping. Measured national concentration would be massively higher in the second country, but consumers might prefer it, because every consumer has two stores to choose from, and there is likely to be more competition in terms of price and variety.

Research by Chang-Tai Hsieh and Esteban Rossi-Hansberg examined the difference between local and national concentration in the United States since 1977. They concluded that national concentration has risen and local concentration has fallen; Lanier Benkard, Ali Yurukoglu, and Anthony Lee Zang find the same.[6] The reason identified by Hsieh and Rossi-Hansberg is a profoundly intangible one: "ICT-based technologies and adoption of new management practices have finally made it possible for firms outside of manufacturing to scale production over a large number of locations."[7] To put it another way, because intangibles are scalable, services businesses with valuable intangibles (such as popular brands, strong management practices, or distinctive product offerings) can spread across many local markets. If that sounds abstract, think of national and international retail chains, which invest heavily in branding, software (for stock control, customer loyalty programmes, and e-commerce), relationships with suppliers (the secret sauce of "fast fashion"), and new product development—all intangible investments. Think of the pub chain JD Wetherspoons, of the midmarket chains that rapidly grow from successful independent restaurants, of Zara and IKEA. A world with lots of these chains, whose business models rely on intangibles in a way most independent stores do not, is likely to have more intense local competition that does not show up in the national figures.

This idea is also borne out in work by Matej Bajgar, Chiara Criscuolo, and Jonathan Timmis at the OECD, who studied the correlation between changes in concentration and intangible intensity.[8] As we saw in chapter 2, rises in concentration have occurred in the most intangible-intensive industries. Turning to markups and profits, as we mentioned in chapters 1 and 2,

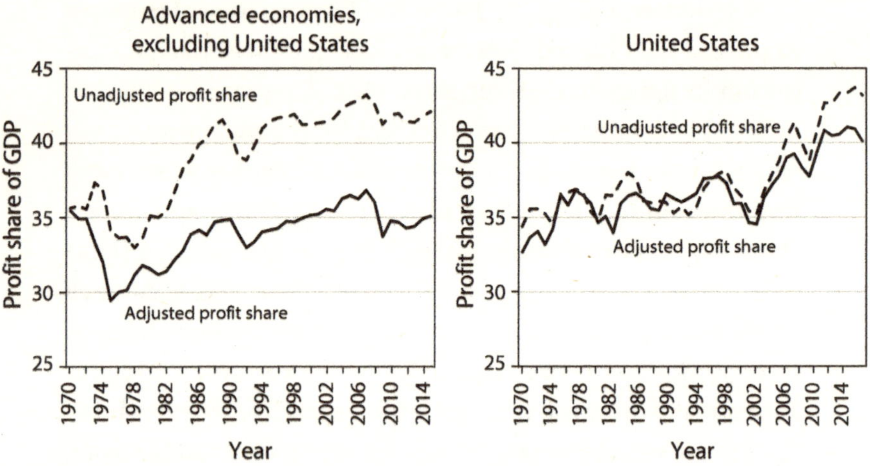

FIGURE 7.2: Profit Shares Inside and Outside the United States. *Note*: Unadjusted line includes corporation-owned dwellings; adjusted line excludes them. *Source*: Gutiérrez and Piton 2019a.

the markups of American firms and the total rate of return are more or less unchanged when one accounts for intangibles in firms' capital. The runaway profitability of businesses is at least partly an artifact of using the wrong denominator, omitting an increasingly important part of the capital stock that businesses invest in.

We see something similar when we look at profits. Measurement here is fraught with difficulty. Profits are a measure of the return to capital, so it seems natural to turn to national accounts that measures wages and salaries (which are the returns to labour) and profits. Figure 7.2, which presents the headline figures, labelled "unadjusted," for the share of GDP accounted for by profits. It shows that both in the United States and elsewhere, the share of profits has risen.

Germán Gutiérrez and Sophie Piton have dug into these data and found a different picture.[9] National accounts break GDP into wages, profits, and payments to the self-employed (which are in practice a mixture of wages and profits). Profits are measured by tax returns from corporations. Profits therefore will change for at least two reasons. First, profits will change if the numbers or treatment of the self-employed as corporations changes. Second, national accounts treat buildings as capital, as would be expected because buildings are durable sources of capital services. Buildings consist of commercial buildings and dwellings, which are residential homes. In the United Kingdom, dwellings are 40 percent of the total capital stock. It turns out, however, that many corporations own houses; and if a commercial corporation owns a stock of houses, then the returns that it makes are part of commercial profits. As Gutiérrez and Piton discovered, outside the United States many houses are classified as "corporations." In fact, in Europe nearly 20 percent of nonfinancial corporations' capital stock is housing (compared with 1 percent in the United States). When we talk about "profits" as a measure of competition between businesses, we surely want to strip this aspect out. As the "adjusted" line in figure 7.2 shows, it makes little difference in the United States: the share of wages has been falling, and so profits have been rising. But at least outside the United States, the share of profits has been stable.

Finally, could the ability of large firms to scale up and exploit synergies explain the growing gap between the leaders and the laggards? As we saw in figure 2.4, Carol Corrado and colleagues find evidence consistent with this suggestion.[10] Controlling for a large number of other factors, industries that are more intangibles intensive have a growing productivity dispersion, which suggests that intangibles are the main driver of productivity dispersion, an argument consistent with that made by Sam Peltzman.[11]

The implication of all these findings is that intangibles help make sense of the crisis of interfirm competition in three ways. First, including intangibles in some measures of market power (such as markups) reduces or eliminates the apparent increases in market power we would otherwise see in the data. Second, the growing importance of intangibles has underpinned the phenomenon of increasing local competition and falling national competition as intangibles-rich national chains open new local establishments. Third, to the extent that concentration has increased, it seems that it has done so in the most intangible-intensive sectors, suggesting that the winner-takes-all characteristics of intangible capital may be to blame, rather than an exogenous deterioration of competition policy.

New Competition Concerns Raised by Intangibles

So far our arguments suggest that, when it comes to interfirm competition, intangibles provide reasons for optimism and for rejecting the concerns of hipster antitrust. Unfortunately, things are not quite so simple. An intangible economy is harder to regulate, requiring changes to the institutions that enforce competition policy.

How does competition affect prices in an intangibles-rich economy? The digital economy goes hand in hand with the growing importance of intangibles (recall that intangible assets include software and databases, for example). There is a lingering suspicion that competition might work differently online. After all, doesn't the information that the internet now gives consumers benefit only the smart and savvy? Those who seek the variety of supply that competition brings will be the winners. Those without the ability or means to seek such bargains, will surely lose out.

This logic needs careful teasing out. The basic textbook economics model suggests the complete opposite. In that world, the smart, savvy consumers spread the benefits of their bargain hunting to everybody else. To understand how that happens, start by thinking about the price of milk at your local supermarket. If you ask people what the price of milk is, most of them are rather hazy about it. Indeed, many politicians get a briefing on the price of milk before they go into the interview room, as it's a standard question that an interviewer might ask in an attempt to embarrass them. (In the United Kingdom, the price is about £1 for 4 pints; in the United States, about $3.59 per gallon). Does a general lack of awareness regarding milk prices mean that supermarkets can simply raise the price of milk, safe in the knowledge that uninformed consumers will not notice the difference? Not necessarily. Suppose there are some consumers who *do* know the difference. If the supermarket raises the price of milk, those consumers will simply go elsewhere, either by physically walking elsewhere or by clicking a button. And if there are enough of them, then the supermarket knows that it's going to lose out if it raises its milk price. Just how much it loses out depends on the responsiveness of demand to its price. It turns out that supermarkets don't need that many "marginal consumers" to make such a price increase unprofitable. For example, suppose typical markups over variable costs of 50 percent. Even if 85 percent of customers remain after a 5 percent price increase, that price increase is unprofitable.

The consequences of this market behaviour are important. When only 15 percent of consumers are responsive, milk prices stay low. Thus, the 85 percent of consumers who either have little idea of milk prices or pay no attention whatsoever get the benefit from those active 15 percent, and the benefits of competition cascade beyond just those savvy consumers. The actions of a few hold the price low for everyone, supporting the textbook model that predicts widely spread benefits of competition.

Another example is hotel minibars.[12] These minibars, with their very high prices, seem to be a prime example of preying on thirsty and hungry consumers (or perhaps those with less self-control). But it's worth remembering that hotels offer minibars to everybody. If the hotel believes that at least some fraction of its guests is going to purchase items from the minibar, it will reduce the base price of its hotel rooms to attract more minibar users. The hotel therefore ends up reducing prices for everyone, and the non-minibar drinkers get the advantage of those who yield to such temptation (who may in any case have good reason to want to pay a premium for a cold drink that is available in their room). Payments for checking baggage at airports work on a similar principle. Savvy consumers who do not incur these costs are subsidised by those who end up paying.

Matters are different, however, if everybody pays a different price. If the supermarket could engineer price changes in such a way that prices stay low for the price-sensitive customers but get raised for the price-insensitive customers, then it might be able to successfully raise prices, even in the face of competition. Such a strategy is difficult to pull off. First, the supermarket must know who is price sensitive and who is price insensitive. And it would have to know that fact not only for the price of milk but also for the price of meat, bread, and the thousands of other products that supermarkets usually stock. Second, the supermarket would have to find a way of segmenting the market and holding prices low just for the more responsive. In the pre-internet days, coupons were used for exactly this purpose. Sensitive customers snipped coupons and got price reductions for which insensitive customers were ineligible, allowing supermarkets to segment the market. But coupons were an inaccurate method of segmentation, and whilst the customers bearing coupons revealed themselves to be the sensitive customers, coupons didn't typically use customers' purchasing histories.

Today, in the internet era, segmentation can be accomplished much more easily. Shops, especially those online, have detailed information about individuals, their shopping habits, their responsiveness to prices, and other contractual details—from online accounts or from loyalty cards for in-store purchases. So, the cost of information, which the market segmentation strategy crucially requires, seems to have come down, which raises an interesting hypothesis. Perhaps in earlier years, with less personalised pricing and less segmentation in markets, the vast bulk of uninformed consumers unknowingly benefitted from the actions of informed consumers. As far as prices were concerned, we were really all in it together. With the move to the internet and increased information in the economy, perhaps the situation has completely changed. Shops can target offers at particular customers. Consumers are now faced with an assault on their attention that the digital economy brings, and uninformed consumers are failing to get any benefit from informed consumers. In this digital marketplace, therefore, we are decidedly not all in it together.

Finding widespread evidence of "personalised" pricing is harder than you might think. One standout area is internet dating. A 2016 mystery shopping exercise organised by WISO, a German consumer organisation, revealed that a dating portal used personalised price segmentation—that is, it offered different prices to different customers. Parship, a large German provider of online dating services that boasts of setting up 55,000 relationships since 2001, uses its detailed sign-up questionnaire to determine the client's monthly membership fee. These fees differed by salary, among other characteristics. A female tester with a fictional annual income of €100,000 was asked to pay a €44.93 monthly fee, while another tester with a lower fictional annual income of €15,000 was offered the membership for €30.02 per month. A male user with an equally low income was offered a lower fee than the female user—only €26.45 per month.

While Parship extensively uses personal information to charge personal prices, less sophisticated efforts are more common. The economist Aniko Hannak and colleagues[13] documented several cases where companies inferred higher ability to pay from the type of computer that the buyer used. For example, researchers found that Mac users can spend up to 30 percent more than PC users for the same room on the US online booking portal Orbitz. In other cases, Staples, a large office supply chain in the United States, charged different prices based on the location of its online shoppers. Search effort can also make a difference; for example, users searching for flights more intensively, by using Google Flights, always paid less.

Price steering, a close cousin of individualised pricing, changes the order of search results, presenting those results based on what the retailer already knows about the customer from previous visits to its site. A good analogy is the way that Netflix presents content to its users. Over the course of time, Netflix learns about its users' preferences, allowing it to tailor suggested content better and better from visit to visit.

Whether these practices are common or not, the rationale and effectiveness of intervention in this marketplace are very complicated. Taking steps to raise competition typically helps all customers. But many suggested interventions in these marketplaces—regulating minibar prices, for example—are steps to change not all prices but rather the structure of prices. Capping minibar prices might help those customers who want a drink or a snack, but it might harm other customers if the general level of prices rises to recover the loss in profits from the minibar. Michael Grubb and Matthew Osborne examined the US Federal Communications Commission's 2013 introduction of "bill-shock" regulation.[14] In response to the mobile phone users who went over their allotted minutes and received enormous bills, a law was passed requiring mobile operators to send a text alert to consumers who are about to go over their text/call limit and so incur "overage" charges. And indeed, this law did reduce the number of consumers who incurred overage charges. But simulations suggested that the operators, which were competing in other parts of the market, regained profits by increasing their standard charges for everyone. Overall, consumers became worse off. What should we conclude? Interventions that end up changing the *structure* of prices are fraught with problems and need to be considered very carefully.

Furthermore, there are situations in which differential pricing improves things for both firms and consumers, particularly when it comes to some intangibles-intensive businesses whose products have fixed costs but near-zero marginal cost, such as software, data, music, or video games. Setting prices for businesses like these is tricky; they need to find a way of covering their fixed costs. One way to do this is to allow businesses to charge different prices to different consumers (often for different versions: free and paid-for Zoom, for example). Consider the market for video games, where sales, deals, bundles, and so forth likely help companies set different prices for many different types of customers (most notably, those willing to wait versus those unwilling to wait). Charging different prices probably increases the amount of games sold compared with what would happen if firms had to set a single price high enough to cover their fixed costs, and it means that more consumers get a game at a price they are willing to pay.

Another issue relates to how we encourage *business dynamism*. There has been a welcome trend in competition policy away from monitoring simple concentration metrics towards ensuring that it remains possible for new firms to enter a market. The entry of new firms is particularly important as the significance of intangibles increases, to the extent that threats to large, intangibles-rich incumbents often come from new entrants. But ensuring that market entry is easy becomes harder in a world of intangibles-intensive businesses. As we saw in chapter 2, intangible capital tends to be heterogeneous: one idea, one brand, one operating process is usually not like any others. One consequence of this heterogeneity is that the tactics that intangibles-rich businesses use to maintain competitive advantage—what Warren Buffett would call the "moats" around their business model—are also highly varied and tend to require bespoke analysis.

When one of the authors worked on intellectual property policy for the UK government, a controversial issue was the rivalry between online platforms and the owners of content such as music videos and sporting rights. The issue was in a broad sense one of competition and market dominance. But the specifics were very specific indeed. For example, how quickly should content platforms such as YouTube be required to take down pirated content? (The answer to this question matters because the faster a platform is required to remove the offending content, the less likely it is to have a permanent "reserve army" of illegal content available to users, which in turn weakens its bargaining position in negotiations with rights holders over how much money the rights holders receive each time their content is viewed.) It may come as no surprise that this issue was dealt with not by the normal regulatory processes but rather with a high-touch negotiation conducted across two government departments.

Another issue is mergers. Critics decry Facebook's purchase of WhatsApp on the basis that the purchase may have stopped future competition. But the prospect of being bought out by another company may be the only way that new intangibles-intensive businesses will start in the first place, especially if they have trouble raising finance through conventional channels (see chapter 5).

These examples are just some of the almost infinite variety of market-dominance questions that regulators may be called on to resolve for intangibles-intensive businesses. Each question presents its own technical challenges, and it is hard to resolve them using the kind of rules-based procedures that work for assessing market dominance in discrete industries dominated by brick-and-mortar assets. Crucially, these policy questions are not ones that would usually be considered to fall into the realm of competition policy or antitrust policy. A whole host of regulatory questions affect business dynamism, so if business dynamism becomes a more important lever of competition policy, it will require a wider range of government competencies to make it work.

Institutions for Competition in an Intangible Economy

Both the many different types of the market-dominance problem in an intangible economy and the way online platforms change the marginal consumer's effect on pricing decisions have implications for the way we regulate competition. Our guiding principle should remain consumer welfare, and ensuring that markets are contestable should remain an important means to achieve consumer protections. However, understanding a wide variety of new business models, market-access dynamics, and the impact of digital technologies on pricing requires significant knowledge on the part of regulators.

The economist John Fingleton has made two interesting suggestions. First,[15] an "n + 1" regulator might sit across all sectors of the economy and aim to support new companies with innovative business ideas that existing laws or regulations cannot accommodate. The "n + 1" name signifies that the regulator would be responsible for radically new business models that do not sit well in the established market framework of the industry; recent examples that an n + 1 regulator may have looked at include peer-to-peer finance businesses or telematic car insurance, both of which faced regulatory challenges. The idea is that the regulator would grant five-year licences to new companies whose business models conflict with existing regulations—the next Uber, for example—and allow the companies to operate for this period whether they are in breach of existing law or not. The companies would be required to take out liability insurance, or in some cases the regulator itself may offer insurance (at a price) if the private sector will not insure an innovative business.

This approach already exists in health care, where treatments that haven't received regulatory approval are allowed to be used under certain circumstances. It also exists to some extent in fintech (innovations in the financial and technology crossover space). The regulator would have two responsibilities here: (1) it would allow into the market innovative companies that would otherwise be blocked by regulation and (2) it would be responsible for negotiating with the sector regulators to change the rules so that those innovative new companies can continue to operate in the long run. This approach dovetails nicely with our earlier framework. It solves a collective-action problem in institutional reform—namely, that many individual companies might want to change regulations (those that block entry for many, for example), but none of these individual firms benefit from spending effort to change the regulations.[16]

In addition, Fingleton suggests that we might reform sectoral regulation so that sector regulators deal with activity rather than industry—for example, on access charges for all utilities rather than access charges on a utility-by-utility basis. Reformed sectoral regulation might also help avoid worries that industry-specialist regulators might be captured by the industries they regulate. It would also provide a forum for thinking about how to regulate intangibles-intensive platform businesses, such as food delivery firms. The expertise required to assess whether it makes sense to compel open access to a utility network could also be applied to networks such as Deliveroo or Uber Eats.

Turning to broad competition questions in the intangible economy and in particular in the digital economy, we are cautious. Sometimes regulators encourage rivalry by intervening in a market, thereby improving its general functioning and encouraging rivalry and entry in the whole market. On other occasions they intervene in only part of the market (often following lobbying from politicians). Interventions around the *structure* of prices, rather than general market functioning, can have unforeseen consequences. As we saw in the bill-shock case, these efforts may backfire.

Further, we think the intangibles lens helps to better evaluate some policy questions. Large companies might very well be a good thing if their scale and synergies, which abound in the digital economy, benefit consumers, providing, for example, a wide network or indirectly encouraging entrants with the prospect of mergers. Breaking up a company like Amazon might dissolve synergies and scale, which could end up being a net loss for consumers if a broken-up firm cannot use them. Does this possible outcome mean that we should do nothing in the digital space?

Not necessarily. First, there might be some harm if large search engines dominate the digital advertising market, in which case action may be taken in that particular market (but even then the "harm" to the economy of having expensive advertisements would have to be calibrated). Second, rather than treating intangibles as a bug, competition authorities should treat them as a feature. The obvious example is the widespread use of online price comparison websites, used by 85 percent of UK consumers with internet access according to the CMA, and accounting for 40 and 60 percent of home and car insurance sales, respectively.[17] The CMA Digital Competition Tools inquiry found that 64 percent of consumers used multiple comparison tools when shopping around. Making sure competition between these sites is strong would be a good use of limited regulatory time. Finally, competition regulators need to keep an eye out for unintended competition consequences of other measures in the digital economy, such as privacy.[18]

These institutional changes are less dramatic than the aggressive upgrading of antitrust rules that many are advocating. Indeed, some might call them downright boring because they involve investing in the skills and capacities of regulators, which is never a rousing political argument. In many cases, they have little to do with competition authorities. But the key point is that in a world of intangibles-intensive businesses that have strong economies of scale and that may often obtain temporary dominance over markets, the best weapon is new firms. Making sure new, innovative businesses have a fair chance to enter markets and dethrone today's monopolists is more effective than the traditional metrics and tools of antitrust.

Intangibles and the Rat Race

Let's turn now to the other dysfunctional aspect of competition in today's economy: the intensification of competition among workers. This trend has been accelerated by the growing importance of intangibles in the economy, and it presents its own institutional challenges. But unlike the question of interfirm competition, it has received relatively little political consideration.

In the words of legal scholar Daniel Markovits, "Today's elite workplace fetishises extreme skill and effort. Super-skills (and hence also the education and degrees that provide and mark skill) become increasingly important not just to securing high incomes and high status but also to avoiding low incomes and low status."[19] The rat race does not affect only elites. Many workers in lower-paid services jobs are increasingly subject to surveillance, enforced work discipline, and punishment for slacking. However, high-status and/or high-skill workers are better placed to win the rat race and to claim a disproportionate share of the rewards.

Anecdotes abound of how the rat race, especially in education, has become pervasive. The 2019 FBI investigation "Operation Varsity Blues" revealed a network of Wall Street and Hollywood personalities paying to get their children into various universities, via bribery of officials and inflation of exam results.[20] Wealthy families in New York are reported to pay vast sums to get their young children into prestigious preschools and kindergartens that will give them the best chance of then getting into prestigious schools, for which they will then pay further vast sums, and so on.

More prosaic, but no less remarkable, academic research has documented the huge difference to life prospects from failing at various academic hurdles, surely adding to the pressures on parents and children. The economists Stephen Machin, Sandra McNally, and Jenifer Ruiz-Valenzuela[21] looked at the consequences of failing to obtain a C grade in English, in the GCSE (General Certificate of Secondary Education) exam in the United Kingdom. The GCSE is an externally marked exam taken by all school students in England at age sixteen. It is marked on a scale from 0 to 300 and the information summarised in a letter grade from A to U. Machin, McNally, and Ruiz-Valenzuela compared pupils with marks just above and below the grade C line (within 10 points) and found that such students have drastically different outcomes. Those who narrowly miss a C grade have much lower chances of achieving any further qualifications and a much higher chance of dropping out altogether. The probability of dropping out of school at age eighteen for the narrow-miss pupils rises by about 4 percentage points. This is a large number when compared with the national dropout average, which is about 12 percent.[22] Such findings are backed by employer surveys. A 2013 survey shows that GCSEs are important shortcuts for employers when hiring: of those surveyed, 43 percent use GCSEs in English and math as a filter.[23] Hiring managers did not see applicants with grades below level C regardless of the applicants' other achievements. Contrast this with blue-collar hiring practices at Ford in the 1960s reported by Acemoglu. In the words of one of Ford's managers, "If we had a vacancy, we would look outside in the plant waiting room to see if there were any warm bodies standing there. If someone was there and they looked physically OK and weren't an obvious alcoholic, they were hired."[24]

To some extent, the rat race is a first-order consequence of the growth of intangible capital. One subset of intangible capital is the software and management systems that enable businesses to track staff performance, reward the high performers, and punish the low performers, whether the workplace is an Amazon warehouse or a corporate law firm. The other aspect of intangibles is that they allow the talented workers to create eye-watering amounts of value, increasing the returns to being the best footballer, quantitative trader, or industrial designer. No wonder, then, that in an intangibles-intensive society, these aspects of the rat race are intensified.

The inequality caused by these first-order effects of intangibles is significant, but in some sense it is familiar and can be addressed by familiar policies and institutions. Redistributive taxation, minimum wage laws, and employment rights are endlessly contested, but there is nothing institutionally new about them. To the extent that the search for great rewards incentivises people to develop useful skills, it also has a positive effect, and passing an exam must say *something* about the student.

But the quote from Markovits reveals a less obvious, second-order effect of an intangibles-rich economy. As Markovits observes, modern workplaces don't just value skills; they "fetishise" them. Educations and degrees are valuable not just because they confer skills but because they "mark" them. In other words, an intangible economy is likely to reward what economists call *human capital signalling*: acquiring credentials not because they are inherently valuable but because they are a credible way to prove that a worker is skillful.

Signalling matters because it is hard for employers to distinguish skillful workers from less skilled workers. Gaining an elite qualification such as a university degree may be valuable not only because it indicates that an employee has learned valuable skills but also because it is a credible signal that a prospective employee is conscientious and intelligent.

To be credible, a signal must be costly, either in cash terms or in terms of the time and effort it takes to obtain; otherwise anyone could get one. This requirement creates a problem. A dollar or hour of work spent gaining a useful qualification not only creates value for the person who earns it; by making that person more productive, it also creates value for the economy as a whole. It is a positive-sum proposition. In contrast, spending the same dollar or hour on a qualification whose only benefit is signalling is a different matter. It creates a private return to the people who earn the qualification, but it does not give them skills that create any additional value. Instead, it merely allows them to get a job that someone else might have got. It is zero-sum investment, or near enough.

Unfortunately, none of the participants in a typical educational transaction have a strong incentive to distinguish between real human capital formation and signalling. From an employer's viewpoint, it does not matter why a degree and certificate are useful, so long as they are. When John Paul Getty was asked why he chose men with classics degrees to run his companies, he replied, "Because they sell more oil"—it was irrelevant to him whether Greek and Latin were useful in the oil business or talented people tended to get classics degrees. Similarly, employees care only about their private return. Even schools, universities, and training establishments have mixed motives. On the one hand, they may have strong intrinsic motivations to ensure that what they teach is rigorous and in good faith; on the other hand, they have little incentive to make themselves redundant by probing too deeply the nature of the benefit they provide.

What is more, it may not be easy for educational establishments to provide real human capital formation even if they want to. Paul Lewis, a political economist who has studied advanced technical skills, interviewed people at dozens of high-tech British firms.[25] They reported that even well-intentioned education providers had trouble providing the right skills for technical recruits. The synergies between intangibles such as R&D and worker skills can often be difficult to realise, requiring close interaction between education providers and employers (or their integration, in the form of apprenticeships or on-the-job training).

In a world where the returns to skills are high and rising but the ability to judge talent is imperfect, and where it is hard for colleges and universities to predict employer needs, we would expect to see a boom in signalling. There is some evidence of such a boom. It is widely observed that a college degree is becoming a prerequisite for many jobs that were once done by nongraduates. Prestigious employers that once recruited candidates with undergraduate degrees are now choosing between candidates with a master's degree and those with a doctorate. These changes might reflect genuine increases in skills, but they might not. Especially in the United States, many jobs that once required no qualifications now require certification or occupational licencing,[26] ostensibly on skills and safety grounds. If more and more jobs are requiring a degree as a way of sorting between potential employees, this could help explain why graduate wage premiums in the United Kingdom have fallen for recent cohorts: graduates born in 1970 enjoyed an average wage premium of 19 percent over nongraduates, compared with only 11 percent for graduates born in 1990.

How much evidence is there for educational signalling? Bryan Caplan has been a vocal proponent of the view that college wage premiums in the United States are significantly about signalling. His main argument is that dropping out one year before graduating involves a large wage penalty, but it seems unlikely that the one additional year is so productivity raising as to justify that wage rise.[27] Thus, the graduation status is signal and not productivity. Noah Smith has argued that the passing of exams is a difficult enough hurdle to justify such wage premiums. Further, he argues, firms are likely to learn about workers' skills when they hire them. If educated workers were really not productive, then the high return to education would decline as firms learnt about their workers' actual abilities: if those students failing their GCSEs are doing worse for extended periods, then their failure must convey some underlying information about their productivity.[28] Caplan counters with US evidence that employers seem to learn quickly about college-educated workers, but remarkably slowly about non-college-educated workers.[29] In a study of US high school graduates, Peter Arcidiacono, Patrick Bayer, and Aurel Hizmo suggest that employers have not learnt about underlying productive attributes of those graduates even after twelve years of employing them.[30]

It is presumably even harder for employers to learn when noncognitive skills become more important. If such skills are crowded out by teaching to the test, then it may be that employers look even harder at student background, raising the scope for wasteful signalling.

One proposed solution is to make the education market work better. If students spent their own money on education, then providers, public or private, would compete to offer courses that really do improve employability and really do offer something useful. This intuition has been the main thrust behind much of the past thirty years of higher education reform in the United Kingdom, in which university education has gone from an entirely state-funded system (with student numbers capped, and places limited to those with the best examination results) to a system of relatively high fees and subsidised loans provided by the government. The government has produced detailed data sets on the future salaries of graduates in different disciplines, along with frameworks and rankings that try to provide this evidence to prospective students in a salient way. The US system has of course gone much further down this road, with most students incurring large amounts of private debt to pay for their studies.

Gallons of ink have been spilled over the merits and demerits of marketising the university system. Critics argue that it is reductionist, increases inequality, and ignores the value of education to the extent that it does not translate into a higher graduate salary, and that many of the metrics used to assess courses and universities are statistically unsound. But neither side of the argument seems to have much of an answer to the question of how to discourage wasteful signalling. Even if market reforms fully achieve their goal of giving prospective students very strong incentives to choose only courses with very high returns, there is still the problem that an individual student is indifferent as to whether that return comes from real human capital formation (that is to say, learning actually useful knowledge and skills) or acts as a signal that they are more intelligent and conscientious than other people.

Another marginal improvement is to expand subsidies to cover more than just a university education. The UK government announced in 2021 that it was extending its loan subsidies to nonuniversity vocational education, a move that was widely welcomed by people worried about the dominance of universities in the British system.[31] American critics of universities point to short, vocational coding schools like Lambda School as possible models for the future, and imply that it would be better if more young people took this route for postsecondary education.

But this route also has risks. The United Kingdom's historical experience of a freer education market in which students have access to cheap loans is not encouraging. In September 2000 the government introduced an Individual Learning Accounts scheme, a sum of money that adults aged nineteen and older could spend on education. An education provider could enrol a student, get the student's account number from the enrolled student, and then claim the student's allowance from the government. To encourage entry by new education providers, the government allowed any institution to enrol students. A host of new "providers" enrolled students and obtained the subsidy. But after fears that bogus providers were walking away with the money, the scheme was scrapped just fifteen months later. It was later found that lack of reporting meant that the government was unaware that just thirteen providers had registered over ten thousand accounts.[32]

The real problem here is that the institutions that govern education and training have relatively few defences against credentialism and signalling. For the most part, government policy sees more education as better, and relatively little consideration is given to what to do about signalling. It is assumed that education providers, employers, and learners have a strong incentive to make sure that education is useful. But, as we have seen, there is no real incentive for any of these groups to prefer real human capital formation over signalling alone. In addition, making policy on this subject is hard. Governments are not well placed to differentiate between degrees or qualifications that generate real skills and those that merely signal. At most, they make very broad-brush attempts to promote science and math degrees—which could involve more human capital formation, but could equally also involve signalling—or focus on student earnings, which could also be the result of signalling.

We believe that policy makers need to invest time and money into studying this problem. If we gathered more data and conducted more experiments, we could understand more about postsecondary education and what types of licencing generate real value rather than signalling. Our hope is that governments equipped with this information will take the idea of wasteful competition through signalling much more seriously and design an education system to discourage it. In some ways, educational reform has strong parallels with the quantity versus quality in public science funding that we discussed in chapter 4. The idea that funneling ever-increasing numbers of students into higher education is sufficient to solve the skills problem is a quantity view, but the solution may be to provide more variety in truly useful skills (quality) rather than just sheer numbers.

Summary

The growing gap between leader and laggard firms in the economy seems to be caused to a great extent by the increasing importance of intangibles rather than by businesses distorting competition regulation. Maximising competition in the economy requires us to increase dynamism, to give challenger firms the best possible chance of dislodging incumbents, rather than embarking on a new wave of trust-busting policy, as some have proposed. The growing importance of intangibles has also increased competition among workers and encouraged an increase of signalling in fields like education, which is wasteful, costly, and stressful. Policy makers have done little to understand this, let alone to reduce it. That should change.

Conclusion

RESTARTING THE FUTURE

Growth needs institutions to provide commitment, collective action, information, and limits to influence activities. In this concluding chapter we set out cross-cutting themes around the institutional reforms that we recommended in this book: designing systems that strike the right balance between quantity and quality of investment, building state capacity, resisting influence activities, and changing culture to lower cognitive load and restore trust.

We began this book by describing the malaise that has affected the economies of the rich world in the twenty-first century. Specific calamities such as the global financial crisis and the COVID-19 pandemic have affected these economies, but our economic problem is longer term and deeply rooted. It is a chronic, systemic illness rather than an acute, specific one.

We argued that this problem is multifaceted and characterised by five symptoms: stagnation, inequality, a combination of decreased and increased competition, fragility, and inauthenticity. We also noted that the way these symptoms manifest themselves is often puzzling or paradoxical. Economic stagnation coexists with low interest rates, high business profits, and a widespread belief that we live in an age of dizzying technological progress. The rise of material inequality has slowed down, but its consequences and sequelae—inequality of status, political polarisation, geographical divides, and deaths of despair—continue to grow. Although business competition seems to have fallen, with fewer new firms and a more persistent performance gap between leader and laggard businesses, working life for managers and workers alike does not feel "fat, dumb, and happy" but rather more frenetic and contested than ever.

The net result is an economy that has been performing poorly—not just quantitatively but also qualitatively—for the better part of two decades. Many of us are accustomed to thinking of modern economic growth as remarkably consistent. After all, the US economy managed an average growth rate of 2.3 percent in GDP per capita per year between 1950 and 2000[1] even though the world changed a great deal over that period. The type of economic growth that the rich world has experienced since the Industrial Revolution, so the story goes, is a new, persistent normal, and pessimists should be distrusted. But longer-run economic history suggests that periods of intensive growth can falter and end.

In chapter 3 we discussed the medieval Italian city-states, which briefly broke out of the Malthusian trap of extensive growth before their golden age ended and they returned to subsistence poverty. The economic historian Jack Goldstone points out that this sort of short-lived economic flourishing was not uncommon. He called these periods "efflorescences" and argued that we should think of them as the opposite of crises, as limited periods of time during which things go right in a self-reinforcing way. Economic historians observe that these efflorescences seem to have occurred repeatedly throughout history, including in Song China, Abbasid Mesopotamia, ancient Greece, and the Dutch Golden Age.[2]

Another economic historian, Joel Mokyr, provides a theory for why efflorescences don't last.[3] He labelled this theory Cardwell's law after the historian of science who pointed out that no country stays at the cutting edge of technology for long. Mokyr's contribution was to describe *why* Cardwell's law occurs. He argues that important new technologies, which often inconvenience established interests, require new institutions to make them work. A society that has the right institutions to thrive in the technological landscape of one time period may not be well positioned to thrive in the next technological era. Indeed, its historical success may render its institutions resistant to change. Bas van Bavel discusses this issue in his book *The Invisible Hand*.[4]

This analysis seems relevant to our current situation. In chapter 2 we showed that the five symptoms of our economic malaise have their origins in a large, gradual change in the capital stock of rich-world economies. Specifically, we have seen a shift from physical, tangible capital to intangible capital, consisting of knowledge, relationships, and expressive content, which behave differently from an economic point of view. This shift has two primary characteristics: much of it has happened already, with the result that more business investment is intangible than tangible; and the growth of intangibles has begun to slow, which in turn has slowed down economic growth.

This narrative is qualitatively different from other explanations for our current economic state. Some of these explanations argue that we have lost a particular societal virtue that we once had. For Marc Andreessen, what has been lost is the urge to build. For Thomas Piketty, it is egalitarianism. For Thomas Philippon, it is intolerance of monopoly. Others, such as

Ross Douthat, argue that we have lost not a specific virtue but rather virtue in general, and that we are gripped by a pervasive decadence that we must cast off. Another group of explanations treats the economic problem as exogenous but unavoidable. Erik Brynjolfsson, Daniel Rock, and Chad Syverson take a more optimistic view: today's lacklustre economy is temporary, and the full potential of new technologies will soon be unleashed and things will improve. The pessimistic version of the exogenous story is summed up by Robert Gordon's argument that our historical growth depended on a technological bounty that will not happen again. Somewhere between Brynjolfsson and Gordon is Dietrich Vollrath, who argues that slow growth is simply something natural that happens to rich, service-based economies.

Our explanation differs from these explanations in two ways. First, it is not based on a falling away from some virtue that abounded in the past. Rather, it is based on the idea that a society faces different challenges when it generates around 2 percent growth in GDP per capita and grows its intangible capital stock by 4 percent than when those figures are 0.5 percent and 2 percent, respectively. Second, although our explanation is based on an exogenous change—specifically, the change in the capital stock that happens as society gets richer—it does not assume that its effects are immutably determined. The link between these changes and the economic malaise is, we argue, an *institutional* one. In chapters 4–7 we looked at four ways in which important institutions are poorly suited to an economy based on intangibles.

The idea that institutions are out of sync with the intangible economy raises a disconcerting possibility: perhaps the long period of growth in the rich world has more in common with Goldstone's efflorescences than we suspect. For a long time our institutions were up to the challenge of overcoming the four problems that typically stand in the way of growth: lack of commitment, too little collective action, constrained information, and influence activities. But as the capital stock has changed, we have encountered different problems that our institutions struggle to deal with.

Chapters 4–7 also put forth a set of institutional reforms that we believe would make a significant difference in fixing the problems that have caused our economic malaise: fixing cities, improving competition and regulation, embracing the public's role in encouraging investment, and changing financial architecture. Getting these changes right is partly about designing effective policies, such as street votes and automatic stabilisers. But achieving institutional change requires more than just policy wonkery. It also requires that we build state capacity, design systems that strike the right balance between quantity and quality of investment, resist influence activities (or rent seeking), and bring about cultural change.

A Framework: Trade-Offs and Institutional Design

Two key graphs can help us understand the impact of improving state capacity, the importance of resisting rent seeking, and how the quantity versus quality of intangibles matters.

The Trade-Off between Collective Goods and Influence and Information Costs

Figure C.1 sets out the key constraint trade-off faced by economies.[5] As you go up the vertical axis, the economy is able to provide more centralised collective goods per spend. In a public-sector context, these collective goods might be security, the science budget, and monetary stability per unit of cost/tax

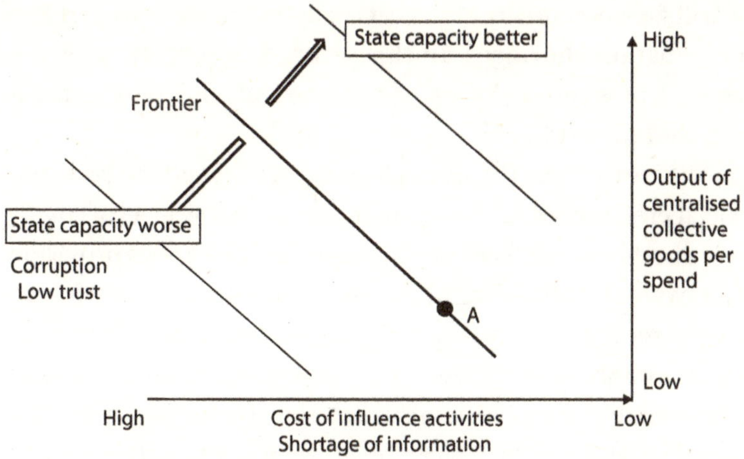

FIGURE C.1: Providing Centralised Goods: The Constraint.

raised. In a private-sector context, these goods might be centralised coordination activities within large enterprises—for example, the ability of a head office to coordinate and direct activity.

Providing centralised goods involves at least two costs. First, as Paul Milgrom and John Roberts[6] have documented, centralised provision might promote wasteful influence activities—for example, large amounts of time spent lobbying or the misrepresentation of private information (such as a scientist overpromising on a project). Second, the act of centralised provision itself might bring a shortage of information. Without experimentation by the market and the revelation of values and usefulness that this brings, information might be scarce. Soviet planners faced just such an information shortage, along with a system riddled with waste due to influence spending.

Thus, with the costs of information shortages and influence spending on the horizontal axis of the figure, we can draw the economy's constraint, illustrated by the thick line. If a society wants to produce high levels of centralised collective goods, it will face potentially high costs from influence activities and information shortages. In this setup, any society faces the choices of where to locate on the trade-off and/or whether it can shift the trade-off.

Where to locate (for example, point A) depends on costs and social preferences. A society might choose a low level of collective goods when it faces very costly collective goods provision (for example, providing health or communication services to a very geographically dispersed population). Or, that society might simply have an aversion to providing collective goods. One source of such aversion might be attribution bias. It is often argued that individuals overweight their own contribution to their success and underweight the collective contribution—for example, bankers who credit their own stock-picking skills rather than the general rise in the market. If such a cognitive bias is widespread, there may be a natural preference against collective goods.

How Steep Is the Trade-Off?

Turning to the shape of the frontier, what determines its slope and position, and how do intangibles change it? Let's start with the slope and use the example of a big science project. Some believe the slope is steep. Centralised direction of science will mean the provision of more collective goods regardless of the project; any project will likely throw off unexpected gains to society so that the sacrifice of information from a centralised project is small. Furthermore, the nonpecuniary objectives of scientists mean that the sacrifice of wasteful influence activities is small. Indeed, some might argue that centralisation itself helps foster common purpose, and again the slope is steep. Others, such as Matt Ridley,[7] argue that the line is flat. The costs of centralised goods are huge: centralisation provokes wasteful influence spending, and the very act of central direction sacrifices valuable information, resulting in very little payoff.

Where Is the Trade-Off?

Turning to the position of the curve, we suggest that it is defined by "state capacity." Consider a line drawn to the left of the bold curve. Such an economy is able to provide the same number of centralised collective goods (per resource) only by incurring high costs of influence activities (and a large shortage of information). Thus, states to the left are corrupt and unable to provide centralised collective goods because they are riven with influence activities. In other words, they have low state capacity.

Two things will shift this line: either the centralised authority gets better or changes in the authority's design permit delegation. We can think of the authority's "getting better" as "building state capacity." That is, the centralised authority is perhaps more trusted and more informed. An example of delegation is the transfer of policy levers, such as monetary policy and competition policy, to independent authorities. Another example might be the successful contracting out of publicly provided goods. For example, the competitive auctioning of contracts for local rubbish collection in the United Kingdom revealed information (the availability of new providers) and likely lowered influence activities, thus shifting the frontier to the right. However, if regulators become more cosy with the industry they regulate, then this curve will shift inwards (to the left).

A more extreme example of delegation policy is charter cities. The economist Paul Romer has suggested that a country might delegate the administration and powers of a city within that country to an outside nation, which would administer the city or region and create its own laws and policies without the control of the host nation.[8] Other examples are trade agreements, in which countries commonly agree to dispute resolution procedures outside those of the particular country: the Stockholm Chamber of Commerce is a leading arbitrator in disputes outside Sweden on, for example, the alleged appropriation of investment by foreign companies in a particular host country.

Delegation can have significant costs, however. Delegation of promotion decisions to a remote committee that promotes by, say, seniority might help decrease the time and money spent on influencing those decisions, but such a committee might make costly, bad decisions. For example, some argue that delegation of science policy to established committees might shift influence activities towards the lobbying of those committees. And such committees might be too inflexible to, for example, take advantage of the synergies of cross-disciplinary opportunities.[9]

The Intangible Economy and the Trade-Off

The shift to an intangible economy worsens the trade-off in two crucial ways, as shown by a flatter curve that is more to the left in figure C.2. First, with more synergies the curve gets flatter. The more that a successful good requires combinations of intangible assets, the more costly is the lack of information. This relationship flattens the curve: at every information point, society can get fewer centralised goods. Second, as the intangible economy grows, it becomes more divided by income, wealth, and esteem. This increased division lowers state capacity—by eroding trust, for example—and the curve shifts to the left. More social division might also shift the curve to the left by weakening the effectiveness of delegation: delegation can likely stop influence activities, but it may be too inflexible to allow for synergies, which may be important.

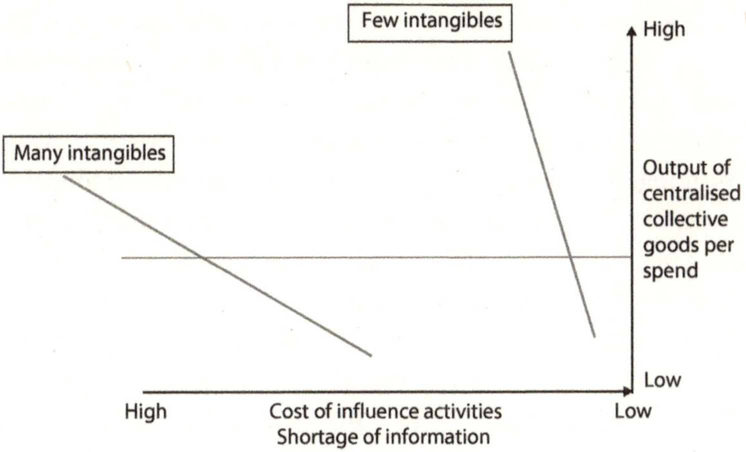

FIGURE C.2: How Intangibles Affect the Trade-Off.

As figure C.2 illustrates, the move to more intangibles has worsened the constraints on the economy. If you wanted to keep the output of collective goods at some fixed level, as shown by the horizontal line (this level of output may not be optimal, but we use it here to illustrate the point), a shift in the line to the left means that society has to tolerate more influence activities and less information.

Improving the Centralisation Trade-Off

We may apply this framework to a number of different questions.

State Capacity

One recurrent constraint that prevents governments from encouraging intangible investment and dealing with its consequences is *inadequate state capacity*, which we can think of as broadly shifting the line to the left in figure C.2.

The idea of state capacity arose in political science and sociology, and it became a hot topic among scholars of political economy and development economics; but it is less commonly applied to modern, developed economies, so let us unpack its meaning. A recent paper by economic historians Noel Johnson and Mark Koyama and defines *state capacity* as "the ability of a state to collect taxes, enforce law and order, and provide public goods."[10] Thus, if we say that Britain in 2022 has greater state capacity than Anglo-Saxon England did in 1022, we mean that the state taxes and spends a greater proportion of output, exercises much greater control through the law, and provides a wealth of public goods unthinkable to King Cnut's subjects.

At this point, readers of a libertarian persuasion may be getting nervous: Is a call for increased state capacity the equivalent of a call for a big state? It is not, because state capacity is not an exact measurement of the size of the state. A classic paper by Douglass North and Barry Weingast framed the success of the English state after the Glorious Revolution in terms of its precocious state capacity—but they noted that an important aspect of this success was the state's ability to effectively constrain itself, which encouraged investment and helped the government borrow because people were less afraid of being expropriated.[11] State capacity also implies the state's ability to do what it does effectively, which is orthogonal to its size. Johnson and Koyama point out that effectively administered states are "better able to overcome vested interests."[12]

To a development economist or an economic historian, most rich countries today, broadly speaking, have high state capacity. Contemporary France and contemporary Japan, for example, are more like one another than either of them is like contemporary South Sudan or Merovingian France, and it is possible to measure this difference quantitatively.[13] But by taking a more finely grained approach, we can see differences in state capacity among modern rich countries, even if those differences are smaller and more debatable than historical comparisons. So, for example, South Korea, Singapore, and Taiwan are all thought to have highly effective "developmental states" that helped to support the emergence of high-value-added industries in the late twentieth century; to the extent that many other countries tried to support such industries and failed, this seems to be a matter not just of policy but also of capacity.

The rich countries' responses to the COVID-19 pandemic made differences in state capacity more obvious. Even allowing for geographical and cultural differences, it appeared that some governments were better able to design and implement new care pathways, tracking protocols, and lockdown processes; better able to adopt strategies and stick to them; and better able to persuade citizens to follow them. The United Kingdom, for example, did a good job of procuring vaccines quickly, drawing on its government's close links with the life sciences sector.

In chapters 4–7, we saw several examples of institutions that are necessary for dealing effectively with an economy based on intangible capital. These institutions rely on state capacity that is often absent. For example, patent offices are unable to filter out low-quality patents. City governments are unable to reform planning or manage congestion. Research funders rely on over-determined systems. Regulators lack the bandwidth or data they need to understand the dynamics of the industries they regulate. In some important areas, such as producing public data, investing in technical training, or understanding innovative new entrants to traditional markets, many governments currently have very little capacity at all.

In one sense, these problems are different, but at heart they are all the same. Encouraging intangible investment (for example, fixing the problem of spillovers) and dealing with its consequences (such as the rise of cities or the growth of platform businesses) require better judgment, more agency, and better analysis on the part of the bureaucrats who make government work and greater receptivity from the politicians for whom they work.

This is a deeply unfashionable policy agenda, for both the Right and the Left. Its unpalatability for conservatives is perhaps obvious: since at least the Reagan and Thatcher eras, many on the right have sought to cut not just the state's size but also its agency and even its knowledge. James Cowperthwait, the architect of Hong Kong's twentieth-century economic success and a hero of laissez-faire economics, has suggested that countries that want to get rich should "abolish their office of national statistics."[14] Grover Norquist, an American conservative activist, famously wanted a state that he could "drown in the bathtub"—a call not just for smallness but also for weakness. New Public Management, the term coined to characterise some of the governmental reforms implemented in Britain in the 1980s and 1990s, involved managerialism, clearer rules, and less discretion: the government created agencies but reduced agency. Improving state capacity looks very much like a charter for pencil pushers and bureaucrats.

In 2019, the economist Tyler Cowen coined the phrase *state capacity libertarianism* to describe what he saw as a growing trend for politicians on the right to recognise that a weak state is no longer in their interests. We believe the economic case for improving state capacity is clear. As we shall see, the political case is still under debate.

Improving state capacity in a general sense is more congenial to those on the left, but more challenging are the specifics of state capacity interactions with the private sector. To understand these challenges, let us consider the next important theme of institutional reform: the trade-off between improving the quantity of intangibles and improving their quality.

The Quality Theory of Intangibles and the Quantity Theory

Increasing state capacity should help drive more, better intangible investment. But which should come first: more or better? In chapter 5, we outlined the tension between attempts to increase the *quantity* of intangibles and attempts to increase their *quality*. Subsidising intangibles—for example, through tax breaks, public funding, or direct government investment in training or R&D—helps solves the *quantity* problem of underinvestment caused by spillovers and typically involves centralisation, either in the provision of R&D by public institutions or in the decisions over the details of the policy (generosity, scope, and so on). But, at the margin, these policies can reduce the *quality* of investment by encouraging gaming or low-quality research, or simply because the funding rules have not kept pace with the latest practices and technologies. We can think of the relative importance of these benefits and costs as giving society a steep (centralisation is good) versus flat (centralisation is costly) curve.

These possibilities explain why increasing state capacity can also prove politically challenging for the Left. A capable state providing generous intangible investment subsidies (such as R&D or student loans) may not on its own be enough to encourage enough *productive* investment, which also requires an active entrepreneurial ecosystem to generate variety and the valuable synergies that arise when you hit upon the right combination. This model differs somewhat from the model of an entrepreneurial state, which sees its role as identifying the goals for innovation. The model of increased state capacity assumes this role will be widely distributed among firms and consumers. It is predicated on the idea that a strong state can coexist with strong businesses.

Resisting Influence Activities and Rent Seeking

An important element of institutional design involves how to stop vested interests from taking the new, more capable state for a ride. The traditional way to guard against vested interests involved rules, delegation, and depoliticisation. The reasoning behind this classic New Public Management model is simple: taking a government function such as monetary policy, intellectual property management, or the collection of geospatial data, putting it in an apolitical, arm's-length body, and lashing it to the mast with clear rules and processes would allow it to resist the siren song of lobbyists. (In terms of figure C.2, successful delegation will shift the line to the right.)

As we have seen, this tactic *can* work well when the rules are clear, when they are well matched to their environment, and when they leave little room for lobbying. But if the circumstances change, or if lobbyists find points of entry, the rules-and-independence tactic can backfire, giving free rein to special interests. Indeed, lobbyists have a strong presence in fields such as intellectual property and the public funding of intangible assets.

The other way to resist influence activities is less elegant from a design point of view but more flexible in the face of changing requirements. Specifically, governments may expend political capital to prioritise the matter in question. For all that governments are often accused of continually giving in to rent seekers, one of the defining activities of politicians is the opposite:

building coalitions and earning political capital in order to do things that they consider important. Thus, the new, high-capacity state will need to be more political, not necessarily in the sense of being ideologically partisan but rather in the sense that governments will need to wield political power to hold them to their mission.

Our menu of institutional reforms includes increasing state capacity (in ways that may prove ideologically difficult), striking a balance between the state and businesses that is likely to annoy activists on both the left and the right, and increasing government's willingness to resist rent seeking by expending political capital. Any politicians reading this paragraph would be forgiven for considering this agenda to be unappealing and difficult to implement. But there are ways to make it work politically, or at least more likely to work, and given the political challenges of institutional change in general, getting the politics right is an integral part of the plan.

Consider one example: automatic stabilisers. When politicians run monetary policy—that is, when monetary policy is centralised—they are subject to lobbying problems as anxious members of Parliament lobby for cheap money near an election. Delegation of monetary policy helps lower this lobbying. And there is another bonus. If politicians could commit to not being influenced by such activities, they can keep the decisions for themselves. Because they can rarely make such commitments credibly, they tend to delegate policy to central bankers.[15] Thus, one can think of the horizontal axis in figure C.2 as having commitment costs along it as well. Delegation therefore shifts the line to the right, but if interest rates are near the lower bound, then delegation becomes less useful and the line shifts to the left again. Automatic stabilisers commit politicians to rescuing the economy and so shift the line to the right again.

A Political Settlement

Faced with a tough set of institutional reforms, governments typically have a few generic options. They can tweak the reforms themselves to make them more palatable, they can use persuasion to change voters' minds, they can link the reforms to positive things that voters care about, or they can accumulate political capital elsewhere and spend it to push the reforms through—ideally without making too much of a fuss.

All of these options may have a role to play. The point of some of the urban reforms set out in chapter 6, such as street and block votes, is to create coalitions that have a vested interest in institutions that are conducive to intangible investment.

Moral suasion was the preferred tactic of France's technophilic En Marche government (elected in 2017) in its early days: its investment in technology formed a big part of its messaging. Since the "Gilets Jaunes" protests (originally against fuel taxes, but later a broader populist movement), tech optimism seems to have been deprioritised in the way the government talks about itself; it continues to develop an ambitious set of pro-tech policies, but more discreetly.

Small countries with a strong external focus (often a polite way of saying "an aggressive neighbour") provide one example of how institutional reform can sometimes be linked to other things that voters like. As we saw in chapter 4, Mark Zachary Taylor points out that countries with a strong external focus (such as Israel, South Korea, and Finland) seem historically to have developed effective institutions relating to intangibles, as demonstrated by all three countries' ability to support world-leading tech sectors, backed up by well-regarded public institutions, from Finland's TEKES to the role of the South Korean government in the international growth of K-Pop.[16]

A big external enemy is a hard thing to invent if it does not already exist, but it seems to us that the success of countries with a clear external goal lies behind the appeal of much mission-oriented innovation. Picking a genuinely charismatic mission that excites people and that they care about is something that politicians have occasionally succeeded at; the archetype is the US Apollo space programme. But these missions are hard to design—the four Grand Challenges designed by Theresa May's government in the United Kingdom gained little traction beyond Whitehall, and too many challenges in general seem too generic and *bien-pensant* to work. The Green New Deal is perhaps the most charismatic mission in recent years, but so far it has failed to take off. Another way to link institutional reform to a charismatic mission entails harnessing local political legitimacy, where it exists. A good example is the institutional success of the Basque Country, as discussed in chapter 6, but of course not all localities have strong local identities and social capital to draw on. In addition, more localities claim to have these things than actually have them.

This leaves the option of earning political legitimacy elsewhere and spending it on institutional reform. To some extent, this is the model that En Marche has now adopted in France. It also has its more bombastic version, in the form of what Lorenzo Castellani and Rowland Manthorpe call *technopopulism*.[17] Castellani coined the term to describe an unusual aspect of Italy's Five Star Movement: in Rome and other places, he saw populist politicians such as Virginia Raggi surrounding themselves not with like-minded Jacobins but rather with "functionaries, magistrates, academics, and other professionals, the likes of whom you would never see at a Five Star meet-up." British readers will recognise something similar in the way that the Brexit referendum and British prime minister Boris Johnson's 2019 election victory have led to a rather technocratic-sounding drive to reform the civil service, to greatly increase public R&D investment, and to reform research funding bodies. These initiatives are backed by Dominic Cummings, who served as chief adviser to Boris Johnson and was associated both with the populist Vote Leave campaign and with a technocratic, technophilic desire to reform British institutions. (His WhatsApp description is "Get Brexit done, then ARPA.") Donald Trump's government paid little regard to technocracy, but the support he received from accelerationist technology investor Peter Thiel perhaps comes from the same place.

It is not clear which, if any, of these political gambits to gain the legitimacy needed to drive institutional change will work. But it is notable that they are being tried—and that politicians are willing to risk reputational damage to see if they work.

Culture, Trust, and Cognitive Load

Institutional design and politics are important to fixing the mess we are in, but on their own they can go only so far. If we are to develop and deploy better institutions for a new type of economy, we will also need cultural change.

Economic historians such as Joel Mokyr and Avner Greif have shown how the prosperity of the modern age depended not just on institutions, technologies, and resources but also on underlying cultural change. In the seventeenth and eighteenth centuries, some people in Britain, the Netherlands, and other places became more curious, more enterprising, and more prosocial—what historian Anton Howes calls the *improving mind-set* spread, somewhat virally. This mind-set was reinforced by technologies and by institutions, but it also made technologies easier to develop and institutions more likely to thrive.

For example, Howes's history of the Royal Society of Arts in London shows that such great Enlightenment organisations were often as much a product of the culture as the culture was a product of them. The artificial intelligence researcher Eliezer Yudkowsky framed this mind-set as the desire to look for "inadequate equilibria" in society—norms and rules that work, but not as well as they should—and having the audacity to try to fix them.

We do not claim that we can predict the manifestations of the new culture that the new economy will call forth. But there may be some clues from cultures and parts of the world where the transition to intangible capital has gone the furthest. Specifically, it seems that the cognitive load on individuals has risen in the digital arena. But solutions to this challenge have arisen, often from the market itself; they include ad blockers, anonymous search engines, and price-comparison sites. Debt also keeps cognitive load low (in periods of no crisis), and so the returns to new financial innovation that will enable intangibles to be securitised will help.

Finally, we saw that one institution is fit for purpose throughout the ages and over all the dimensions of exchange: trust and reciprocity. The long-run determinants of this institution are a source of ongoing debate; see, for example, the work of Francis Fukuyama and Robert Putnam.[18] In the meantime, the software industry has developed tools, practices, and working norms that make it perhaps the most remote-work-friendly high-skilled job. Perhaps people who grew up playing online video games or socialising and dating over smartphones have developed ways of communicating at a distance that replicate much of the emotional and psychological quality of face-to-face interactions. The open-source-software movement has created a new field where people recognise the value of spillovers and receive credit for producing them for others. Perhaps reciprocity and reputation are making a comeback.

Where, then, does all this leave us, as citizens concerned about how to make the world we live in fairer and more prosperous? We began the book by describing the "Lost Golden Age" story that many people use to understand what is happening to the economy today. This narrative has pessimistic and optimistic versions: either historical levels of growth are gone for good and we have to learn to live with it, or the good times will return again if we somehow rediscover certain lost civic virtues of the past. In one sense, we side with the optimists: the disappointments of today's economy are not unchangeable facts but specific failures to put in place the right institutions for growth and human flourishing.

But these answers will not be found by patiently waiting or by recapturing past virtues. The problems arise because the nature of the economy has changed—the shift of our capital stock from tangible to intangible represents a quiet revolution that is still playing out. And our institutions, from our financial system to our planning rules and from our patent courts to our educational establishments, have not kept pace.

If we want higher growth and a fairer economy, we need the courage and determination to rebuild and refresh these institutions. Restarting tomorrow is within our grasp.

Summary

Entities such as states and corporations need authority and centralised control to provide the collective goods that will benefit their citizens and employees. But a basic trade-off exists. The greater the spending on providing these collective goods, the more the temptation to create influence activities and the greater the likelihood that important information will be sacrificed. Indeed, some extremely corrupt societies find it almost impossible to provide any collective goods because they are all absorbed by influence activities. For example, it was widely reported in 2021 that the central bank governor in Lebanon had been embezzling money even as the country suffered from hyperinflation.

The intangible economy has two effects on this trade-off. First, it worsens the slope of the trade-off. If synergies become more important in an intangible economy, then additional spending on centralised collective goods is less effective and efficient because of the sacrifice of synergies is more acutely detrimental in the face of complexity. Second, to the extent that the intangible economy raises inequality in various dimensions, it makes it more difficult for any given degree of centralised spending to be politically acceptable (that is, it shifts the trade-off curve to the left).

In this chapter we reviewed at least two possible changes to help us solve these problems. The first is to build state capacity to support the economy, and the second is to spend political capital. Both of those challenges are becoming more urgent as the economy stagnates and the feedback loop of declining support for intangibles persists, holding societies back.

These issues, building state capacity and spending political capital, are cross-cutting suggestions around the themes in this book. We have tried to document how the change to a more intangible-intensive economy better explains the problems our economies face: of stagnation, inequality, dysfunctional competition, fragility, and inauthenticity. Like any change in underlying economic structure, such a change needs a fresh set of institutions to solve the problems of an intangible economy—for example, collective action, information, commitment, and deterring wasteful influence activities.

We have highlighted the needed institutional reforms around support for research, cities, monetary and financial policy, and competition. The exact details of the suggested reforms will differ from country to country. But we hope that our diagnosis of the problem, and the generic framework for understanding how a more intangible economy puts institutions under strain, will stand the test of time and offer a new perspective for how to meet the challenges of the modern economy.

NOTES

Introduction

1. US patent 549,160 is available at "Road-engine," Google Patents, https://patents.google.com/patent/US549160A/en, accessed July 31, 2021.
2. Furman and Summers 2020.
3. Graeber 2018, xviii.
4. Baudrillard 1994.
5. Douthat 2020.
6. Case and Deaton 2020.

Chapter 1

1. Gross and Sampat 2020, 2021.
2. Congressional Budget Office 2007.
3. Schwartz and Leyden 1997.
4. Krugman 1997.
5. Keynes 2010.
6. Wilkinson and Pickett 2009.
7. Piketty 2014.
8. McRae 1995.
9. Moretti 2012.
10. Jennings and Stoker 2016.
11. Case and Deaton 2020.
12. Decker et al. 2018.

13. The rise in Tobin's Q and the rise in this markup are somewhat different measures of rising corporate profitability. The exact relation between these measures is set out in Haskel (2019).

14. Philippon 2019.

15. Cowen 2017, 1.

16. Malcolm Baldrige, quoted in "Fat, Dumb, Happy," *New York Times*, October 4, 1981, sec. 3, p. 20, https://www.nytimes.com/1981/10/04/business/fat-dumb-happy.html.

17. Markovits 2019, 158.

18. Kuhn and Lozano 2005.

19. Furman and Summers 2020.

20. De Veirman, Hudders, and Nelson 2019.

21. Shiller 2019.

22. Leamer 2008; Harari 2015; Kay and King 2020.

23. Cowen 2011; Gordon 2016.

24. Vollrath 2020.

25. Brynjolfsson and McAfee 2014.

26. Harvey 2007; Hutton 1995.

27. Cohen and DeLong 2016.

28. Philippon 2019.

29. Sichel 2016.

30. Mokyr 2018. See also Branstetter and Sichel 2017.

31. In table 4.1, on page 48 of his book, Vollrath (2020) reports slightly different numbers for the contribution of physical capital per capita for the United States. His contribution between the years 2000 and 2016 is 0.27 percent. He documents a similar fall in the contribution of human capital per capita. With this different contribution in physical capital he gets a slowdown in TFP growth from 1 percent to 0.8 percent. This means that the slowdown in the growth of human capital per capita (in his data, 0.7 percent) accounts for most of the slowdown in GDP per capita of 1.3 percent in his data. The difference in the contributions in table 1.1 and Vollrath's calculations results from the fact that Vollrath uses capital stocks, whereas our calculation uses capital services. As Vollrath notes, one could also use capital services; see the discussion on page 224 of his book.

32. Byrne, Corrado, and Sichel 2017.

33. Byrne and Sichel 2017.

34. Corrado, Haskel, and Jona-Lasinio 2021.

35. Traina 2018.

36. Syverson 2019.

37. Haskel and Westlake 2017.

38. Davis 2018.

39. It is perfectly possible for a firm to have an intangible asset that does not involve a relationship: an expressive intangible evokes an emotion, so a design or work of art could evoke pathos, catharsis, awe, excitement, and so on. The contrast is that a

relational intangible promises or hints at a future social exchange. Thus, Apple's supply chain relationship is akin to an informal semi-promise that it will buy Gorilla-glass screens from a manufacturer for many years to come, pay them on time, treat them honestly, and so on.

40. Simon 1995.

41. Benmelech et al. 2021.

42. Scott 1999.

43. Schumacher 1980.

44. McAfee 2019.

45. In *Capitalism without Capital* we speculated that when we look at the investment share of intangibles in GDP over the long run, we are looking not just at the level of intangible spending but also at how much such spending costs. The phenomenon that economists call *Baumol's cost disease* probably plays a role in the rise in the investment share, to the extent that much physical capital is manufactured (such as a shipping container or a lathe) and hence falls in price over time, whereas the main cost of producing intangible capital is human labour—the salaries of the marketing department or the R&D lab, the delivery of training courses—which gets more expensive as society gets richer.

46. Adler et al. 2017; Duval 2017.

47. Arquié et al. 2019; Demmou, Stefanescu, and Arquié 2019.

48. Wise and Turnbull 2019.

49. Uncertainty will also affect tangible investment (Abel et al. 1996; Dixit 1992; Dixit and Pindyck 1995). But tangible investment might be less irreversible if it can be sold off. And because intangible investment can be scaled up, it is likely more expansible than tangible investment, so the nature of uncertainty matters differently: the expectation of bad news depresses investment in intangibles and tangibles (because firms are worried about the downside), whereas the expectation of good news raises investment in tangibles (because firms want to exploit the possible upside). Thus, a transition to a period where bad news is expected disproportionately affects intangibles.

50. Bessen et al. 2020.

Chapter 2

1. The economist Michael Kremer (1993) used the term "O ring" to describe the gap between a successful space shuttle mission and a failed one.

2. Brynjolfsson, Rock, and Syverson 2021.

3. There are two quite separate arguments here that we need to be careful to distinguish. If intangibles are booming but unmeasured, then measured TFP falls during the initial investment period until the new output comes onstream, when TFP rises again; vice versa if they are falling. If intangibles have a spillover effect on TFP growth, then TFP rises and falls respectively.

4. Vollrath 2020.

5. See Bajgar, Criscuolo, and Timmis 2020.

6. Corrado et al. 2019.

7. Markovits 2019.

8. Garicano 2000.

9. The reason income inequality has not risen more in the United Kingdom in the twenty-first century is that the UK benefits system has to some extent restrained it. For an excellent summary of recent trends in UK income inequality, pre- and posttax, see Francis-Devine 2020.

10. Garicano and Hubbard 2007.

11. Rognlie 2015.

12. Hsieh and Moretti 2019.

13. Department for Business, Energy & Industrial Strategy 2019, table 1.

14. Douthat 2020.

Chapter 3

1. Daron Acemoglu and James Robinson (2019, 126ff) draw attention to this fresco as an example of an institutional system whereby the state had sufficient power to provide communal goods (supervisors of public buildings and weights and measures, six "good men" who oversaw taverns and prevented swearing) but not too much power to become autocratic.

2. North 1993.

3. Smith 1904, 1:xxxv.

4. Marx and Engels 2002 [1848].

5. Acemoglu, Johnson, and Robinson 2004, 395.

6. Kling and Schultz 2009.

7. North 1993, 97.

8. The "transactions costs" approach to exchange notes that exchange is affected by the transactions costs in each situation. This analysis is often, but not always, applied to a situation in which two parties are trading but face the problems that the assets they bring to the match are specific, there is uncertainty, and exchange might be infrequent (Milgrom and Roberts 2009; Williamson 2009). We wish to step back from this approach and make sure we include in the process of exchange the finding of a partner in the first place. We also think that, following Milgrom and Roberts (2009), treating the exchange as the unit of analysis, rather than the transactions costs of the matched transaction, helps us be more specific about what the transactions costs are. In conditions of incomplete contracts with asset specificity, uncertainty and infrequent trade arise because these conditions induce high bargaining costs, problems of commitment and information, and the like.

9. Milgrom and Roberts 1990.

10. Hart 2017.

11. This argument is set out in Demsetz (1967).

12. Hayek 1945.

13. A more modern example of property rights is the compulsory military draft. A society without a compulsory military draft is a society that has assigned to potential draftees a private property right over their labour power. Once potential draftees have the private property right, then the society can bargain with them for the supply of their labour, which is of course voluntary military service. Therefore, to those opposed to compulsory military service, the institution of private property rights is a solution.

14. One might therefore argue that trust and reciprocity are not an institution within themselves but rather a subset of the institution that is a mechanism for collective decision-making. We have assigned its own institutional heading to trust and reciprocity, given its historical and anthropological importance.

15. Regarding transactions costs, Mançur Olson (1965) (discussed in more detail below) pointed out that the benefits of many policies are concentrated, whereas the costs are dispersed. So, for example, all London taxi drivers benefit from regulators setting a high price for a taxi ride. This benefit is concentrated in comparison with the dispersed benefit of low prices for the much broader community of taxi riders. But it's very expensive for the taxi riders to arrange themselves in a coalition and push for low taxi prices; in economists' language, the transactions costs of organising the large community who benefit from such low prices are simply too high. Thus, institutions might well evolve based on the relative degrees of transactions costs.

16. Acemoglu, Johnson, and Robinson 2004, 428.

17. Acemoglu, Johnson, and Robinson (2004) stress the constraints on the executive.

18. Acemoglu and Robinson 2019.

19. Weingast (1995) opens as follows: "The fundamental political dilemma of an economic system is this: A government strong enough to protect property rights and enforce contracts is also strong enough to confiscate the wealth of its citizens. Thriving markets require not only the appropriate system of property rights and a law of contracts, but a secure political foundation that limits the ability of the state to confiscate wealth." He continues, "The fundamental political dilemma forces us to ask what form of political system is required so that a viable, private market economy is a stable policy choice of that political system? The answer concerns the design of political institutions that credibly commit the state to preserving markets. . . . The central component of a credible commitment to limited government is that these limits must be self-enforcing. For limits on government to be sustained, political officials must have an incentive to abide by them" (1). His answer is that some degree of federalism in a country restricts governments from too much interference in markets because activity can move elsewhere.

20. Anton Howes (private communication) has suggested to us that an additional dimension of the conditions needed for exchange is recognition of the right to the good (of which property rights or respectfulness/reciprocity might be the appropriate institution). In the example of someone trying to use intellectual property for which they have not paid, we think that recognition of the right is implied in the condition of "need to solve collective-action problem" or the condition of "commitment" (i.e., the good will not be simply confiscated).

21. Posner and Weyl 2018.

22. One of their many fascinating suggestions is to make property much more tradable by having it registered at a self-declared value and taxed but also eligible for purchase at that value. Owners declaring a low value pay a low tax but would potentially have to sell at that low value. Whatever the desirability of this scheme, table 3.1 suggests that this plan would require low haggling costs to succeed.

23. Acemoglu, Johnson, and Robinson 2004.

24. See Tim Taylor's wonderful blog post "An Update Concerning the Economics of Lighthouses," July 24, 2020, https://conversableeconomist.blogspot.com/2020/07/updates-for-economics-of-lighthouses.html, which brought to our attention the fascinating work of Theresa Levitt, David van Zandt, and Erik Lindberg on lighthouses.

25. Modern-day lighthouses provide such a service, but radio transmission has mostly superseded light as a navigation aid.

26. For those who studied economics, you will have encountered the lighthouse example in almost any textbook. It was first used in Samuelson's famous economic textbook in 1948. The economist Ronald Coase pointed out the fact that lighthouses were privately provided; nonetheless, the lighthouse, as an example of a public good, seems to have remained in many textbooks.

27. Levitt 2020.

28. Van Zandt 1993. The economist Kenneth Arrow (1962) argued that there is a second economic difficulty: unless the lighthouse owner could commit to an acceptable price in advance (for example, by publishing a price schedule), the ship owner might worry about being charged a high price and so not use the lighthouse at all.

29. Lindberg (2013) notes that King James I did not recognise Trinity House's exclusive right to build lighthouses. By 1700, Lindberg says, Trinity House started to sell the rights to operate a lighthouse.

30. Indeed, the motive for public lighthouse ownership had originally come from the fact that the private lighthouses were charging *too much* for their services, just as Arrow had feared, not that they were unable to charge at all. Indeed, Lindberg (2013) argues that the private lighthouses were extremely profitable—so profitable, in fact, that ship owners began pressing for nationalisation.

31. As van Zandt (1993) notes, by the nineteenth century, almost every nation except Britain provided lighthouse services from general tax revenues. In the United States, for example, "One of the first acts of Congress brought all existing lighthouses and beacons under the control of the secretary of the Treasury. . . . By 1875, France, Russia all provided for lighthouses from government funds and charged no user fees" (70). In fact, the argument about the public/private provision of lighthouses in the economics textbooks, at least in the United Kingdom, is nuanced. Before 1836 there was a mix of public and private ownership, with the private ones nationalised in 1836 and brought under the control of Trinity House, which had a licence from the public sector. However, the lighthouses were financed from local port charges. In 1834 a Parliamentary Select Committee recommended keeping local lights under private or Trinity House control and funding seaview lights by general levies. Parliament ended

up granting Trinity House exclusive ownership, but with compulsory charges for all ships everywhere to fund the seacoast lights they passed (Levitt 2020).

32. Weingast 1995.

33. Mokyr 2002.

34. Howes 2020.

35. De Soto 2000; Hornbeck 2010; van Bavel 2016.

36. Nelson 1994.

37. Ostrom 2005, 12.

38. Liebowitz and Margolis (1990) strongly contest this.

39. Greif 2006.

40. Edgerton 2018.

41. Lerner and Nanda 2020.

42. Johnson 2004.

43. Wing warping is a system of cables and pulleys that twist the wing to stop the aircraft from rolling over; ailerons—from the French for "little wings"—are hinged surfaces on the wing. The breadth of the Wright Brothers' patent was enough to hold up Glenn Curtiss's aileron invention.

44. Katznelson and Howells (2015) dispute the details of who held up whom. Nonetheless, the point that the whole ecosystem was decided by these institutions remains.

45. Olson 1965.

46. Van Bavel 2016, 21.

47. See Broadberry 2013, section 4.4.

48. What is the difference between a spillover and synergy? You can think of the former as an institutional feature around excludability and the latter as technological. For example, a regime of perfectly enforced intellectual property rights would stop spillovers. But there would still be synergies from, for example, the combination of a film script and software to make an animated movie.

Chapter 4

1. Arrow 1962; Nelson 1959.

2. Mazzucato 2013.

3. David Willetts, personal communication with the authors, 2019.

4. Matt Ridley, "Don't Look for Innovations before Their Time," *Wall Street Journal*, September 14, 2012. See also Ridley (2020) or Syed (2019).

5. Lachmann 1956.

6. Lachmann described a number of associated problems arising from the observation that combinations of capital mattered. One was to stress the role of the entrepreneur experimenting in light of the impossibility of knowing what combinations of capital were best. Another was how to measure combinations of capital of different types and ages, a problem taken up in the Cambridge Capital Controversy

(a lively discussion is in a podcast by Noah Smith and Brad DeLong, "Hexapodia XII: The Cambridge Capital Controversy," May 5, 2021, https://www.bradford-delong.com/2021/05/podcast-hexapodia-xii-%C3%BEe-cambridge-capital-controversy.html). A solution to this question, used by statistical agencies today, is weighting together capital types by their rental rates, proposed by the economists Robert Hall and Dale Jorgenson (1967). Erwin Diewert (1976) showed how such a solution can be applied when capital was used in combination (a retail building and a supply vehicle in traditional retail) or substitution (a retail building versus a warehouse and delivery van in e-commerce).

7. Goldin and Katz 2008.

8. See the discussion in, for example, Cowen and Southwood (2019).

9. Wilsdon et al. 2015.

10. The Augar review, "Independent Panel Report to the Review of Post-18 Education and Funding," May 2019, https://assets.publishing.service.gov.uk/government/uploads/system/uploads/attachment_data/file/805127/Review_of_post_18_education_and_funding.pdf, 31.

11. Campbell 1979; Goodhart 1981.

12. Nielsen 2013.

13. Williamson et al. 2020.

14. Ritchie 2020.

15. Aarts et al. 2015.

16. For example, Dattani and Bechhofer 2021.

17. Bessen and Meurer 2009.

18. Boldrin and Levine 2013.

19. Justin Tranter quoted in "To Succeed in a Business That Doesn't Really Want Anyone to Succeed, You Have to Be Quite Confident," interview by Dave Roberts, Music Business Worldwide, May 21, 2020, https://www.musicbusinessworldwide.com/justin-tranter-to-succeed-in-a-business-that-doesnt-really-want-anyone-to-succeed-you-have-to-be-quite-confident/?fbclid=IwAR3IPUzTde8xVdy8bjZlKOKqHtDcNSlRwNC7fXvZWUJODOIG0Ez8T4sLV-w.

20. Heller 2008.

21. Khan 2014.

22. Hall et al. 2014.

23. See Kleiner (2006). Forth et al. (2011) estimate that at least 20 percent of the US workforce is subject to licensing. Six percent of the US workforce is certified, and 14 percent of the UK workforce is certified.

24. Phelps 2013; Ridley 2020.

25. Mazzucato 2021.

26. This idea is developed further in Mazzucato (2021).

27. Discussed in Jeffrey Mervis, "U.S. Lawmakers Unveil Bold $100 Billion Plan to Remake NSF," *Science*, May 26, 2020, https://www.sciencemag.org/news/2020/05/us-lawmakers-unveil-bold-100-billion-plan-remake-nsf.

28. In Cowen and Southwood 2019.

29. Eghbal 2016.

30. Quoted in "Good Data: With Ben Goldacre," Digital Health, January 14, 2016, https://www.digitalhealth.net/2016/01/good-data-with-ben-goldacre/.

31. Dan Davies, "Midsummer in Midwinter," *Crooked Timber* (blog), March 22, 2015, https://crookedtimber.org/2015/03/22/the-world-is-squared-episode-6-midsummer-in-midwinter/.

32. Kremer 1998. For more on prizes and other innovation-encouraging mechanisms applied to vaccines, see Kremer and Snyder (2020).

33. Gans 2020.

34. Milgrom and Roberts 1988.

35. Taylor 2016.

36. Johnstone 1999.

Chapter 5

1. Whitehead 1911, 46.

2. Lowenstein 2001.

3. McLean and Elkind 2005.

4. There are differences between countries here. Broadly speaking, compared with US companies, European companies rely much more on bank loans for debt rather than bonds, and much less on equity (see, e.g., de Fiore and Uhlig 2011). Porta et al. (1997) argue that, compared with Europe, the United States and the United Kingdom have common-law traditions that offer more protection of shareholders and creditors, hence favouring equity and bonds rather than bank loans. De Fiore and Uhlig (2011) also argue that there is less public information in Europe about company creditworthiness, thus raising the importance of banks, which have to gather information about the firms to which they lend.

5. Davies 2014.

6. For a formal discussion, see Holmstrom (2015). Holmstrom discusses the simplest collateralisable debt contract: a pawnbroker lending money against a watch. The pawnbroker has to figure out the value of the watch and then lend that value minus an allowance for default. But that lower bound is established by one party to the contract and is not necessarily the value of the watch. This debt contract doesn't require both parties to agree on a common value, a maximum value, or a share of resulting cash flow. And once the debt is paid back to the pawnbroker, the watch is restored: nobody needs to agree on what the value of the watch is now or might have been. Debt contracts with collateral are therefore highly information saving. Further, when times are bad and lenders think the principal will not be paid, a substantial crisis can emerge because lenders now demand the very information that the structure is designed to economise on.

7. Cecchetti and Schoenholtz 2018.

8. Drechsel (2021), Greenwald (2019), and Lian and Ma (2021) have highlighted the pervasive use of loan covenants related to earnings. And Lim, Macias, and Moeller (2020) show that after an accounting change that booked intangible assets, borrowing

rose; importantly, borrowing rose after the accounting change when identified intangibles assets rose, not all intangible assets. (Assets were identified by a record of the purchase price paid for them and consisted of things like trademarks, domain names, and mineral rights.) An unidentified intangible asset was acquisition goodwill.

9. Lian and Ma 2021.

10. Dell'Ariccia et al. 2017.

11. Kaoru, Daisuke, and Miho 2017.

12. Lim, Macias, and Moeller 2020.

13. Ampudia, Beck, and Popov 2021.

14. "Box 4, The Supply of Finance for Productive Investment," in Bank of England, Financial Policy Committee 2020.

15. Wyman and British Business Bank 2019, 23.

16. "Patient Capital Review, Industry Panel Response, October 2017," https://assets.publishing.service.gov.uk/government/uploads/system/uploads/attachment_data/file/661397/PCR_Industry_panel_response.pdf.

17. Brazier 2020.

18. Duval 2017; Duval, Ahn, and Can 2018.

19. Lakonishok, Shleifer, and Vishny 1994.

20. See Daniel Finkelstein, The Fink Tank, accessed July 31, 2021, https://extras.thetimes.co.uk/web/interactives/7da9de56f480e009b5e9f18b279859d7.html.

21. Lev and Gu 2016.

22. Lev and Srivastava 2019, 24.

23. Brav, Jiang, and Ma 2018.

24. As Brav and colleagues are careful to point out, this does not mean that hedge fund investment is the cause of these effects, because hedge funds might invest in the very firms where the opportunities for such changes are easy to realise.

25. Arora, Belenzon, and Patacconi 2015, 2018; Arora, Belenzon, and Sheer 2021.

26. Arora, Belenzon, and Sheer 2021.

27. Arora, Belenzon, and Sheer 2021, 878.

28. Brav, Jiang, and Ma 2018.

29. Edmans 2009.

30. Kay and King 2020.

31. There is an additional path, via consumption. Changes in interest rates change savings for those who can easily borrow and lend, with a lowering of rates typically helping with spending as people save less. For those who cannot borrow and lend easily, there is a potentially much larger effect: if rates are lower on whatever borrowing they have made or might have to make to tide them over, then those lower rates free up some cash for them to spend. Finally, low interest rates depreciate the exchange rate, other things being equal, as money flows to countries with higher rates, raising a country's competitiveness and net exports.

32. Bean, Larsen, and Nikolov 2002.

33. Gilson and Altman, 2010.

34. A recent review of the US position is Del Negro et al. (2020) and, for the UK position, Cunliffe (2017). Some dispute that the Phillips curve has become flatter (McLeay and Tenreyro 2020), but this issue has been widely discussed.

35. Subir Lall and Li Zeng (2020) find that rising investment in intangibles across countries is associated with a flattening aggregate supply curve, arguing that this trend is consistent with a flattening Phillips curve.

36. This section is based on Haskel (2020a).

37. Daly 2016; Rachel and Smith 2015.

38. See Kevin Daly "A Higher Global Risk Premium and the Fall in Equilibrium Real Interest Rates," VoxEU, November 18, 2016, https://voxeu.org/article/higher-global-risk-premium-and-fall-equilibrium-real-interest-rates.

39. Implicit in this argument is that interest rates go "too negative," that is, they cannot decline much below zero.

40. Brassell and King 2013.

41. Nanda and Kerr 2015.

42. Lerner and Nanda 2020.

43. NESTA 2016.

44. Davies 2015.

45. Dell'Ariccia et al. 2017.

46. Bahaj et al. 2021.

47. Thais Jensen, Soren Leth-Petersen, and Ramana Nanda (2014) find a rise in entrepreneurship following a Danish mortgage reform that allowed unlocking of home equity.

48. Bank of England, Financial Policy Committee 2020, table D.B.

49. Davies 2015.

50. Bell et al. 2019.

51. Mirrlees and Adam 2011; OECD 2021.

52. Kortum and Lerner 2000.

53. The Investment Association 2020.

54. See Wyman and British Business Bank 2019.

55. Such changes would be, for example, relaxing regulations around investing in illiquid assets. See the Productive Finance Working Group, Minutes of the First Technical Expert Group (TEG) Meeting, 12 February 2021, https://www.bankofengland.co.uk/-/media/boe/files/minutes/2021/productive-working-group-minutes-february-2021.pdf?la=en&hash=1D243F9291E0B92562F762D69787ACBA28798D08.

56. Brazier (2020) writes, "No one is suggesting moving all pension assets to illiquid equity assets; rather, the goal is to enable more, and more diversified, assets from the current almost-zero base. Indeed, young members and older members have different liquidity preferences. As long as liquidity and longevity/maturity of assets and liabilities are well thought through and aligned, there should not be an "unwarranted risk."

57. Ahn, Duval, and Sever 2020.

58. What is the difference between this arrangement and QE? QE means that the central bank issues interest-bearing central bank reserves, which pay Bank Rate, and buys interest-bearing (long-dated) government bonds. Thus the central bank's assets are long-dated bonds, and liabilities are central bank reserves. Currently, the interest rate on such long-dated bonds is higher than Bank Rate, so the central bank is remitting money to the Treasury. If Bank Rate were to rise, the central bank would have to get money from the Treasury or some other source to pay the rates due. The result is a potential loss but not a guaranteed loss in the sense of a subsidy to commercial banks.

59. Blanchard, Dell'Ariccia, and Mauro 2010; Smith et al. 2019.

60. Feyrer and Sacerdote 2013.

61. Blanchard, Dell'Ariccia, and Mauro 2010.

62. The responsiveness of the economy to spending programs is bigger when the citizens who benefit spend and invest more. In adverse economic circumstances, consumers in low-income jobs typically have few resources to draw from or find it difficult to borrow. The impact of stabilisation-type policies, such as temporary tax cuts, on their consumption is likely to be very large, which makes fiscal policy potentially extremely potent.

63. For the mathematically minded, the equation is

$$\left(\frac{\text{Debt}}{\text{GDP}}\right)_t - \left(\frac{\text{Debt}}{\text{GDP}}\right)_{t-1} \approx (r_t - g_t)\left(\frac{\text{Debt}}{\text{GDP}}\right)_{t-1} + \left(\frac{\text{Primary Deficit}}{\text{GDP}}\right)_t$$

where r is the real interest rate, g is the real growth rate of GDP, and the primary deficit is the difference between noninterest spending and revenues.

64. Furman and Summers 2020.

Chapter 6

1. As discussed in Clay Jenkinson, "Thomas Jefferson, Epidemics and His Vision for American Cities," Governing, April 1, 2020, https://www.governing.com/context/Thomas-Jefferson-Epidemics-and-His-Vision-for-American-Cities.html.

2. Letter from Thomas Jefferson to Benjamin Rush, September 23, 1800, in National Archives, Founders Online, https://founders.archives.gov/documents/Jefferson/01-32-02-0102.

3. Letter from Thomas Jefferson to Benjamin Rush, September 23, 1800.

4. Haskel 2021.

5. Duranton and Puga 2014.

6. Glaeser 2011.

7. Clancy 2019.

8. Jaffe, Trajtenberg, and Henderson 1993.

9. Berkes and Gaetani 2019.

10. An active debate in the United Kingdom looks at whether the rise in house prices since the 1980s has been driven by restrictive supply, unanticipated lower real

interest rates, or a combination of both. The regional dispersion, with higher growth in London than elsewhere, suggests that supply also plays a role. Furthermore, there are periods where real rates fell but house prices didn't move, and vice versa. See Lisa Panigrahi and Danny Walker, "There's More to House Prices than Interest Rates," Bank Underground, June 3, 2020, https://bankunderground.co.uk/2020/06/03/theres-more-to-house-prices-than-interest-rates/. For differing views, see David Miles and Victoria Monro, "What's Been Driving Long-Run House Price Growth in the UK?," Bank Underground, January 13, 2020, https://bankunderground.co.uk/2020/01/13/whats-been-driving-long-run-house-price-growth-in-the-uk/.

11. Fischel 2005. See also Pennington 2001.

12. Max Nathan and Henry Overman discuss the impacts of COVID-19 on cities in "Will Coronavirus Cause a Big City Exodus?," Economics Observatory, September 22, 2020, https://www.coronavirusandtheeconomy.com/question/will-coronavirus-cause-big-city-exodus.

13. Forth 2018.

14. Paul Krugman, "The Gambler's Ruin of Small Cities (Wonkish)," *New York Times*, December 30, 2017, https://www.nytimes.com/2017/12/30/opinion/the-gamblers-ruin-of-small-cities-wonkish.html.

15. Moretti 2012.

16. See Waldrop 2018.

17. Cairncross 1997.

18. Cheshire and Buyuklieva 2019.

19. Leunig and James Swaffield 2007.

20. Myers 2020.

21. Ostrom 2005.

22. Hughes and Southwood 2021.

23. This discussion is drawn from Bowman and Westlake (2019).

24. See, respectively, Robert Nelson 1999; Royal Town Planning Institute 2020; and Building Better, Building Beautiful Commission 2020.

25. Glaeser 2020.

26. Walker 2011.

27. As Bogart (2005) discusses, the funding of roads and road repairs is not a new problem. In the seventeenth century, local parishes were unable to charge road users for maintenance and investment. For example, in 1693 Bethnal Green appealed for assistance from county magistrates because its repair expenses amounted to the substantial sum of £200 per year on two major roads to London. However, Bethnal Green had only 200 inhabitants and so did not have the local tax base to pay for road repair. The problem was solved by delegating funding of road building to turnpike trusts, private organisations with a body of trustees with the authority to levy tolls and borrow against toll revenues, which could therefore charge road users and charge for the whole length of the road. Parish records indicate that turnpike trusts boosted road investment relative to parishes with no trusts between 1730 and 1840. This is yet another example of how institutional reform (in this case, collective property rights) helped overcome problems of exchange (in this case, collective-action problems).

28. Shoup 2018.

29. Ostrom 2005. In the United Kingdom, local parking revenues are remitted back to the locality.

30. Skelton 2019, 16.

31. Quoted in Will Tanner, "The Tories May Have Captured 'Workington Man,' but This Is How They Make Sure the Red Wall Turns Blue," *The Sun*, December 17, 2019, https://www.thesun.co.uk/news/10566847/tories-workington-man-red-wall.

32. Swinney, McDonald, and Ramuni 2018.

33. Kerr and Robert-Nicoud 2020, 66.

34. Centre for Local Economic Strategies 2019.

35. This discussion is based on Haskel (2020b).

36. Sawhill and Guyot 2020.

37. Bloom et al. 2013.

38. Gibbs, Mengel, and Siemroth 2021.

39. Deming 2017. Work by the economists Philippe Aghion, Antonin Bergeaud, Richard Blundell, and Rachel Griffith has shown that soft skills, particularly teamwork, are very important for helping wage progression for low-skilled workers and are all the more important if such workers are in high-tech firms (Aghion et al. 2019).

Chapter 7

1. Subcommittee on Antitrust, Commercial and Administrative Law of the Committee on the Judiciary 2020.

2. European Union 2020.

3. De Loecker and Eeckhout 2018.

4. Andrews, Criscuolo, and Gal 2016.

5. Schumpeter 1942, 83.

6. Benkard, Yurukoglu, and Zhang 2021; Hsieh and Rossi-Hansberg 2019.

7. Hseih and Rossi-Hansberg 2019, 2.

8. Bajgar, Criscuolo, and Timmis 2020.

9. Gutiérrez and Piton 2019a.

10. Corrado et al. 2021.

11. Peltzman 2020.

12. Armstrong 2015.

13. Hannak et al. 2014.

14. Grubb and Osborne 2015.

15. The following discussion is based on Bowman and Westlake (2019).

16. It is also a counterbalance to the influence costs that might otherwise be incurred by incumbent firms lobbying widely to protect their current status.

17. CMA 2017.

18. Aridor, Che, and Salz (2020) studied the competition consequences of the General Data Protection Regulation, the EU regulation that, among other things, requires

people to actively accept the use of cookies on websites. They found a 12 percent reduction in cookie use. However, most people who opted out had previously been using ad blocker or privacy devices, which randomised their ISP addresses. Opting out gave rise to an interesting effect. For a firm collecting information across *all* users, some of whom were using the ad blocker technology and others who were not, the ad blocker randomness generated a lot of noise, reducing the value of these data. Once those consumers who had previously been using ad blockers opted out, no information about their ISPs was given to the firm. That made the remaining customers *more* easily trackable and identifiable. Thus, whilst the regulation may have helped with the privacy of the people opting out, it decreased the privacy of the remaining parties even more.

19. Markovits 2019, 5.

20. Emma Jones, "Operation Varsity: How the Rich and Famous Cheated the US University System," BBC News, March 18, 2020, https://www.bbc.co.uk/news/entertainment-arts-56427793.

21. Machin, McNally, and Ruiz-Valenzuela 2020.

22. It is interesting to investigate what causes students to underachieve in high-stakes exams. Robert Metcalfe, Simon Burgess, and Steven Proud (2019) find that students taking GCSEs during a World Cup year underperform significantly. These students are 12 percent less likely to achieve Cs in at least five subjects, compared with those taking GCSEs during a non–World Cup year. The problem is even worse for boys from a poor background, whose grades suffer by as much as a third. In addition, transitory spikes in air pollution significantly lower long-term school achievement among pupils in Israel (Ebenstein, Lavy, and Roth 2016), and high summer heat lowers exam scores among New York high school students, with impacts on graduation status (Park 2020).

23. BMG Research, "New GCSE Grades Research amongst Employers," report for the Office of Qualifications and Examinations Regulation (Ofqual), Ofqual/13/5334, November 2013, https://assets.publishing.service.gov.uk/government/uploads/system/uploads/attachment_data/file/529390/2013-11-01-bmg-research-with-employers-on-new-gcse-grades.pdf.

24. Acemoglu 1999, 1270.

25. Lewis 2000.

26. Department of the Treasury Office of Economic Policy, the Council of Economic Advisers, and the Department of Labor 2015.

27. Caplan 2018.

28. See Noah Smith, "College Isn't a Waste of Time," Bloomberg, December 2017, https://www.bloomberg.com/opinion/articles/2017-12-11/college-isn-t-a-waste-of-time.

29. Caplan 2017.

30. Arcidiacono, Bayer, and Hizmo 2010.

31. Sibieta, Tahir, and Waltmann 2021.

32. National Audit Office 2002.

Conclusion

1. Vollrath 2020.

2. Goldstone 2002.

3. Mokyr 1994.

4. Van Bavel 2016.

5. For those with an economics background, you can think of an underlying production function describing the output of collective goods. Such goods might be classic public goods (e.g., streetlights), but they might also be private collective goods (e.g., coordination activities within firms). Assume that collective output requires capital and hours of productive labour as is conventional plus coordination activities. (Coordination activities do not appear in a classic production function in a firm that specifies only capital and labour, but that is because a firm is viewed as a set of blueprints efficiently combining capital and labour inputs with no assumed costs of coordinating such inputs.) So there is an upward-sloping curve, not drawn in figure C.1, reflecting this production relation: the output of goods to coordination activities and information. The downward-sloping curve drawn in figure C.1 assumes that the more collective and centralised the output, the greater the incentive to allocate time to influence activities and distort information, or the more that information is lacking owing to collective provision lessening experimentation. Thus, the drawn curve describes not the underlying production of collective goods but rather the constraints to such production.

6. Milgrom and Roberts 1988, 1990.

7. Ridley 2020.

8. Paul Romer, "Why the World Needs Charter Cities," July 1, 2009, https://paulromer.net/video-why-the-world-needs-charter-cities-ted/.

9. In addition, the algorithm they use (for example, scientific publications) might dissuade synergies.

10. Johnson and Koyama 2017, 2.

11. North and Weingast 1989.

12. Johnson and Koyama 2017, 3.

13. O'Reilly and Murphy 2020.

14. Quoted by Alex Singleton, "Sir John Cowperthwaite: Free-Market Thinking Civil Servant behind Hong Kong's Success," *The Guardian*, February 8, 2006, https://www.theguardian.com/news/2006/feb/08/guardianobituaries.mainsection.

15. The argument is delicate: politicians typically delegate operational policy but set the targets for a central bank.

16. Taylor 2016.

17. Lorenzo Castellani, "L'ère du technopopulisme," *Le Grand Continent*, March 16, 2018, https://legrandcontinent.eu/fr/2018/03/16/lere-du-technopopulisme/?utm_campaign=Matt%27s%20Thoughts%20In%20Between&utm_medium=email&utm_source=Revue%20newsletter.

18. Fukuyama 1995; Putnam 1994.

REFERENCES

Aarts, Alexander A., Joanna E. Anderson, Christopher J. Anderson, Peter R. Attridge, Angela Attwood, Jordan Axt, Molly Babel, et al. 2015. "Estimating the Reproducibility of Psychological Science." *Science* 349 (6251). https://doi.org/10.1126/science.aac4716.

Abel, A. B., A. K. Dixit, J. C. Eberly, and R. S. Pindyck. 1996. "Options, the Value of Capital, and Investment." *Quarterly Journal of Economics* 111 (3): 753–77. https://doi.org/10.2307/2946671.

Acemoglu, Daron. 1999. "Changes in Unemployment and Wage Inequality: An Alternative Theory and Some Evidence." *American Economic Review* 89 (5): 1259–78.

Acemoglu, Daron, Simon Johnson, and James Robinson. 2004. "Institutions as the Fundamental Cause of Long-Run Growth." National Bureau of Economic Research working paper no. 10481. https://doi.org/10.3386/w10481.

Acemoglu, Daron, and James A. Robinson. 2019. *The Narrow Corridor: States, Societies, and the Fate of Liberty*. New York: Penguin.

Adler, Gustavo, Romain A. Duval, Davide Furceri, Sinem Kılıç Çelik, Ksenia Koloskova, and Marcos Poplawski Ribeiro. 2017. "Gone with the Headwinds; Global Productivity." International Monetary Fund Staff Discussion Notes, April. https://ideas.repec.org/p/imf/imfsdn/2017-004.html.

Aghion, Philippe, Antonin Bergeaud, Richard W. Blundell, and Rachel Griffith. 2019. "The Innovation Premium to Soft Skills in Low-Skilled Occupations." *SSRN Electronic Journal*, November. https://doi.org/10.2139/ssrn.3489777.

Ahn, JaeBin, Romain Duval, and Can Sever. 2020. "Macroeconomic Policy, Product Market Competition, and Growth: The Intangible Investment Channel." International Monetary Fund working paper no. 20/25. https://www.imf.org/en/Publications/WP/Issues/2020/02/07/Macroeconomic-Policy-Product-Market-Competition-and-Growth-The-Intangible-Investment-Channel-49005.

Alvardero, Facundo, Lucas Chancel, Thomas Piketty, Emmanuel Saez, and Gabriel Zucman. 2020. *World Inequality Report 2018*. https://wir2018.wid.world/files/download/wir2018-full-report-english.pdf.

Ampudia, Miguel, Thorsten Beck, and Alexander Popov. 2021. "Out with the New, in with the Old? Bank Supervision and the Composition of Firm Investment." Centre for Economic Policy Research working paper no. DP16225. https://cepr.org/active/publications/discussion_papers/dp.php?dpno=16225#.

Andrews, Dan, Chiara Criscuolo, and Peter N. Gal. 2016. "The Best versus the Rest: The Global Productivity Slowdown, Divergence across Firms and the Role of Public Policy" OECD Productivity working paper no. 5. https://www.oecd-ilibrary.org/economics/the-best-versus-the-rest_63629cc9-en.

Arcidiacono, Peter, Patrick Bayer, and Aurel Hizmo. 2010. "Beyond Signaling and Human Capital: Education and the Revelation of Ability." *American Economic Journal: Applied Economics* 2 (4): 76–104. https://doi.org/10.1257/app.2.4.76.

Aridor, Guy, Yeon-Koo Che, and Tobias Salz. 2020. "The Economic Consequences of Data Privacy Regulation: Empirical Evidence from GDPR." National Bureau of Economic Research working paper no. 26900. https://doi.org/10.3386/w26900.

Armstrong, Mark. 2015. "Search and Ripoff Externalities." *Review of Industrial Organization* 47 (3): 273–302. https://doi.org/10.1007/s11151-015-9480-1.

Arora, Ashish, Sharon Belenzon, and Andrea Patacconi. 2015. "Killing the Golden Goose? The Changing Nature of Corporate Research, 1980–2007." Fuqua Business School, working paper. https://www.semanticscholar.org/paper/Killing-the-Golden-Goose-The-changing-nature-of-%2C-Arora-Belenzon/c24b06fcfe989cd4ba2df14eb93f7f2146129a29.

———. 2018. "The Decline of Science in Corporate R&D." *Strategic Management Journal* 39 (1): 3–32. https://doi.org/10.1002/smj.2693.

Arora, Ashish, Sharon Belenzon, and Lia Sheer. 2021. "Knowledge Spillovers and Corporate Investment in Scientific Research." *American Economic Review* 111 (3): 871–98. https://doi.org/10.1257/AER.20171742.

Arquié, Axelle, Lilas Demmou, Guido Franco, and Irina Stefanescu. 2019. "Productivity and Finance: The Intangible Assets Channel—A Firm Level Analysis." OECD Economics Department working paper no. 1596. https://doi.org/10.1787/d13a21b0-en.

Arrow, Kenneth. 1962. "Economic Welfare and the Allocation of Resources for Invention." In *The Rate and Direction of Inventive Activity: Economic and Social Factors*, edited by Universities-National Bureau, 609–26. National Bureau of Economic Research. http://ideas.repec.org/h/nbr/nberch/2144.html.

Bahaj, Saleem, Angus Foulis, Gabor Pinter, and Jonathan Haskel. 2021. "Intangible Investment and House Prices." Unpublished working waper.

Bajgar, Matej, Chiara Criscuolo, and Jonathan Timmis. 2020. "Supersize Me: Intangibles and Industry Concentration." Draft working paper. https://www.aeaweb.org/conference/2020/preliminary/paper/iGtrhyEZ. Accessed August 30, 2021.

Bank of England, Financial Policy Committee. 2020. *Financial Stability Report*. August. https://www.bankofengland.co.uk/-/media/boe/files/financial-stability-report/2020/august-2020.pdf.

Baudrillard, Jean. 1994. *Simulacra and Simulation*. Translated by S. F. Glaser. Ann Arbor: University of Michigan Press. (Original work published in 1981.)

Bean, Charles R., Jens Larsen, and Kalin Nikolov. 2002. "Financial Frictions and the Monetary Transmission Mechanism: Theory, Evidence, and Policy Implications." European Central Bank working paper no. 113. https://econpapers.repec.org/RePEc:ecb:ecbwps:2002113.

Bell, Alex, Raj Chetty, Xavier Jaravel, Neviana Petkova, and John Van Reenen. 2019. "Who Becomes an Inventor in America? The Importance of Exposure to Innovation." *Quarterly Journal of Economics* 134 (2): 647–713. https://doi.org/10.1093/qje/qjy028.

Benkard, C. Lanier, Ali Yurukoglu, and Anthony Lee Zhang. 2021. "Concentration in Product Markets." National Bureau of Economic Research working paper no. 28745. https://papers.ssrn.com/abstract=3838512.

Benmelech, Efraim, Janice Eberly, Dimitris Papanikolaou, and Joshua Krieger. 2021. "Private and Social Returns to R&D: Drug Development and Demographics." *AEA Papers and Proceedings* 111 (May): 336–40. https://doi.org/10.1257/pandp.20211104.

Bergeaud, Antonin, Gilbert Cette, and Rémy Lecat. 2015. "GDP per Capita in Advanced Countries over the 20th Century." Banque de France working paper no. 549. https://papers.ssrn.com/sol3/papers.cfm?abstract_id=2602267.

Berkes, Enrico, and Ruben Gaetani. 2019. "The Geography of Unconventional Innovation." *SSRN Electronic Journal*, July. https://doi.org/10.2139/ssrn.3423143.

Berlingieri, G., Carol A. Corrado, C. Criscuolo, Jonathan Haskel, Alex Himbert, and Cecilia Jona-Lasinio. 2021. "New Evidence on Intangibles, Diffusion and Productivity." OECD Science, Technology and Industry working paper no. 2021/10. https://doi.org/10.1787/de0378f3-en.

Bessen, James, and Michael Meurer. 2009. *Patent Failure*. Princeton, NJ: Princeton University Press.

Bessen, James E., Erich Denk, Joowon Kim, and Cesare Righi. 2020. "Declining Industrial Disruption." *SSRN Electronic Journal*, February. https://doi.org/10.2139/ssrn.3682745.

Blanchard, Olivier, Giovanni Dell'Ariccia, and Paolo Mauro 2010. "Rethinking Macroeconomic Policy." International Monetary Fund Staff Position Note no. 10/03. https://www.imf.org/external/pubs/ft/spn/2010/spn1003.pdf.

Bloom, Nicholas, James Liang, John Roberts, and Zichun Jenny Ying. 2013. "Does Working from Home Work? Evidence from a Chinese Experiment." National Bureau of Economic Research working paper no. 18871. https://www.nber.org/papers/w18871.

Bogart, Dan. 2005. "Did Turnpike Trusts Increase Transportation Investment in Eighteenth-Century England?" *Journal of Economic History* 65 (2): 439–68. http://www.jstor.org/stable/3875068.

Boldrin, Michele, and David K. Levine. 2013. "The Case against Patents." *Journal of Economic Perspectives* 27 (1): 3–22. https://doi.org/10.1257/jep.27.1.3.

Bowman, Sam, and Stian Westlake. 2019. *Reviving Economic Thinking on the Right: A Short Plan for the UK.* https://revivingeconomicthinking.com.

Branstetter, Lee, and Daniel Sichel. 2017. "The Case for an American Productivity Revival." Peterson Institute for International Economics Policy Brief no. 17-26. https://ideas.repec.org/p/iie/pbrief/pb17-26.html.

Brassell, Martin, and Kelvin King. 2013. *Banking on IP?* https://www.gov.uk/government/publications/banking-on-ip.

Brav, Alon, Wei Jiang, and Song Ma. 2018. "How Does Hedge Fund Activism Reshape Corporate Innovation?" *Journal of Financial Economics* 130 (2): 237–64. https://doi.org/10.1016/j.jfineco.2018.06.012.

Brazier, Alex. 2020. "Protecting Economic Muscle: Finance and the Covid Crisis." Bank of England, July 23. https://www.bankofengland.co.uk/speech/2020/alex-brazier-keynote-dialogue-at-the-cfo-agenda.

Broadberry, Stephen. 2013. "Accounting for the Great Divergence." *Economic History Working Papers* 184:2–33. https://doi.org/10.1017/CBO9781107415324.004.

———. 2020. "The Industrial Revolution and the Great Divergence: Recent Findings from Historical National Accounting." Centre for Economic Policy Research, discussion paper no. DP15207. https://cepr.org/active/publications/discussion_papers/dp.php?dpno=15207.

Brynjolfsson, Erik, and Andrew McAfee. 2014. *The Second Machine Age.* New York: W. W. Norton.

Brynjolfsson, Erik, Daniel Rock, and Chad Syverson. 2021. "The Productivity J-Curve: How Intangibles Complement General Purpose Technologies." *American Economic Journal: Macroeconomics* 13 (1): 333–72.

Building Better, Building Beautiful Commission. 2020. *Living with Beauty: Promoting Health, Well Being and Sustainable Growth.* January. https://assets.publishing.service.gov.uk/government/uploads/system/uploads/attachment_data/file/861832/Living_with_beauty_BBBBC_report.pdf.

Byrne, David M., Carol A. Corrado, and Daniel E. Sichel. 2017. "Own-Account IT Equipment Investment." FEDS Notes, Board of Governors of the Federal Reserve System, October 4. https://www.federalreserve.gov/econres/notes/feds-notes/own-account-it-equipment-investment-20171004.htm.

Byrne, David M., Stephen D. Oliner, and Daniel E. Sichel. 2017. "How Fast Are Semiconductor Prices Falling?" *Review of Income and Wealth,* April. https://doi.org/10.1111/roiw.12308.

Byrne, David, and Dan Sichel. 2017. "The Productivity Slowdown Is Even More Puzzling than You Think." *VoxEU,* August 22. https://voxeu.org/article/productivity-slowdown-even-more-puzzling-you-think.

Cairncross, F. 1997. *The Death of Distance: How the Communications Revolution Is Changing Our Lives.* Cambridge, MA: Harvard Business School Press.

Campbell, Donald T. 1979. "Assessing the Impact of Planned Social Change." *Evaluation and Program Planning* 2 (1): 67–90. https://doi.org/10.1016/0149-7189(79)90048-X.

Caplan, Bryan. 2017. "Reply to Noah on *The Case Against Education*." Blog post, EconLog, December 18. https://www.econlib.org/archives/2017/12/reply_to_noah_o.html.

———. 2018. *The Case against Education: Why the Education System Is a Waste of Time and Money*. Princeton, NJ: Princeton University Press.

Case, Anne, and Angus Deaton. 2020. *Deaths of Despair and the Future of Capitalism*. Princeton, NJ: Princeton University Press.

Cecchetti, Stephen, and Kim Schoenholtz. 2018. "Financing Intangible Capital." *VoxEU*, February 22, 2018. https://voxeu.org/article/financing-intangible-capital.

Centre for Local Economic Strategies. 2019. "Community Wealth Building 2019: Theory, Practice and Next Steps." September. https://cles.org.uk/wp-content/uploads/2019/09/CWB2019FINAL-web.pdf.

Cheshire, Paul, and Boyana Buyuklieva. 2019. "Homes on the Right Tracks: Greening the Green Belt to Solve the Housing Crisis." Centre for Cities, September. https://www.centreforcities.org/wp-content/uploads/2019/09/Homes-on-the-Right-Tracks-Greening-the-Green-Belt.pdf.

Clancy, Matt. 2019. "Innovation and the City: Are Local Knowledge Spillovers Getting Weaker?" New Things under the Sun, December 19. https://mattsclancy.substack.com/p/innovation-and-the-city.

CMA. 2017. *Digital Comparison Tools Market Study: Final Report*. https://assets.publishing.service.gov.uk/media/59c93546e5274a77468120d6/digital-comparison-tools-market-study-final-report.pdf.

Cohen, Stephen S., and J. Bradford DeLong. 2016. *Concrete Economics: The Hamilton Approach to Economic Growth and Policy*. Cambridge, MA: Harvard Business Review Press.

Congressional Budget Office. 2007. *The Budget and Economic Outlook: Fiscal Years 2008 to 2017*. Washington, DC. https://www.cbo.gov/sites/default/files/110th-congress-2007-2008/reports/01-24-budgetoutlook.pdf.

Corrado, Carol, Jonathan Haskel, Massimiliano Iommi, and Cecilia Jona-Lasinio. 2019. "Intangible Capital, Innovation, and Productivity à La Jorgenson: Evidence from Europe and the United States." In *Measuring Economic Growth and Productivity: Foundations, KLEMS Production Models, and Extensions*, edited by Barbara M. Fraumeni, 363–86. London: Academic Press.

Corrado, Carol A., Chiara Criscuolo, Jonathan Haskel, Alex Himbert, and Cecilia Jona-Lasinio. 2021. "New Evidence on Intangibles, Diffusion and Productivity." OECD Science, Technology and Industry working paper no. 2021/10. Paris: OECD Publishing. https://doi.org/https://doi.org/10.1787/de0378f3-en.

Corrado, Carol A., Jonathan E. Haskel, and Cecilia Jona-Lasinio. 2021. "Artificial Intelligence and Productivity: An. Intangible Assets Approach." *Oxford Review of Economic Policy*, forthcoming. Available at https://spiral.imperial.ac.uk/bitstream/10044/1/89036/2/Innov_J_curve_17Mar21.pdf.

Cowen, Tyler. 2011. *The Great Stagnation*. New York: E. P. Dutton.

———. 2017. *The Complacent Class: The Self-Defeating Quest for the American Dream*. New York: St. Martin's Press.

Cowen, Tyler, and Ben Southwood. 2019. "Is the Rate of Scientific Progress Slowing Down?" https://docs.google.com/document/d/1cEBsj18Y4NnVx5Qdu43cKEHMaVBODTTyfHBa8GIRSec/edit.

Cunliffe, Jon. 2017. "The Phillips Curve: Lower, Flatter, or in Hiding?" Bank of England, November 14. https://www.bankofengland.co.uk/-/media/boe/files/speech/2017/the-phillips-curve-lower-flatter-or-in-hiding-speech-by-jon-cunliffe.

Daly, Kevin. 2016. "A Higher Global Risk Premium and the Fall in Equilibrium Real Interest Rates." *VoxEU*, November 18. https://voxeu.org/article/higher-global-risk-premium-and-fall-equilibrium-real-interest-rates.

Dattani, Saloni, and Nathaniel Bechhofer. 2021. "The Speed of Science." Works in Progress, February 8. https://worksinprogress.co/issue/the-speed-of-science/.

Davies, Dan. 2014. "The World Is Squared—Episode 3: The Greek Calends." Crooked Timber, October 11. https://crookedtimber.org/2014/10/11/the-world-is-squared-episode-3-the-greek-calends/.

———. 2015. "Flat Whites, Hipsters, and the Post-mortgage British Economy." Medium, March 13. https://medium.com/bull-market/flat-whites-hipsters-and-the-post-mortgage-british-economy-6a8ea2a39478.

Davis, Jerry. 2018. "Apple's $1 Trillion Value Doesn't Mean It's the 'Biggest' Company." The Conversation, August 10. https://theconversation.com/apples-1-trillion-value-doesnt-mean-its-the-biggest-company-101225.

Decker, Ryan A., John Haltiwanger, Ron S. Jarmin, and Javier Miranda. 2018. "Changing Business Dynamism and Productivity: Shocks vs. Responsiveness." Board of Governors of the Federal Reserve System. https://doi.org/10.17016/FEDS.2018.007.

De Fiore, Fiorella, and Harald Uhlig. 2011. "Bank Finance versus Bond Finance." *Journal of Money, Credit and Banking* 43 (7): 1399–1421. https://doi.org/10.1111/j.1538-4616.2011.00429.x.

Dell'Ariccia, Giovanni, Dalida Kadyrzhanova, Camelia Minoiu, and Lev Ratnovski. 2017. "Bank Lending in the Knowledge Economy." International Monetary Fund working paper no. 2017/234. https://econpapers.repec.org/RePEc:imf:imfwpa:17/234.

De Loecker, Jan, and Jan Eeckhout. 2018. "Global Market Power." National Bureau of Economic Research working paper no. 24768. https://www.nber.org/papers/w24768.

Del Negro, Marco, Michele Lenza, Giorgio Primiceri, and Andrea Tambalotti. 2020. "Why Has Inflation in the United States Been So Stable since the 1990s?" *Research Bulletin*, no. 74. https://www.ecb.europa.eu/pub/economic-research/resbull/2020/html/ecb.rb200917~3bc072ea95.en.html.

Deming, David J. 2017. "The Value of Soft Skills in the Labour Market." *The Reporter*, December. https://www.nber.org/reporter/2017number4/value-soft-skills-labor-market#N_6_.

Demmou, Lilas, Irina Stefanescu, and Axelle Arquie. 2019. "Productivity Growth and Finance: The Role of Intangible Assets-a Sector Level Analysis." OECD Library. https://doi.org/10.1787/e26cae57-en.

Demsetz, Harold. 1967. "Toward a Theory of Property Rights." *American Economic Review* 57 (2): 347–359.

Department for Business, Energy & Industrial Strategy. 2019. "2018 UK Greenhouse Gas Emissions, Provisional Figures." March 28. https://assets.publishing.service.gov.uk/government/uploads/system/uploads/attachment_data/file/790626/2018-provisional-emissions-statistics-report.pdf.

Department of the Treasury Office of Economic Policy, the Council of Economic Advisers, and the Department of Labor. 2015. *Occupational Licensing: A Framework for Policymakers*. July. https://obamawhitehouse.archives.gov/sites/default/files/docs/licensing_report_final_nonembargo.pdf.

De Soto, Hernando. 2000. *The Mystery of Capital: Why Capitalism Triumphs in the West and Fails Everywhere Else*. New York: Basic Books.

De Veirman, Marijke, Liselot Hudders, and Michelle R. Nelson. 2019. "What Is Influencer Marketing and How Does It Target Children? A Review and Direction for Future Research." *Frontiers in Psychology* 10 (December). https://doi.org/10.3389/fpsyg.2019.02685.

Diewert, W. E. 1976. "Exact and Superlative Index Numbers." *Journal of Econometrics* 4 (2): 115–45. https://doi.org/10.1016/0304-4076(76)90009-9.

Diez, Federico, Jiayue Fan, and Carolina Villegas-Sanchez. 2019. "Global Declining Competition." International Monetary Fund working paper no. 19/82. https://papers.ssrn.com/sol3/papers.cfm?abstract_id=3397540.

Dixit, Avinash. 1992. "Investment and Hysteresis." *Journal of Economic Perspectives* 6 (1): 107–32. http://www.aeaweb.org/articles?id=10.1257/jep.6.1.107.

Dixit, Avinash, and Robert S. Pindyck. 1995. "The Options Approach to Capital Investment." *Harvard Business Review* 73 (3) (May–June): 105–15. https://hbr.org/1995/05/the-options-approach-to-capital-investment.

Douthat, Ross. 2020. *The Decadent Society: How We Became the Victims of Our Own Success*. New York: Avid Reader Press / Simon & Schuster.

Drechsel, Thomas. 2021. "Earnings-Based Borrowing Constraints and Macroeconomic Fluctuations." University of Maryland, Department of Economics, March 15. http://econweb.umd.edu/~drechsel/papers/jmp_drechsel.pdf.

Duranton, Gilles, and Diego Puga. 2014. "The Growth of Cities." In *Handbook of Economic Growth*, edited by Phillipe Aghion and Steven Durlauf, 781–853. Amsterdam: Elsevier.

Duval, Romain. 2017. "Financial Frictions and the Great Productivity Slowdown." International Monetary Fund working paper no. 17/129. https://www.imf.org/en/Publications/WP/Issues/2017/05/31/Financial-Frictions-and-the-Great-Productivity-Slowdown-44917.

Duval, Romain, JaeBin Ahn, and Can Sever. 2018. "Product Market Competition, Monetary Policy, and Intangible Investment: Firm-Level Evidence from the Global Financial Crisis." 1 St IMF-OECD-World Bank Conference on Structural Reforms, Paris, June 11. https://www.oecd.org/eco/reform/joint-imf-wb-oecd-conf-structural-reform-2018/Product_market_competition_monetary_policy_and_ intangible_investment.pdf.

Ebenstein, Avraham, Victor Lavy, and Sefi Roth. 2016. "The Long-Run Economic Consequences of High-Stakes Examinations: Evidence from Transitory Variation in

Pollution." *American Economic Journal: Applied Economics* 8 (4): 36–65. https://doi.org/10.1257/app.20150213.

Edgerton, David. 2018. *The Rise and Fall of the British Nation: A Twentieth-Century History*. London: Allen Lane.

Edmans, Alex. 2009. "Blockholder Trading, Market Efficiency, and Managerial Myopia." *Journal of Finance* 64 (6): 2481–513. https://doi.org/10.1111/j.1540-6261.2009.01508.x.

Eghbal, Nadia. 2016. *Roads and Bridges: The Unseen Labor behind Our Digital Infrastructure*. New York: Ford Foundation. https://www.fordfoundation.org/media/2976/roads-and-bridges-the-unseen-labor-behind-our-digital-infrastructure.pdf.

European Union. 2020. "Speech by Executive Vice-President Margrethe Vestager: Building Trust in Technology." October. https://ec.europa.eu/commission/commissioners/2019-2024/vestager/announcements/speech-executive-vice-president-margrethe-vestager-building-trust-technology_en.

Feyrer, James, and Bruce Sacerdote. 2013. "How Much Would US Style Fiscal Integration Buffer European Unemployment and Income Shocks? (A Comparative Empirical Analysis)." *American Economic Review* 103:125–28. https://doi.org/10.1257/aer.103.3.125.

Fischel, William A. 2005. *The Homevoter Hypothesis*. Cambridge, MA: Harvard University Press. https://www.hup.harvard.edu/catalog.php?isbn=9780674015951.

Forth, John, Alex Bryson, Amy Humphris, Lse Maria Koumenta, Morris Kleiner, and Paul Casey. 2011. "A Review of Occupational Regulation and Its Impact." UK Commission for Employment and Skills, Evidence Report no. 40. https://assets.publishing.service.gov.uk/government/uploads/system/uploads/attachment_data/file/306359/ER40_Occupational_regulation_impact_-_Oct_2011.pdf.

Forth, Tom. 2018. "The UK Government Is Not Investing More in Transport in North England than London and the Wider South East." August 21. https://www.tomforth.co.uk/transportspending/.

Forth, Tom, and Richard Jones. 2020. *The Missing Four Billion: Making R&D Work for the Whole UK*. London: NESTA.

Francis-Devine, Bridig. 2020. "Income Inequality in the UK." 7484. House of Commons Briefing Paper no. 7484. London. https://researchbriefings.files.parliament.uk/documents/CBP-7484/CBP-7484.pdf.

Fukuyama, Francis. 1995. *Trust: The New Foundations of Global Prosperity*. New York: Free Press.

Furman, Jason, and Lawrence Summers. 2020. "A Reconsideration of Fiscal Policy in the Era of Low Interest Rates." Discussion draft. https://www.brookings.edu/wp-content/uploads/2020/11/furman-summers-fiscal-reconsideration-discussion-draft.pdf.

Gans, Joshua. 2020. *Economics in the Age of COVID-19*. Cambridge, MA: MIT Press.

Garicano, Luis. 2000. "Hierarchies and the Organization of Knowledge in Production." *Journal of Political Economy* 108 (5): 874–904. https://doi.org/10.1086/317671.

Garicano, Luis, and Thomas N. Hubbard. 2007. "Managerial Leverage Is Limited by the Extent of the Market: Hierarchies, Specialization, and the Utilization of Lawyers' Human Capital." *Journal of Law and Economics* 50 (1): 1–43.

Gibbs, Michael, Feirderike Mengel, and Christop Siemroth. 2021. "Work from Home & Productivity: Evidence from Personnel & Analytics Data on IT Professionals." Becker Friedman Institute for Economics working paper no. 2021-56. https://papers.ssrn.com/sol3/papers.cfm?abstract_id=3843197#.

Gilson, S. C., and E. I. Altman. 2010. *Creating Value through Corporate Restructuring: Case Studies in Bankruptcies, Buyouts, and Breakups*. 2nd ed. Hoboken, NJ: Wiley.

Glaeser, Edward L. 2011. *Triumph of the City*. New York: Macmillan.

———. 2020. "Urbanization and Its Discontents." *Eastern Economic Journal* 46 (2): 191–218. https://doi.org/10.1057/s41302-020-00167-3.

Goldin, Claudia, and Lawrence Katz. 2008. *The Race between Education and Technology*. Cambridge, MA: Harvard University Press.

Goldstone, Jack A. 2002. "Efflorescences and Economic Growth in World History: Rethinking the 'Rise of the West' and the Industrial Revolution." *Journal of World History* 13 (2): 327–89. https://doi.org/10.1353/jwh.2002.0034.

Goodhart, Charles A. E. 1981. "Problems of Monetary Management: The U.K. Experience." In *Inflation, Depression, and Economic Policy in the West*, edited by Anthony S. Courakis, 91–109. Totowa, NJ: Barnes and Noble Books.

Gordon, Robert J. 2012. "Is U.S. Economic Growth Over? Faltering Innovation Confronts the Six Headwinds." National Bureau of Economic Research working paper no. 18315. https://doi.org/10.3386/w18315.

———. 2016. *The Rise and Fall of American Growth: The U.S. Standard of Living since the Civil War*. Princeton, NJ: Princeton University Press.

Graeber, David. 2018. *Bullshit Jobs: A Theory*. London: Allen Lane.

Greenwald, Daniel. 2019. "Firm Debt Covenants and the Macroeconomy: The Interest Coverage Channel." Society for Economic Dynamics, 2019 Meeting Papers 520. https://ideas.repec.org/p/red/sed019/520.html.

Greif, Avner. 2006. *Institutions and the Path to the Modern Economy: Lessons from Medieval Trade*. Cambridge: Cambridge University Press. https://doi.org/DOI:10.1017/CBO9780511791307.

Gross, Daniel P., and Bhaven N. Sampat. 2020. "Organizing Crisis Innovation: Lessons from World War II." National Bureau of Economic Research working paper no. 27909. https://doi.org/10.3386/w27909.

———. 2021. "The Economics of Crisis Innovation Policy: A Historical Perspective." National Bureau of Economic Research working paper no. 28335. https://ideas.repec.org/p/nbr/nberwo/28335.html.

Grubb, Michael D., and Matthew Osborne. 2015. "Cellular Service Demand: Biased Beliefs, Learning, and Bill Shock." *American Economic Review* 105 (1): 234–71. https://doi.org/10.1257/aer.20120283.

Gutiérrez, Germán, and Sophie Piton. 2019a. "Is There Really a Global Decline in the (Non-housing) Labour Share?" Bank Underground, August 7. https://bankunderground

.co.uk/2019/08/07/is-there-really-a-global-decline-in-the-non-housing-labour-share/.

———. 2019b. "Revisiting the Global Decline of the (Non-housing) Labor Share." http://www.centreformacroeconomics.ac.uk/Discussion-Papers/2019/CFMDP2019-13-Paper.pdf.

Hall, Bronwyn, Christian Helmers, Mark Rogers, and Vania Sena. 2014. "The Choice between Formal and Informal Intellectual Property: A Review." *Journal of Economic Literature* 52 (2): 375–423. https://doi.org/10.1257/jel.52.2.375.

Hall, Robert E., and Dale W. Jorgenson. 1967. "Tax Policy and Investment Behavior." *American Economic Review* 57 (3): 391–414. http://www.jstor.org/stable/1812110.

Hannak, Aniko, Gary Soeller, David Lazer, Alan Mislove, and Christo Wilson. 2014. "Measuring Price Discrimination and Steering on E-Commerce Web Sites." In *Proceedings of the ACM SIGCOMM Internet Measurement Conference*, 305–18. New York: Association for Computing Machinery. https://doi.org/10.1145/2663716.2663744.

Harari, Yuval Noah. 2015. *Sapiens: A Brief History of Humankind*. New York: Harper.

Hart, Oliver. 2017. "Incomplete Contracts and Control." *American Economic Review* 107 (7): 1731–52. https://doi.org/10.1257/aer.107.7.1731.

Harvey, David. 2007. *A Brief History of Neoliberalism*. Oxford: Oxford University Press.

Haskel, Jonathan E. 2019. "Capitalism without Capital: Understanding Our New 'Knowledge' Economy—Speech by Jonathan Haskel." Bank of England, May 16. https://www.bankofengland.co.uk/speech/2019/jonathan-haskel-ken-dixon-lecture-at-university-of-york.

———. 2020a. "Monetary Policy in the Intangible Economy—Speech by Jonathan Haskel." Bank of England, February 11. https://www.bankofengland.co.uk/speech/2020/jonathan-haskel-lecture-at-the-university-of-nottingham.

———. 2020b. "Remarks by Jonathan Haskel on COVID-19 and Monetary Policy." Bank of England, July 1. https://www.bankofengland.co.uk/speech/2020/jonathan-haskel-brighton-hove-chamber-of-commerce.

———. 2021. "What Is the Future of Working from Home?" Economics Observatory, April 20. https://www.economicsobservatory.com/what-is-the-future-of-working-from-home.

Haskel, Jonathan, and Stian Westlake. 2017. *Capitalism without Capital: The Rise of the Intangible Economy*. Princeton, NJ: Princeton University Press.

Hayek, F. A. 1945. "The Use of Knowledge in Society." *American Economic Review* 35 (4): 519–30.

Heller, Michael. 2008. *The Gridlock Economy: How Too Much Ownership Wrecks Markets, Stops Innovation, and Costs Lives*. New York: Basic Books.

Holmstrom, Bengt. 2015. "Understanding the Role of Debt in the Financial System." Bank for International Settlements working paper no. 479. https://economics.mit.edu/files/9777.

Hornbeck, Richard. 2010. "Barbed Wire: Property Rights and Agricultural Development." *Quarterly Journal of Economics* 125 (2): 767–810. https://doi.org/10.1162/qjec.2010.125.2.767.

Howes, Anton. 2020. *Arts and Minds*. Princeton, NJ: Princeton University Press.

Hsieh, Chang-Tai, and Enrico Moretti. 2019. "Housing Constraints and Spatial Misallocation." *American Economic Journal: Macroeconomics* 11 (2): 1–39. https://doi.org/10.1257/MAC.20170388.

Hsieh, Chang-Tai, and Esteban Alejandro Rossi-Hansberg. 2019. "The Industrial Revolution in Services." *SSRN Electronic Journal*, July. https://doi.org/10.2139/ssrn.3404309.

Hughes, Samuel, and B. Southwood. 2021. *Strong Suburbs*. London: Policy Exchange.

Hutton, Will. 1995. *The State We're In*. London: Jonathan Cape.

The Investment Association. 2020. *IA UK Funds Regime Working Group, Final Report to HM Treasury Asset Management Taskforce, 6 June 2019, Addendum on Onshore Professional Fund Proposals—11 March 2020*. https://www.theia.org/sites/default/files/2020-04/20200330-ukfrwgfinalreport.pdf.

Jaffe, A. B., M. Trajtenberg, and R. Henderson. 1993. "Geographic Localization of Knowledge Spillovers as Evidenced by Patent Citations." *Quarterly Journal of Economics* 108 (3): 577–98. https://doi.org/10.2307/2118401.

Jennings, Will, and Gerry Stoker. 2016. "The Bifurcation of Politics: Two Englands." *Political Quarterly* 87 (3): 372–82. https://doi.org/10.1111/1467-923X.12228.

Jensen, Thais Laerkholm, Soren Leth-Petersen, and Ramana Nanda. 2014. "Housing Collateral, Credit Constraints and Entrepreneurship—Evidence from a Mortgage Reform." *SSRN Electronic Journal*, October. https://doi.org/10.2139/ssrn.2506111.

Johnson, Herbert. 2004. "The Wright Patent Wars and Early American Aviation." *Journal of Air Law and Commerce* 69 (1). https://scholar.smu.edu/jalc/vol69/iss1/3.

Johnson, Noel D., and Mark Koyama. 2017. "States and Economic Growth: Capacity and Constraints." *Explorations in Economic History* 64 (April): 1–20. https://doi.org/10.1016/j.eeh.2016.11.002.

Johnstone, Bob. 1999. *We Were Burning: Japanese Entrepreneurs and the Forging of the Electronic Age*. New York: Basic Books.

Jorda, Oscar, Moritz Schularik, and Alan Taylor. 2017. "Macrofinancial History and the New Business Cycle Facts." In *NBER Macroeconomics Annual*, vol. 31, edited by Martin Eichenbaum and Jonathan A. Parker, 213–63. Chicago: University of Chicago Press.

Kaoru, Hosono, Daisuke Miyakawa, and Miho Takizawa. 2017. "Intangible Assets and Firms' Liquidity Holdings: Evidence from Japan." Research Institute of Economy, Trade and Industry discussion paper no. 17053. https://ideas.repec.org/p/eti/dpaper/17053.html.

Katznelson, Ron D., and John Howells. 2015. "The Myth of the Early Aviation Patent Hold-Up: How a US Government Monopsony Commandeered Pioneer Airplane Patents." *Industrial and Corporate Change* 24 (1): 1–64. https://doi.org/10.1093/icc/dtu003.

Kay, John, and Mervyn King. 2020. *Radical Uncertainty: Decision-Making for an Unknowable Future*. London: Bridge Street Press.

Kerr, William R., and Frédéric Robert-Nicoud. 2020. "Tech Clusters." *Journal of Economic Perspectives* 34 (3): 50–76. https://doi.org/10.1257/jep.34.3.50.

Keynes, John Maynard. 2010. "Economic Possibilities for Our Grandchildren." In *Essays in Persuasion*, 321–32. London: Palgrave Macmillan. (Original work published in 1930.)

Khan, Zorina. 2014. "Facts and Fables: A Long-Run Perspective on the Patent System." *Cato Unbound*, September 10. https://www.cato-unbound.org/browse?searchquery=facts+and+fables.

Kleiner, Morris M. 2006. *Licensing Occupations: Ensuring Quality or Restricting Competition?* Kalamazoo, MI: W.E. Upjohn Institute. https://doi.org/10.17848/9781429454865.

Kling, Arnold, and Nick Schulz. 2009. *From Poverty to Prosperity: Intangible Assets, Hidden Liabilities and the Lasting Triumph over Scarcity*. New York: Encounter Books.

Kortum, Samuel, and Josh Lerner. 2000. "Assessing the Contribution of Venture Capital to Innovation." *RAND Journal of Economics* 31 (4): 674. https://doi.org/10.2307/2696354.

Kremer, Michael. 1993. "The O-Ring Theory of Economic Development." *Quarterly Journal of Economics* 108 (3): 551–75. https://doi.org/10.2307/2118400.

———. 1998. "Patent Buyouts: A Mechanism for Encouraging Innovation." *Quarterly Journal of Economics* 113 (4): 1137–67. https://doi.org/10.1162/003355398555865.

Kremer, Michael, and Christopher Snyder. 2020. "Strengthening Incentives for Vaccine Development." National Bureau of Economic Research *Reporter* no. 4 (December). https://www.nber.org/reporter/2020number4/strengthening-incentives-vaccine-development.

Krugman, Paul. 1997. *The Age of Diminished Expectations*. Cambridge, MA: MIT Press.

Kuhn, Peter, and Fernando Lozano. 2005. "The Expanding Workweek? Understanding Trends in Long Work Hours among U.S. Men, 1979–2004." National Bureau of Economic Research working paper no. 11895. https://ideas.repec.org/p/nbr/nberwo/11895.html.

Lachmann, Ludwig M. 1956. *Capital and Its Structure*. London: Bell and Sons. https://mises.org/library/capital-and-its-structure.

Lakonishok, Josef, Andrei Shleifer, and Robert W. Vishny. 1994. "Contrarian Investment, Extrapolation, and Risk." *Journal of Finance* 49 (5): 1541–78. https://doi.org/10.1111/j.1540-6261.1994.tb04772.x.

Lall, Subir, and Li Zeng. 2020. "Intangible Investment and Low Inflation: A Framework and Some Evidence." International Monetary Fund working paper no. 20/190. https://papers.ssrn.com/abstract=3695369.

Leamer, Edward E. 2008. *Macroeconomic Patterns and Stories: A Guide for MBAs*. Berlin: Springer.

Lerner, Josh, and Ramana Nanda. 2020. "Venture Capital's Role in Financing Innovation: What We Know and How Much We Still Need to Learn." *Journal of Economic Perspectives* 34 (3): 237–61. https://doi.org/10.1257/jep.34.3.237.

Leunig, Tim, and James Swaffield. 2007. *Cities Unlimited: Making Urban Regeneration Work*. London: Policy Exchange. https://www.policyexchange.org.uk/wp-content/uploads/2016/09/cities-unlimited-aug-08.pdf.

Lev, Baruch, and Feng Gu. 2016. *The End of Accounting*. Hoboken, NJ: Wiley.

Lev, Baruch, and A. Srivastava. 2019. "Explaining the Recent Failure of Value Investing." NYU Stern School of Business. https://ssrn.com/abstract=3442539.

Levitt, Theresa. 2020. "When Lighthouses Became Public Goods: The Role of Technological Change." *Technology and Culture* 61 (1): 144–72. https://doi.org/10.1353/tech.2020.0035.

Lewis, Paul. 2020. *Flying High? A Study of Technician Duties, Skills and Training in the UK Aerospace Industry*. London: Gatsby Charitable Foundation. https://www.gatsby.org.uk/uploads/education/reports/pdf/gatsby-flying-high.pdf.

Lian, Chen, and Yueran Ma. 2021. "Anatomy of Corporate Borrowing Constraints." *Quarterly Journal of Economics* 136 (1): 229–91. https://doi.org/10.1093/qje/qjaa030.

Liebowitz, S. J., and Stephen E. Margolis. 1990. "The Fable of the Keys." *Journal of Law and Economics* 33 (1): 1–25. https://doi.org/10.1086/467198.

Lim, Steve C., Antonio J. Macias, and Thomas Moeller. 2020. "Intangible Assets and Capital Structure." *Journal of Banking and Finance* 118 (September): 105873. https://doi.org/10.1016/j.jbankfin.2020.105873.

Lindberg, Erik. 2013. "From Private to Public Provision of Public Goods: English Lighthouses between the Seventeenth and Nineteenth Centuries." *Journal of Policy History* 25 (4): 538–56. https://doi.org/10.1017/S0898030613000298.

Lowenstein, Roger. 2001. *When Genius Failed*. New York: Penguin Random House.

Machin, Stephen, Sandra McNally, and Jenifer Ruiz-Valenzuela. 2020. "Entry through the Narrow Door: The Costs of Just Failing High-Stakes Exams." *Journal of Public Economics* 190 (October): 104224. https://doi.org/10.1016/j.jpubeco.2020.104224.

Markovits, Daniel. 2019. *The Meritocracy Trap*. London: Allen Lane.

Marx, Karl, and Frederick Engels. 2002 [1848]. *The Communist Manifesto*. London: Penguin Books.

Mazzucato, Mariana. 2013. *The Entrepreneurial State: Debunking Public vs. Private Sector Myths*. London: Anthem Press.

———. 2021. *Mission Economy: A Moonshot Guide to Changing Capitalism*. London: Allen Lane.

McAfee, Andrew. 2019. *More from Less*. New York: Simon and Schuster.

McLean, Bethany, and Peter Elkind. 2005. *The Smartest Guys in the Room: The Amazing Rise and Scandalous Fall of Enron*. New York: Portfolio.

McLeay, Michael, and Silvana Tenreyro. 2020. "Optimal Inflation and the Identification of the Phillips Curve." *NBER Macroeconomics Annual* 34:4–255. https://doi.org/10.1086/707181.

McRae, Hamish. 1995. *The World in 2020: Power, Culture and Prosperity*. Cambridge, MA: Harvard Business Review Press.

Metcalfe, Robert, Simon Burgess, and Steven Proud. 2019. "Students' Effort and Educational Achievement: Using the Timing of the World Cup to Vary the Value of

Leisure." *Journal of Public Economics* 172 (April): 111–26. https://doi.org/10.1016/j.jpubeco.2018.12.006.

Milgrom, Paul, and John Roberts. 1988. "An Economic Approach to Influence Activities in Organizations." *American Journal of Sociology* 94:S154–79. http://www.jstor.org/stable/2780245.

———. 1990. "Bargaining Costs, Influence Costs, and the Organization of Economic Activity." In *Perspectives on Positive Political Economy*, edited by James E. Alt and Kenneth A. Shepsie, 57–89. Cambridge: Cambridge University Press.

———. 2009. "Bargaining Costs, Influence Costs, and the Organization of Economic Activity." In *The Economic Nature of the Firm: A Reader*, 3rd ed., edited by Louis Putterman and Randall S. Kroszner, 143–55. Cambridge: Cambridge University Press.

Mirrlees, J., and S. Adam. 2011. *Tax by Design: The Mirrlees Review*. London: Institute for Fiscal Studies.

Mokyr, Joel. 1994. "Cardwell's Law and the Political Economy of Technological Progress." *Research Policy* 23 (5): 561–74. https://doi.org/10.1016/0048-7333(94)01006-4.

———. 2002. *The Gifts of Athena : Historical Origins of the Knowledge Economy*. Princeton, NJ: Princeton University Press.

———. 2018. "The Past and the Future of Innovation: Some Lessons from Economic History." *Explorations in Economic History* 69: 13–26. https://doi.org/10.1016/j.eeh.2018.03.003.

Moretti, Enrico. 2012. *The New Geography of Jobs*. Boston: Houghton Mifflin Harcourt.

Myers, John. 2020. "Fixing Urban Planning with Ostrom: Strategies for Existing Cities to Adopt Polycentric, Bottom-Up Regulation of Land Use." Mercatus Research, Mercatus Center at George Mason University, Arlington, VA, February. https://www.mercatus.org/system/files/myers_-_mercatus_research_-_fixing_urban_planning_with_ostrom_-_v1.pdf.

Nanda, Ramana, and William Kerr. 2015. "Financing Innovation." *Annual Review of Financial Economics* 7 (1): 445–62.

National Audit Office. 2002. *Individual Learning Accounts*. https://www.nao.org.uk/wp-content/uploads/2002/10/01021235.pdf.

Nelson, Richard R. 1959. "The Simple Economics of Basic Scientific Research." *Journal of Political Economy* 67 (3): 297–306. https://doi.org/10.1086/258177.

———. 1994. "The Co-evolution of Technology, Industrial Structure, and Supporting Institutions." *Industrial and Corporate Change* 3 (1): 47–63. https://doi.org/10.1093/icc/3.1.47.

Nelson, Robert. 1999. "Privatizing the Neighborhood: A Proposal to Replace Zoning with Private Collective Property Rights to Existing Neighborhoods." *George Mason Law Review* 7. HeinOnline, https://heinonline.org/HOL/LandingPage?handle=hein.journals/gmlr7&div=37&id=&page=.

NESTA. 2016. "Pushing Boundaries: The 2015 UK Alternative Finance Industry Report." https://www.nesta.org.uk/report/pushing-boundaries-the-2015-uk-alternative-finance-industry-report/.

Nielsen, Michael. 2013. *Reinventing Discovery: The New Era of Networked Science*. Princeton, NJ: Princeton University Press.

North, Douglass C. 1993. "Douglass C. North—Prize Lecture: Economic Performance through Time." Nobel Prize Lecture, December 9. https://www.nobelprize.org/prizes/economic-sciences/1993/north/lecture/.

North, Douglass C., and Barry R. Weingast. 1989. "Constitutions and Commitment: The Evolution of Institutions Governing Public Choice in Seventeenth-Century England." *Journal of Economic History* 49 (4): 803–32. http://www.jstor.org/stable/2122739.

OECD. 2021. *Bridging the Gap in the Financing of Intangibles to Support Productivity: A Policy Toolkit*. Paris: OECD Publishing.

O'Reilly, Colin, and Ryan Murphy. 2020. "A New Measure of State Capacity, 1789–2018." *SSRN Electronic Journal*, August. https://doi.org/10.2139/ssrn.3643637.

Olson, Mançur. 1965. *The Logic of Collective Action*. Cambridge, MA: Harvard University Press.

Ostrom, Elinor. 2005. *Understanding Institutional Diversity*. Princeton, NJ: Princeton University Press.

Park, R. Jisung. 2020. "Hot Temperature and High Stakes Performance." *Journal of Human Resources*, March. https://doi.org/10.3368/jhr.57.2.0618-9535r3.

Peltzman, Sam. 2020. "Productivity, Prices and Productivity in Manufacturing: A Demsetzian Perspective." *SSRN Electronic Journal*, August. https://doi.org/10.2139/ssrn.3655762.

Pennington, Mark. 2001. *Planning and the Political Market: Public Choice and the Politics of Government Failure*. London: Athlone Press.

Phelps, Edmund. 2013. *Mass Flourishing: How Grassroots Innovation Created Jobs, Challenge, and Change*. Princeton, NJ: Princeton University Press.

Philippon, Thomas. 2019. *The Great Reversal: How America Gave Up on Free Markets*. Cambridge, MA: Belknap Press of Harvard University Press.

Piketty, Thomas. 2014. *Capital in the Twenty-First Century*. Cambridge, MA: Harvard University Press.

Porta, Rafael La, Florencio Lopez-De-Silanes, Andrei Shleifer, and Robert W. Vishny. 1997. "Legal Determinants of External Finance." *Journal of Finance* 52 (3): 1131. https://doi.org/10.2307/2329518.

Posner, Eric, and E. Glen Weyl. 2018. *Radical Markets: Uprooting Capitalism and Democracy for a Just Society*. Princeton, NJ: Princeton University Press.

Putnam, Robert. 1994. *Making Democracy Work: Civic Traditions in Modern Italy*. Princeton, NJ: Princeton University Press.

Rachel, Lukasz, and Thomas Smith. 2015. "Secular Drivers of the Global Real Interest Rate." Bank of England working paper no. 571. https://doi.org/10.2139/ssrn.2702441.

Ridley, Matt. 2020. *How Innovation Works: And Why It Flourishes in Freedom*. London: 4th Estate.

Ritchie, Stuart. 2020. *Science Fictions: Exposing Fraud, Bias, Negligence and Hype in Science*. New York: Penguin.

Rognlie, Matthew. 2015. "Deciphering the Fall and Rise in the Net Capital Share." *Brookings Papers on Economic Activity* 46: 1–69. https://doi.org/10.1353/eca.2016.0002.

Royal Town Planning Institute. 2020. "Priorities for Planning Reform in England." April 23. https://www.rtpi.org.uk/policy/2020/april/priorities-for-planning-reform-in-england/.

Sawhill, Isabel V., and Katherine Guyot. 2020. *The Middle Class Time Squeeze*. Washington, DC: Brookings Institution. https://www.brookings.edu/wp-content/uploads/2020/08/The-Middle-Class-Time-Squeeze_08.18.2020.pdf.

Schumacher, E. F. 1980. *Small Is Beautiful*. London: Blond & Briggs. https://www.amazon.co.uk/Small-Beautiful-F-Schumacher/dp/B0010365XW/ref=tmm_hrd_swatch_0?_encoding=UTF8&qid=&sr=.

Schumpeter, Joseph A. 1942. *Capitalism, Socialism and Democracy*. New York: Harper.

Schwartz, Peter, and Peter Leyden. 1997. "The Long Boom: A History of the Future, 1980–2020." *Wired*, July 1. https://www.wired.com/1997/07/longboom/.

Scott, James. 1999. *Seeing Like a State: How Certain Schemes to Improve the Human Condition Have Failed*. New Haven, CT: Yale University Press.

Shiller, Robert. 2019. *Narrative Economics*. Princeton, NJ: Princeton University Press.

Shoup, Donald. 2018. *Parking and the City*. New York: Routledge.

Sibieta, Luke, Imran Tahir, and Ben Waltmann. 2021. "Big Changes Ahead for Adult Education Funding? Definitely Maybe." Institute for Fiscal Studies Briefing Note BN325. https://ifs.org.uk/uploads/BN325-Big-changes-ahead-for-adult-education-definitely-maybe.pdf.

Sichel, Daniel E. 2016. "Two Books for the Price of One: Review Article of *The Rise and Fall of American Growth* by Robert J. Gordon." *International Productivity Monitor* 31:57–62. https://ideas.repec.org/a/sls/ipmsls/v31y20164.html.

Simon, Hermann. 1995. *Hidden Champions of the Twenty-First Century: The Success Strategies of Unknown World Market Leaders*. Cambridge, MA: Harvard University Press.

Skelton, David. 2019. *Little Platoons: How a Revived One Nation Can Empower England's Forgotten Tows and Redraw the Political Map*. London: Biteback Publishing.

Smith, Adam. 1904. *An Inquiry into the Nature and Causes of the Wealth of Nations*. Edited by Edwin Cannan. 2 vols. London: Methuen & Co.

Smith, James, Jack Leslie, Cara Pacitti, and Fahmida Rahman. 2019. "Recession Ready? Assessing the UK's Macroeconomic Framework." Resolution Foundation. https://www.resolutionfoundation.org/publications/recession-ready/.

Subcommittee on Antitrust, Commercial and Administrative Law of the Committee on the Judiciary. 2020. "Investigation of Competition in Digital Markets." https://judiciary.house.gov/uploadedfiles/competition_in_digital_markets.pdf.

Swinney, Paul, Rebecca McDonald, and Lahari Ramuni. 2018. "Talk of the Town: The Economic Links between Cities and Towns," London: Centre for Cities. https://www.centreforcities.org/publication/talk-of-the-town/.

Syed, Matthew. 2019. *Rebel Ideas: The Power of Diverse Thinking*. London: John Murray.

Syverson, Chad. 2019. "Macroeconomics and Market Power: Context, Implications, and Open Questions." *Journal of Economic Perspectives* 33 (3): 23–43. https://doi.org/10.1257/jep.33.3.23.

Tabarrok, Alex. 2013. "The Tabarrok Curve in the WSJ." Marginal Revolution, June 23. https://marginalrevolution.com/marginalrevolution/2013/06/the-tabarrok-curve-in-the-wsj.html.

Taylor, Mark Zachary. 2016. *The Politics of Innovation: Why Some Countries Are Better than Others at Science and Technology*. Oxford: Oxford University Press.

Traina, James. 2018. "Is Aggregate Market Power Increasing? Production Trends Using Financial Statements." Available at SSRN, https://doi.org/10.2139/ssrn.3120849.

Van Bavel, Bas. 2016. *The Invisible Hand? How Market Economies Have Emerged and Declined since AD 500*. New York: Oxford University Press.

Van Zandt, David E. 1993. "The Lessons of the Lighthouse: 'Government' vs. 'Private' Provision of Goods." *Journal of Legal Studies* 22 (1): 47–72.

Vollrath, Dietrich. 2020. *Fully Grown: Why a Stagnant Economy Is a Sign of Success*. Chicago: University of Chicago Press.

Waldrop, M. Mitchell. 2018. *The Dream Machine*. 4th ed. San Francisco: Stripe Press.

Walker, John. 2011. *The Acceptability of Road Pricing*. London: RAC Foundation, May. https://www.racfoundation.org/wp-content/uploads/2017/11/acceptability_of_road_pricing-walker-2011.pdf.

Weingast, Barry R. 1995. "The Economic Role of Political Institutions: Market-Preserving Federalism and Economic Development." *Journal of Law, Economics, & Organization* 11 (1): 1–31. http://www.jstor.org/stable/765068.

Whitehead, Alfred North. 1911. *An Introduction to Mathematics*. London: Williams and Norgate.

Wilkinson, Frank, and Kate Pickett. 2009. *The Spirit Level: Why More Equal Societies Almost Always Do Better*. London: Allen Lane.

Williamson, Elizabeth J., Alex J. Walker, Krishnan Bhaskaran, Seb Bacon, Chris Bates, Caroline E. Morton, Helen J. Curtis, et al. 2020. "Factors Associated with COVID-19-Related Death Using OpenSAFELY." *Nature* 584 (7821): 430–36. https://doi.org/10.1038/s41586-020-2521-4.

Williamson, Oliver E. 2009. "Prize Lecture by Oliver E. Williamson." Nobel Foundation. https://www.nobelprize.org/prizes/economic-sciences/2009/williamson/lecture/.

Wilsdon, James, Liz Allen, Eleonora Belfiore, Philip Campbell, Stephen Curry, Steven Hill, Richard Jones, et al. 2015. *The Metric Tide: Report of the Independent Review of the Role of Metrics in Research Assessment and Management*. https://doi.org/10.13140/RG.2.1.4929.1363.

Wise, Tom, and Kenney Turnbull. 2019. "How Has Trade Policy Uncertainty Affected the World Economy?" Bank of England, September 10. https://www.bankofengland.co.uk/bank-overground/2019/how-has-trade-policy-uncertainty-affected-the-world-economy.

Wyman, Oliver, and British Business Bank. 2019. "The Future of Defined Contribution Pensions: Enabling Access to Venture Capital And Growth Equity." British Business Bank, September. https://www.british-business-bank.co.uk/wp-content/uploads/2019/09/Oliver-Wyman-British-Business-Bank-The-Future-of-Defined-Contribution-Pensions.pdf.

INDEX

Note: Page numbers followed by *f* and *t* indicate figures and tables.

ABOUT THE AUTHORS

Jonathan Haskel is professor of economics at Imperial College Business School, Imperial College London, and an external member of the Bank of England Monetary Policy Committee.

Stian Westlake is the chief executive of the Royal Statistical Society.